"*Wonderment* takes readers on a deep dive into the world of spirituality, psychology, and mysticism by opening our minds to the magic that exists in our everyday lives. Guiding us by the hand is author Amber Snider, whose thoroughly researched book is backed by years of studies and experiences. *Wonderment* combines personal anecdotes, fascinating history and concepts, with thoughtful techniques meant to enhance our lives, whether it's journaling for self-awareness or learning to embrace our inner child. . . . *Wonderment* is a testament to the divinity that surrounds us and is perhaps never more needed than at this exact moment in history when, as the author writes, the world seems more like a battlefield than a holy site and having novel techniques in your psychic arsenal is paramount."
—**NIKKI VARGAS,** travel editor and author of *Call You When I Land*

"*Wonderment* is an alchemical experiment, a journey through the labyrinth, a rite of passage that we take with the author close by our side, learning and evolving as we go—Snider at times both the sorcerer and the apprentice. Perhaps the most resonant message of the book is the potent reminder of our own magic, the inherent enchantment of the everyday, and the affirmation of the ability we all possess to manifest true transformation."
—**JESSICA HUNDLEY,** creator and editor of Taschen's the Library of Esoterica series, from the foreword

"In *Wonderment*, a warm embrace of a book, I hear Amber's knowledgeable, open, and curious voice as she guides the reader through her vast and personal stories, toward awakening their own spiritual calling. . . . *Wonderment* is a sublime journey of a book and, most importantly, a reminder of the threads of connective wisdom that hold us together. . . . I loved how Amber brings such intelligence, personal narrative, religious history, spirituality, and magic all together!"
—**CAT CABRAL,** author of *The Spells Deck*

"An exciting book that allows us to understand the complexities of magic and spirituality on a profound level. By reading this book, you'll be able to explore the depths of your mind, heart, and consciousness. A must for the seeker in all of us."
—LISA STARDUST, author of *Saturn Return Survival Guide*

"Amber Snider's beautiful words will transport you on a magical journey around the world. She has written a book of magical introduction that will delight novices and seasoned practitioners alike....It is enhanced with vivid recollections of her own magical experiences in her travels around the world."
—STACY RAPP, owner of Enchantments NYC

"At a time when everything from our attention spans to our creativity is being co-opted by technology, *Wonderment* is a celebratory reminder of the unique mystery and magic of being human. Guiding the reader through topics like the nature of consciousness and the importance of myth, ritual, and storytelling, Snider brings us back to ourselves just when we need it most. Besides leaving me with a list of actionable ways to put my new knowledge into practice, this book left me with a comforting sense of awe, gratitude, and optimism."
—ESME BENJAMIN, wellness and travel journalist and editor

"A literary elixir of sage guidance, multidisciplinary scholarship, evocative storytelling, and empowering exercises, this enchanting read is lovingly created for any and all seekers of magic and meaning."
—RACHEL GOULD, art writer and creator of the Art Tourist

"Snider offers a captivating journey into spirituality—with guidance and insights that inspire—making this book a must-read for anyone exploring their spiritual path."
—DAPHNE CHOULIARAKI MILNER, culture director of *Atmos* magazine

WONDERMENT

ABOUT THE AUTHOR

Amber C. Snider is an New York City–based journalist, editor, and university educator specializing in culture, travel, design, and spirituality. Her bylines can be found in the *New York Times, HuffPost, Teen Vogue, Atmos, Lonely Planet, Fodor's Travel, Refinery29, Zagat Stories, Architectural Digest,* and more. She received a Master of Arts degree in liberal studies from the City University of New York Graduate Center, where her research focused on ancient and modern mythologies, esoteric symbolism, goddess worship, and the Divine Feminine. She's also editor in chief and creator of *Enchantments,* a digital publication from NYC's oldest witchcraft store. You can read more of her work at www.ambercsnider.com.

WONDERMENT

AN ECLECTIC GUIDE TO AWAKENING YOUR DIVINE GIFTS AND INHERENT POTENTIAL

AMBER C. SNIDER

LLEWELLYN
WOODBURY, MINNESOTA

First Edition
First Printing, 2025

Cover design by Shannon McKuhen

Llewellyn Publications is a registered trademark of Llewellyn Worldwide Ltd.

Library of Congress Cataloging-in-Publication Data
Names: Snider, Amber C., author.
Title: Wonderment : an eclectic guide to awakening your divine gifts and
   inherent potential / Amber C. Snider.
Description: First edition. | Woodbury, MN : Llewellyn Publications, a
   Division of Llewellyn Worldwide Ltd., [2025] | Includes bibliographical
   references. | Summary: "Using philosophy, science, and experiential
   learning, Wonderment encourages you to embark on a journey of profound
   spiritual change"— Provided by publisher.
Identifiers: LCCN 2024046924 (print) | LCCN 2024046925 (ebook) | ISBN
   9780738773445 (paperback) | ISBN 9780738773490 (ebook)
Subjects: LCSH: Spirituality—Miscellanea.
Classification: LCC BF1999 .S559 2025 (print) | LCC BF1999 (ebook) | DDC
   204—dc23/eng/20241121
LC record available at https://lccn.loc.gov/2024046924
LC ebook record available at https://lccn.loc.gov/2024046925

Llewellyn Worldwide Ltd. does not participate in, endorse, or have any authority or responsibility concerning private business transactions between our authors and the public.
   All mail addressed to the author is forwarded but the publisher cannot, unless specifically instructed by the author, give out an address or phone number.
   Any internet references contained in this work are current at publication time, but the publisher cannot guarantee that a specific location will continue to be maintained. Please refer to the publisher's website for links to authors' websites and other sources.

Llewellyn Publications
A Division of Llewellyn Worldwide Ltd.
2143 Wooddale Drive
Woodbury, MN 55125-2989
www.llewellyn.com

Printed in the United States of America

For all the women who've walked before and beside me.
And for Dr. John Miller III, who showed me the light.

CONTENTS

FOREWORD

A deep seeking, an open-minded, openhearted curiosity, journalistic objectivity, and empathetic understanding of both the esoteric and material realms—this is the alchemical formula that makes *Wonderment* such a wonder. Poetic inquiry into the meaning of life, our place in this cosmos, and the existence of a godhead are matched with practical answers and pragmatic solutions with the marriage of science, magic, and spirit, core to Amber C. Snider's philosophical exploration. *Wonderment* weaves a silken web of personal experience, travelogue, and memoir with a profound understanding of history, mythology, and scientific theory. Snider has an intuitive grasp of everything from the extensive dialogues of the Greek philosopher Plato and existentialist writings of Friedrich Nietzsche to the sharp-witted musings of Joan Didion and the principles of modern quantum physics. A discussion on the concept of dark matter and mycelium networks sits gracefully alongside ponderings on global religious dogmas, Indigenous myths, Celtic rituals, the archetype of the Divine Feminine, and animism. Snider is adept at eloquently lifting the veil to highlight core truths buried in plain sight—the sacredness of nature and the integral need for connection with our inner worlds and our outer communities, with the earth, with Source, and with self.

Each chapter of *Wonderment* culminates in ways in which to integrate these esoteric and philosophical ideas and methodologies into daily life—through meditation, movement, journaling, and much more. Art and creativity as powerful tools for transformation are central themes for Snider, and the reader is reminded often of the sublime power that comes with concept alchemized into form. The writing of a book itself is just such a magical act, a repository of the author's thoughts, feelings, and wisdom, resonating with personal catharsis. *Wonderment* is an alchemical experiment, a journey through the labyrinth, a rite of passage that we take with the author close by our side, learning and evolving as we go—Snider at times both the sorcerer and the apprentice. Perhaps the most resonant message of the book is the potent reminder of our own magic, the inherent enchantment of the everyday, and the affirmation of the ability we all possess to manifest true transformation.

Yet the ways to connect to our magic and to the many methods of harnessing our powers have too often been hidden and sublimated, dulled by the drone of modernity. But dig deep into Snider's explorations, into her essays and exercises, and what you will find is that these tools remain at our disposal—these wands, these flaming swords, these philosophies, these alchemical formulas. Sulfur, salt, mercury—body, mind, and spirit. The knowledge Snider shares is the key that unlocks the door to self, that allows us to connect with our inner depths, with Source, with the earth beneath us, with the skies above, and most importantly, with each other.

And all of us are alchemists, Snider seems to say, all of us magicians, capable of marrying our bodies and our blood-filled hearts with the brilliant illuminations of our minds, able to channel dreams into creations and to transmute thought into form. We can turn base materials into gold, into enlightenment, into the storied philosopher's stone. Transmutation, creativity, art, ideas, collective communing, ritual, meditation, worship—*Wonderment* posits that these are all ways to perform the true alchemy that we—and the world—most need.

—Jessica Hundley, creator and editor of
Taschen's The Library of Esoterica series

INTRODUCTION

From as far back as I can remember, my spiritual journey began with a simple question: Who am I and what is my purpose? The steps I've taken to unearth the answers are part of a larger journey, one that is, in a sense, just beginning. And I think that may be true for everyone, too.

As a small girl, I was always fascinated with what lies beyond the guise of things, beyond the threshold of our known reality. I struggled with trying to understand my psychic abilities but didn't have the tools or the language to do so—I just had questions. I could feel and read strong currents of energy in people, places, and objects, but I couldn't see the future, find missing people, or know *exactly* what was going to happen. I could sense things, specific details, that *had* happened in a place, in visions or sometimes like memories that I couldn't have possibly known, or find ailments in a person's body with the palms of my hand. For a long time, I tried to shut out these sensitivities, not wanting to be weird or different from my peers, but over time, I learned to embrace them as gifts. It's my hope that you, too, will embrace your own psychic sensitivities and use them to empower both yourself and others.

I've spent nearly twenty years researching, studying, and practicing the metaphysical arts, mysticism, and magic, and although I do not ascribe to one definitive religion or practice, I have learned from a variety of traditions. My spiritual path has been carved out by a range of traditions and practices, including theology, modern witchcraft, goddess worship, paganism, hermeticism, Wicca, Catholicism, Santería, gnosticism, Buddhism, Pythagorean numerology, sacred geometry and symbolism, philosophy, psychology, mythology, and more. I contain pieces of all this knowledge, learned, acquired, passed down, remembered, and restored. I am an eclectic witch, a seeker, a curious, creative being with magic in my bones.

I've been lucky enough to incorporate a fraction of this into my day job as a culture and travel journalist, editor, and educator. My work has enabled me to travel to distant lands, encountering wild places and wonderful people along the way, and it's fortified my understanding of the vast interconnectivity among all things. Travel requires a sense of curiosity, surrender, and trust in the universe, but it is *certainly not the only way to achieve your spiritual goals*. You don't have to go anywhere to experience the wonders of Spirit, both within and beyond.

While working as the editor for New York City's oldest witchcraft shop, Enchantments, I recognized just how much people craved answers and magical knowledge, as well as the importance of destigmatizing witchcraft, paganism, and even the word *witch*. At the request of the shop owner, I created a digital publication dedicated to intention-based empowerment rituals for the shop, which included stories on the ancient art of candle magic, plant and herbal magic, spells, and interviews with practitioners from a variety of paths. We set out to build a platform to help others use magic to enhance their life and unlock their potential. At the shop, the motto was always "We provide the tools, but only you can do the magic," and the same goes for this book.

I'm here as a guide and teacher, with the understanding that any spiritual journey, like time itself, is never a straight line but a never-ending spiral. No two paths are alike. I have never been satisfied with simple answers and over the years have learned to embrace contradictions. Truth as a handy, ready-to-go order isn't possible. It can be an elusive, tricky thing; as soon as it's within your grasp, it slips away and transforms into something else. One series of answers always opens up yet a new set of questions.

My path has led me to finally embrace something I've known since I was a little girl yet didn't have the language for yet: my gifts as a witch. For some, the word *witch* may conjure negative imagery, rooted in patriarchal shame and oppression, but a witch has always been a teacher, a wise one, a healer, an energy and light worker, one who communes with the spirit world and sees beyond the outer guise of things, trusting in the universe and helping others along the way. A witch is a seeker: a seeker of knowledge, a seeker of magic in the everyday and mundane. A witch is someone who taps into their innate power and helps others find their own. A witch is a creator, a creative, a radical—a person who makes *something from nothing*.

It may not be everyone's path, but it's been part of mine. And although no single label, word, or phrase can possibly contain the wonderful spectrum of personal spirituality and the infinite pathways to the Divine, it's my hope that we all realize our innate power and magic that is just waiting to be explored. It is my hope that this book helps you tap into your own sacred calling, manifest your highest intentions, and unlock your magical potential. As you read and perform the following techniques, I hope you experience some flicker of remembrance, some universal truth, a slow aha moment, or a distant call that awakens your spirit. We all have unique gifts to share with the world, and by tuning in to the hidden, mysterious currents around and within us, we can fully realize them. This book is about ways to uncover the elusive spark that permeates all things, awaken your psychic senses, and tap into your own sacred, creative force with the help of nature, magic, and the spirit world. At its core, this is a book about the interconnectivity of all things, illuminating questions of the soul and the life-death-rebirth cycle, accessing your own divine light, reviving curiosity, and remembering the vast possibilities of magic within.

We're at an age in humanity that requires turning our attention inward in order to make sense of what's going on *out there*. The macrocosm—the cosmos, the universe at large—is a mirror of the microcosm—our inner world. The more we discover about our spiritual potential, the more we'll understand humanity's potential. We've done plenty of space exploration, but what of the human soul and mind? Our progress as a species absolutely depends on science, but it also depends on our spiritual growth, too. We are not robots or algorithms. We are complex, creative beings with an entire universe within us.

Our lived experiences serve as evidence that there's something higher than ourselves and that we're all a part of a vast, cosmic dance. Divinity resides in everything—it's the spark that permeates all of nature. We are a microcosm of this grand macrocosm, and just as scientists use telescopes and satellites to study the infinite expanse out there, it's time to take a metaphysical microscope to look at the expanse within. Perhaps one day soon, we'll collectively understand, beyond a shadow of doubt, that we are spiritual beings having a physical experience—and not the other way around. Perhaps one day, we'll understand that not only are supernatural and psychic experiences very real, but also everything in the universe is conscious. And the universe, nature, and the spirit world listen to our call.

The universe is more mysterious than we can possibly imagine. It's my hope that the following experiences, stories, and techniques will help you realize your higher calling, awaken a sense of mystical remembrance, and tap into the divine current both within and around you.

You are a small part of the vast, infinite, mysterious whole. And you, too, contain infinite mysteries.

CHAPTER 1

THE NATURE OF CONSCIOUSNESS

Long before the birth of modern science in the seventeenth century, our ancient ancestors looked up at the stars and made observations about the cosmos in order to understand something deeper about the human experience. They looked to the sky for answers, whether in the form of gods and celestial beings, mathematical patterns and planetary trajectories, or symbols within the heavenly bodies that signify our fate. Our collective reach for celestial knowledge, through the lens of a telescope or astronomical charts, has ultimately been about our search for answers to life's most fundamental questions: Who am I? Where did I come from? What happens after death? What is the source of all life? Is there a God? What is the nature of the soul?

For thousands, if not tens of thousands, of years, human beings have sought the truth *out there*, in the vast, glittering cosmos, in order to make sense of life here on Earth. Both the mystic and the scientist alike seek to uncover our origins and place within the universe, and they have found that chaos and order, perfect symmetries and abysses, beauty and terror, are at the pulsing heart of existence. Truth lies somewhere in these contradictions, chasms, and extremes.

Our collective fascination with the stars has ultimately been a search for answers to distinctly spiritual questions, too: How was the universe created? What is the energetic force that holds the universe together? Is there conscious life out there? What is consciousness anyway? By looking outward into the cosmos, we seek a reflection of ourselves and understanding of the intangible, invisible forces at play.

What we call magic, in many ways, is simply undiscovered science. Much of what we call the paranormal or supernatural can't be measured, tested, and duplicated according to the same scientific method we use today—or at least using the same tools. Our experiences seem restricted to our five senses, but that doesn't mean there isn't a far greater reality beyond them. We can't see electromagnetic waves, yet they're all around us and we benefit from them every day. We can't hear high frequency sound waves, yet other animals can. We can't touch the internet and many of us can't write computer code, and yet we use the results of these technologies every day. Just as we type in a phone number to FaceTime someone or change the dial on a radio, we can also tune in and tap into other energy frequencies, and maybe even other realms around us. Perhaps one day, communicating with the spirit world and higher energies will be as easy as dialing a friend on the phone. Maybe, just maybe, we need to learn the codes.

Imagine going back in time and showing someone an iPhone or the internet. Even one hundred years ago, the technology would seem impossible! To be connected to anyone, anywhere on Earth, and see their face pop up in real time on a screen, to use Google Maps to view the street you once grew up on, to research any topic with the click of a few keys. It would indeed seem like magic. And what we call magic today may not seem as such in the future.

The word *supernatural* contains the word *natural*—what we call supernatural is just an especially amazing or awe-inspiring aspect of nature; it's not *against* nature, it is nature. Dismissing the unseen world—the spirit world—is just as dangerous as dismissing electromagnetic waves or gravity just because we can't see it. With time, science, as precious and necessary as it is for human evolution, progress, and well-being, will catch up with the idea that our planet, all the life it contains, and the entire universe is conscious, living, and sentient.

Spirituality, intuition, and creativity do not have to be at odds with analytical or rational thinking, nor do they have to exist on opposite ends of the proverbial spectrum. What we call the supernatural or mystical actually fuels some of the most important scientific and mathematical questions of all, widening its frontiers and pushing boundaries. In order to realize our full potential, and that of the natural world, we must stay open to new possibilities and discoveries and integrate all our faculties (senses, feelings, intuitions, spirit, analytic thinking) to see beyond.

Now, it may seem futile to conflate science and spirituality or to use one to understand the other. Religion, after all, has often found itself at odds with science. However, there is a serious difference between organized religion and spirituality. Organized religion oftentimes relies on dogma, a prescribed path and doctrine that one must adhere to, with guidelines outlined by men. There's nothing wrong with religion itself, but when it's used as an instrument of power, as a means to control others, it becomes a destructive force. When religion is used to harm or kill others in the so-called name of God, when it's used to steer people away from their spiritual gifts, or when it's used as a tool to oppress and repress, then it becomes antispiritual. Spirituality, on the other hand, is a journey that involves embracing questions and curiosity; it asks that we stay open to possibility, not harden ourselves against it.

Needless to say, it's necessary to separate church and state, religious dogma from science, and sometimes even spirituality and religion. I am certainly not talking about combining religion and science yet again (we've endured and continue to endure the devastating effects of that) but rather proposing a symbiotic, interdisciplinary relationship between all fields of inquiry. Perhaps we should reexamine the questions, some of which are ancient and primal, and seek new answers outside the confines of binary restrictions and silos of thought. Science and spirituality have more in common than we may think, and the two fields can learn much from each other. And although awakening one's spiritual calling and potential isn't a scientific process, it does require a leap of faith into the unknown, diving into uncharted territories, and turning the telescope back around to look within.

STORY: A LIFE OF QUESTIONING

Maryland, 1990s

Growing up in a Christian household, I was taught that heaven and hell were distinct places. I was taught that anyone who didn't believe in Jesus Christ as their personal savior would be condemned for all eternity in a fiery hellscape. But even to my six-year-old mind, something about that just didn't sit right. How could millions—billions— of people on the planet be forever condemned because they believed or thought differently? Isn't the nature of God unconditional love? What we call God didn't seem to be up there in the sky but *right here*.

Heaven and hell seemed more like human constructs or even psychic states of being, and if they were distinct places (or realms), I certainly did not feel we were meant to stay in one or the other for all eternity. The only constant in the universe is change, so why would anything be fixated in a single place forever? I saw the biblical texts as cryptic parables gleaming with hidden lessons, rather than literal ones. There seemed to be more to it all. I had countless questions, and in my relentless pursuit of them, I somehow knew the search for answers would become a lifelong endeavor.

Christianity did, however, offer that very first seed of knowledge, imprinting certain truths about the nature of the soul and concepts of the Divine: One, the soul was eternal. Two, the divine essence is love. And three, life itself is a miraculous gift. I felt that what we call God lives within all of us, pulsing and churning, boundless and immeasurable. We all contain this divine pulse, like a seed waiting to sprout up to reveal itself. Even the heart beneath our chests, sustaining our bodies without conscious effort or control, is a miracle. And if there is a God, a source, a creator, we are all a part of it and also connected to everything else in creation.

Then, something shifted again around the age of seventeen when I first encountered philosophy. A new depth began to emerge in my thinking, a slow restructuring of everything I thought I knew as accepted truth. Something new began to stir, this time allowing for a rational discussion of the questions that fascinated me the most: What is the soul? What is the mind? Is there a universal code of ethics and morals? What is consciousness? Philosophy—Plato, Beauvoir, Benjamin, Nietzsche, Aristotle, Descartes, Camus, Aquinas, Kant, Schopenhauer—presented the possibility of understanding life through a calculated, studied lens.

Philosophy was the strange freedom I had been seeking, giving me permission to finally question and explore, while not blindly relying on dogma. In fact, it required questioning and validated a deep hunger for hidden knowledge and esoteric mysteries. It empowered my sense of wonder, offering a new lens through which to view the world. But here's the beautiful catch: just when philosophy offered clues to answers, those answers ultimately led to new questions. And for the first time in my life, I realized that sometimes the questions were just as important as the answers.

Science, too, offered its own clues to unlock the strange forms of the universe and its mysteries. Albert Einstein once sought to find a unifying theory that explains this great cosmic dance of which we're all a part, and in his pursuit of the singular grand equation, an explanation for how everything in the universe functions, he led humanity down a remarkable path. Even his blunders and errors became breadcrumbs for those who'd follow, to be picked up by future minds with the same goal. His mathematical revelations helped bind a once-fragmented understanding of reality: to know that space and time are interconnected, dependent and inseparable from each other, shattered our previous notions of how reality works.

The space-time continuum seemed, at first, to me, like something out of a fairy tale or sci-fi novel, with too fantastical implications to actually be true. Yet the union of space-time is very real—not just a theory but a fact of nature that engineers have since used countless times over, including in space exploration. Even Einstein's most well-known formula, $E=MC^2$, a beautifully concise theory of special relativity, dashed previously held conceptions of how the universe functions. It showed that mass and energy are essentially different forms of the same thing.

Even with all his mathematical breakthroughs, the genius himself could not, however, find the singular thread—that elusive, mathematical formula—that ties everything together in a neat, palatable package. And when quantum physics came on the scene, it shook things up even further, contradicting again much of what we knew to be true about the universe. If the macrocosm functions according to precise, universal, orderly physical laws that can be applied and relied upon (that is, predictable behavior governed by mathematical truths), the microcosm functions on an entirely different level. To Einstein's initial chagrin, some of the same physical laws that govern matter and energy break down and become wildly strange on the sub-subatomic (or quantum) level. When confronted with these new findings, proving that chaos and probability, not rational order, also ruled the universe, he wrote, "I, at any rate, am convinced that *He* [God] is not playing at dice."[1]

Just because we can't see, measure, or test psychic phenomena, transcendent experiences, or spirit encounters doesn't make them any less real. The reality is that reality is far stranger than we can fathom. Even Einstein himself marveled at the mysteries of the universe and encouraged standing in awe at what we don't fully grasp: "The most beautiful thing that we can experience is the mysterious. It is the

1. Max Born, ed., *The Born-Einstein Letters: The Correspondence between Albert Einstein and Max and Hedwig Born from 1916 to 1955*, trans. Irene Born (New York: Macmillan, 1971), 90–91.

source of all true art and all science. He to whom this emotion is a stranger, who can no longer pause to wonder and stand rapt in awe, is as good as dead; his eyes are closed. … It is enough for me to contemplate the mystery of conscious life perpetuating itself through all eternity, to reflect upon the marvelous structure of the universe which we can dimly perceive, and to try humbly to comprehend even an infinitesimal part of the intelligence manifested in nature."[2]

If intelligence is manifested in nature itself, I believe that magic is that which dwells within the seemingly contradictory space between the sublime and the rational. What we can't ascribe physical laws and verifiable truths to we call *magic*, but it goes by other names, too: the supernatural, paranormal phenomena, ESP, energy work, and yes, even spooky action at a distance. And sometimes when we look closely at things and examine our reality, it morphs and shifts into something else.

DEEP DIVE: IN THE BEGINNING WAS THE WORD

One of the most interesting questions to consider, one that spurs countless new questions, is seemingly very basic: What is consciousness? Is it a distinctly human quality, or does it exist all around us? Is it a force, and can it be measured? Does it extend to plants, animals, trees? Chances are, if you ask a series of people what consciousness means to them, you'll get a slightly different response from each one. If you ask a theologian, mystic, biologist, mathematician, shaman, or AI engineer, you'll probably get entire volumes on the subject, albeit with distinctly different approaches to the question. Many of us have a vague idea of what consciousness is, but surprisingly, there's no consensus on what it actually entails.

Just as we learn more about the nature of the universe every day, we're also constantly constructing and reconstructing language in order to understand our experience of the world. Language—like the universe itself—is in perpetual motion. It's always evolving, expanding, morphing,

2. Albert Einstein, *Living Philosophies* (New York: Simon and Schuster, 1931), 6–7.

conceding, and absorbing the influences around it. Our human histories are etched out within the confines, borders, and expanses of language, and within language, we also catch glimpses of our cultural, geographical, tribal, and historical origins.

The term *consciousness* was first used in the early seventeenth century to denote "internal knowledge," deriving from the Latin word *conscius*, meaning "knowing, aware."[3] The *Oxford English Dictionary* defines consciousness in a number of ways:

- Internal knowledge or conviction; the state or fact of being mentally conscious or aware of something.
- The faculty or capacity from which awareness of thought, feeling, and volition and of the external world arises; the exercise of this.
- The totality of the impressions, thoughts, and feelings, which make up a person's sense of self or define a person's identity.
- The state of being aware of and responsive to one's surroundings, regarded as the normal condition of waking life.[4]

Many of these definitions focus on one word: *awareness*. That is, awareness of the self and one's surroundings. Consciousness is sentience. Yet our anthropocentric ideas on what it means to be aware, sentient, or conscious rarely extend to other life forms, and therein lies a big problem.

We know, for instance, that plants react and respond to their surroundings, as do animals, yet we bristle at extending the term to them. And what about water? What about air? What about trees? What about light? What about the ground beneath our feet, Mother Earth? Could, perhaps, all of life—and the universe—be *conscious*?

3. Online Etymology Dictionary, s.v. "consciousness," by Douglas Harper, last modified March 5, 2018, https://www.etymonline.com/word/consciousness#etymonline_v_28666.

4. *Oxford English Dictionary*, s.v. "consciousness," last modified December 2023, https://www.oed.com/viewdictionaryentry/Entry/39477;jsessionid=711F45ACF928243A7EED 846F75CE8575.

Panpsychism, a term first coined in the sixteenth century by scientist and philosopher Francesco Patrizi from the Republic of Venice, is the idea that "all things have a mind or mind-like quality."[5] Patrizi posited that there was a "divine mental light pervading the universe," a kind of grand, illuminating mind or a "world soul."[6] Today there's growing evidence that the entire universe is, in fact, conscious.[7] Mathematicians at universities such as Oxford are studying panpsychism, which claims that "consciousness is inherent in even the tiniest pieces of matter," suggesting not only that consciousness can be found throughout the universe, but also that the "fundamental building blocks of reality have conscious experience."[8]

According to an article penned by science journalist David Crookes, a prominent Oxford physicist and Nobel Prize physicist named Sir Roger Penrose was among the first academics to propose looking beyond neuroscience when examining consciousness and considering the role of quantum physics. Working with psychologist Stuart Hameroff, together they developed a hypothesis called orchestrated objective reduction, which, at the highest level, suggests a "connection between the brain's biomolecular processes and the basic structure of the universe."[9] Similarly, "neuroscientist and psychiatrist Giulio Tononi, distinguished chair in Consciousness Studies at the University of Wisconsin," developed a theory called integrated information theory (IIT), which posits that "consciousness is a fundamental aspect of reality; that it exists and is structured, specific, unified and definite."[10]

5. David Skrbina, "Panpsychism," Internet Encyclopedia of Philosophy, accessed June 4, 2024, https://iep.utm.edu/panpsych/.

6. Bernardine Bonansea and Godehard Bruentrup, "Panpsychism," *New Catholic Encyclopedia Supplement* (2012–13): 1, https://core.ac.uk/download/pdf/131204105.pdf.

7. David Skrbina, "Panpsychism."

8. David Crookes, "Can Our Brains Help Prove the Universe Is Conscious?" Space.com, February 23, 2022, https://www.space.com/is-the-universe-conscious.

9. Crookes, "Can Our Brains Help Prove the Universe Is Conscious?"

10. Crookes, "Can Our Brains Help Prove the Universe Is Conscious?"

Crookes goes on to paraphrase the core of the IIT theory in his article: "[It] suggests consciousness will emerge when information moves between the subsystems of an overall system: to be conscious, an entity has to be single and integrated and must possess a property called 'phi' which is dependent on the interdependence of the subsystems. In other words, you could have a bunch of coins on your desk, on top of each sits a bunch of neurons. If information which travels along those pathways [is] crucial for those coins, then you've got a high phi and therefore consciousness."[11] In this way, we can think of consciousness as an interdependent process, or interconnected flow of information, happening between all living things.

When trying to understand the nature of reality and the self, the seventeenth-century French philosopher and mathematician Rene Descartes employed rationalized doubt as a tool to tackle existential questions, finally declaring in the now-famous maxim, "Dubito, ergo cogito, ergo sum," or "I doubt, therefore I think, therefore I am." Descartes exists because he is conscious, aware, and sentient. But maybe he was off the mark a bit. Maybe it's "The universe thinks, therefore I am."

A Vast Mystery: Light

If the universe itself is conscious, what about light? Imagine the birth of the universe during the big bang and the intense light emitted in that genesis, propelling and spurring the first inklings of life into being. Consider our central star and light source, the sun, which makes all of physical life on this planet possible: everything we consume and contain, from the food we eat to the bones in our body, is made possible through its power. Without the sun, life on Earth would simply cease to exist. It's no wonder then why ancient peoples across cultures worshiped the sun god or goddess in myriad forms, whether it was Apollo or Helios in ancient Rome and Greece, Lugh for the Celts, or Aten from the pharaoh Akhenaten in ancient Egypt.

---

11. Crookes, "Can Our Brains Help Prove the Universe Is Conscious?"

In Religion

We see an emphasis of light in nearly every world religion, too. In Buddhism, luminosity (light) is associated with the Buddha-nature and enlightenment. In the Upanishads, part of the sacred Vedic texts that shaped Hinduism, light is also spiritually significant: *Atman*, or the soul and true essence of self, is light; light is part of the Supreme Soul (*Brahma*) and Creator. Diwali, the religious holiday called the Festival of Lights, is essentially a celebration of light and its triumph and victory over darkness. In Christianity, Jesus is referred to as the "Light of the World," as both the son of God and God incarnate.

Consider the Gnostic Gospels, or the fifty-two ancient codices (i.e., texts or manuscripts), rediscovered in 1945 in Nag Hammadi in upper Egypt, which were hidden in earthenware for 1,600 years before a group of farmers found them.[12] Written in Coptic (the language of the Egyptian Christians), some of these codices date back to around second century CE of the early Christian era and emphasize a "belief that salvation came through the receiving of a secret 'gnosis' or knowledge."[13] Although the canonical books of the New Testament were ratified many times over years by several church councils, contents of the Nag Hammadi library, which include the Gospel of Thomas and the Gospel of Philip, were strangely enough never included.[14]

The Greek word *gnōsis* means "knowledge." Within these gnostic texts, there's also a compelling emphasis on light and its connection to divine knowledge, as well as knowledge as a map for the path to enlightenment.

---

12. Nag Hammadi Archive, Claremont Colleges Digital Library, https://ccdl.claremont.edu /digital/collection/nha.

13. Elaine Pagels, "The Gnostic Gospels," PBS, accessed June 4, 2024, https://www.pbs.org /wgbh/frontline/article/gnostic-gospels/; Hector Llanes, "Are the Gnostic Gospels Reliable Sources?" Grand Canyon University, March 3, 2015, https://www.gcu.edu/blog /theology-ministry/are-gnostic-gospels-reliable-sources.

14. Daniel Becerra, "The Canonization of the New Testament," in *New Testament History, Culture, and Society: A Background to the Texts of the New Testament*, ed. Lincoln H. Blumell (Salt Lake City: Deseret Book, 2019), 772–86, https://rsc.byu.edu/new -testament-history-culture-society/canonization-new-testament.

Spiritual knowledge, in this sense, is one potential path for salvation or evolution of the soul, which contradicts the canonized Christian teaching. And while the word *light* is used as a cryptic metaphor for spiritual knowledge, these early authors may have also been quite literal in their use of the word. In one translation of the Gospel of Thomas, *light* is mentioned thirteen times, appearing twenty-nine times in the Gospel of Sophia of Jesus Christ and thirty-three times in the Gospel of Philip.[15]

Consider, also, the first words of God in the canonical book of Genesis: "Let there be light."[16] Within the gnostic texts, specifically the Gospel of Thomas, Jesus alludes to the light as humanity's divine source and place of origin: "If they say to you, 'Where did you come from?', say to them, 'We came from the light, the place where the light came into being on its own accord and established itself and became manifest through their image.' If they say to you, 'Is it you?', say, 'We are its children, we are the elect of the living father.' If they ask you, 'What is the sign of your father in you?', say to them, 'It is movement and repose.'"[17] If God is light, which "came into being on its own accord," then we, too, come from that light. Light then, may be not only part of the fundamental fabric of our reality but also our divine center, dwelling within each of us.

In Science

On a scientific level, light is also extremely mysterious—in ways that scientists still haven't completely understood. Imagine going out into the night and looking up at the stars, at these giant balls of burning gasses. Technically speaking, with the right tools and calculations, you could measure a star's distance from Earth and pinpoint its exact location in space.

15. Thomas Lambdin, trans., "Gospel of Thomas," Marquette University, accessed October 30, 2023, https://www.marquette.edu/maqom/Gospel%20of%20Thomas%20 Lambdin.pdf; Douglas M. Parrott, trans., "The Sophia of Jesus Christ," the Gnostic Society Library, http://gnosis.org/naghamm/sjc.html; Wesley W. Isenberg, trans., "The Gospel of Philip," the Gnostic Society Library, accessed June 4, 2024, http://gnosis.org /naghamm/gop.html.

16. Genesis 1:3 (King James Version).

17. Lambdin, trans., "Gospel of Thomas," verse 50.

But experiments at the quantum level show that light—or more precisely, particles of light called photons—changes its behavior depending on whether or not it's being observed. Quantum physicists found that when light is measured and observed as a wave, it will behave like a wave. But when it's measured and observed as a particle, it will behave like a particle. And even more perplexing, if photons are *not* observed, they exist in several places simultaneously, a principle known as superposition.[18] It's only when a photon is observed that it can be measured in a single point. It was a baffling discovery, one that has disturbed some of the greatest minds of our history, including Albert Einstein.

Let's say you throw a dart at a wall. You know it's going to hit one spot—whether that's on the floor or a place on the board. But certainly, that dart cannot hit several or all spots at once. It's physically impossible for a single dart to hit—and exist—at all points on the target at once. But light (or particles of light) functions in a different way altogether: Without an observer, the exact location of a photon isn't certain; it exists in all places at once. In fact, particles may not even have a physical property at all until they're observed.[19]

What does this potentially mean on a spiritual or metaphysical level? For starters, it brings up several new questions: Does reality also require an observer to become manifest? If light changes its behavior when it's observed, does it have consciousness? Does our own spiritual (psychic, vibratory) energy exist in all places at once, until we observe (or channel) it?

And then there's the logic-defying fact of entanglement. Consider this: When two particles of light are entangled and then separated, even over large distances, they will still react to each other. What you do to one of them, the other one will react to as well, almost like psychic lovers

18. Alessandro Fedrizzi and Massimiliano Proietti, "Quantum Physics: Our Study Suggests Objective Reality Doesn't Exist," Phys.Org, November 14, 2019, https://phys.org/news/2019-11-quantum-physics-reality-doesnt.html.

19. "Einstein's Quantum Riddle," NOVA, PBS, January 9, 2019, video transcript, https://www.pbs.org/wgbh/nova/video/einsteins-quantum-riddle/.

across the miles. Let's say a scientist changes something in the conditions of photon A; its entangled particle, or photon B, even thousands of miles away, will react to the *same* stimuli. So what you do to one entangled particle affects the other. "Entangled particles are somewhat like twins still joined by an umbilical cord (their wave function) which can be light-years across," physicist Michio Kaku wrote in his book *Parallel Worlds*. "[These pairs] act as if they were a single object, although they may be separated by a large distance."[20] Quantum entanglement is what Einstein called "spooky action at a distance," revealing just how mystifying, strange, and uncanny the universe truly is.[21] On a spiritual level, we have to wonder: Could quantum entanglement explain psychic phenomena like ESP or telepathy? And can we, too, as beings of light, transmute our energy to several places simultaneously? Could multiple realities be playing out at once? While many warn against so-called magical thinking, quantum physicists are chiseling away at the very idea that an *objective* reality even exists at all.[22]

If reality changes according to our perceptions and observations, perhaps we can move beyond our limited senses to glimpse something higher within ourselves and the world around us. Or at the very least, in our everyday lives, we can become fully aware of how our individual perceptions and observations shape our experience of the world. As physicist Michio Kaku pointed out, Nobel laureates such as Eugene Wigner and others have advocated that "consciousness determines existence," since the phenomena seen in quantum physics experiments require an observer.[23]

However, although our perceptions and observations may shape our individual experience, there is still a vast interconnectivity at play: "There is a cosmic 'entanglement' between every atom of our body and atoms that

20. Michio Kaku, *Parallel Worlds: A Journey through Creation, Higher Dimensions, and the Future of the Cosmos* (New York: Vintage, 2006), 177.

21. "Einstein's Quantum Riddle."

22. Fedrizzi and Proietti, "Quantum Physics."

23. Kaku, *Parallel Worlds*, 165.

are light-years distant. Since all matter came from a single explosion, the big bang, in some sense the atoms of our body are linked with some atoms on the other side of the universe in some kind of cosmic quantum web," writes Kaku.[24] We were all once part of a blazing star out there in the cosmos. And we all quite literally come from the stars. Billions of years have passed, and yet we still contain that very same stardust within us.

A Vast Mystery: Darkness

One cannot discuss light without acknowledging its opposite counterpart. Light and darkness are interdependent. They are mirrors of one another; one cannot exist without the other. So much of modern spirituality has focused on light, while shunning darkness—that is, emphasizing a life rooted entirely on seeking light without also acknowledging the necessity of its opposite, precious counterpart. Like finding the mean between extremes, we need the darkness to recognize our inner light, nature, and potential, too.

As humans, we're diurnal creatures, living out our lives during the day and retreating to our dreams in the darkness. Just as we need light, we also need darkness, both materially and spiritually. I don't mean darkness as in evil, not at all, but rather the mysterious qualities of the void, abyss, and unknown. Although the dark may leave us feeling vulnerable, potentially conjuring a sense of fear (we're always afraid of the unknown), its function is just as important as light for physical survival of life on this planet. Darkness allows for rest, reflection, and growth. Simply look at the negative effects of artificial light pollution on our ecosystem—the natural world needs darkness to thrive, too.

In Religion

Going back to the texts found at the Nag Hammadi library, consider these words found in the Gospel of Philip: "Light and Darkness, life and death, right and left, are brothers of one another. They are inseparable.

24. Kaku, *Parallel Worlds*, 176–77.

Because of this neither are the good good, nor evil evil, nor is life life, nor death death. For this reason each one will dissolve into its earliest origin. But those who are exalted above the world are indissoluble, eternal."[25] In order to understand and recognize the light within us, we must understand and recognize its opposite, too; that darkness is a necessary component for life and part of the fundamental fabric of the universe.

In Science

New findings in quantum physics show that all matter may have a counterpart—a vast, mysterious, invisible substance that we cannot see, touch, or truly understand (yet)—called dark matter. It makes up a whopping 27 percent of the entire universe.[26] Although, the Department of Energy says it makes up 85 percent of the universe, showing there's still much to learn on the subject.[27] But just as there's no definitive consensus on the nature of consciousness, dark matter remains elusive. According to CERN, the European Organization for Nuclear Research and one of the world's largest centers for scientific research, "one idea is that [dark matter] could contain 'supersymmetric particles'—hypothesized particles that are partners to those already known in the Standard Model."[28] In other words, dark matter could be a mirror image of our known material reality. Could it be, from a spiritual perspective, that our material world is a reflection of a higher realm? Does the presence of so-called "dark matter" in the universe signify an interplay or interconnectivity between what we refer to metaphysically as light and dark?

The overwhelming presence of dark matter in our universe also suggests, according to CERN, the real possibility of supersymmetry and

25. Isenberg, trans., "The Gospel of Philip."

26. "Dark Matter," CERN, accessed October 11, 2023. https://home.cern/science/physics/dark-matter.

27. "DOE Explains … Dark Matter," Office of Science, US Department of Energy, accessed July 23, 2024, https://www.energy.gov/science/doe-explainsdark-matter.

28. "Dark Matter."

extra dimensions.[29] While the Large Hadron Collider at CERN is at the helm of studying dark matter, everything we see and typically understand as physical matter—the stars, the galaxies, the earth, all of life—still only makes up about 5 percent of the entire content of the universe.[30]

If that's not enough mystery, consider dark energy, which is different from dark matter and makes up approximately 68 percent of the entire universe.[31] Yes, the entire universe! According to physicist Kaku, "dark energy, or the energy of nothing or empty space, is now re-emerging as the driving force in the entire universe." Still, scientists today don't know for certain what dark energy is either, but they do know that it's (1) evenly distributed, across space and time, throughout the universe and (2) a "repulsive force, which tends to accelerate the expansion of the universe."[32] To add to that, "dark energy is now believed to create a new antigravity field which is driving the galaxies apart. The ultimate fate of the universe itself will be determined by dark energy," Kaku writes.[33]

All of this goes to show how our material world may mirror (what we call in metaphysics, religion, etc.) other spiritual realms. There are layers of other realities all around us, and what we call dark energy or matter could be an entire universe waiting to be explored, or at least be a key to opening the doors of that exploration. For now, practically speaking, we know that both light and dark are necessary, essential forces for life in the universe. The point here is to stay open to that which we do not fully know—what would seem like science fiction even a hundred years ago, ridiculous and mind boggling, is perhaps more akin to the truth of reality than we previously thought.

29. "Dark Matter."
30. "Dark Matter."
31. "Dark Matter."
32. "Dark Matter."
33. Kaku, *Parallel Worlds*, 12.

WORKING WITH LIGHT AND SHADOW

Many spiritual masters in various traditions have observed that light is the essence of our ultimate reality—whether you call that the Source, God/Goddess, Creator, or the Grand Design of the Universe. Darkness, too, is another source of knowledge: through meditation, the act of turning inward, retreating into darkness, finding space for rest and reflection, we get closer to the understanding of unity in all things.

Turning inward—like using a microscope rather than a telescope—into the unknown, we also uncover our human potential. When we confront the difficult parts of ourselves, the so-called ugliness, and unravel the root of shame, anger, and unwanted patterns in our life, this is sometimes called shadow work. Shadow work helps shed light on the hidden aspects of ourselves that we need for both clarity and soul growth. It's not about just embodying light and love, but finding a sense of balance, since we cannot know or understand the light without the darkness, and vice versa. By coupling this inner reflection with a sense of creativity and play, shadow work can be a cathartic avenue for both healing and soul exploration, as well as examining the recesses of your consciousness.

This work begins with curiosity coupled with self-compassion and acceptance. Shadow work is about integrating all the parts of yourself that you turn away from, that you hide from, and finding strength and strange beauty there instead. Just as nature retreats into itself during the winter months, we too must retreat into the inner recesses of our minds, deep into the unconscious, to unlock sacred and perhaps dormant truths. The spiritual idea of "light and love" or "good vibes only" has gotten a bad rap lately and perhaps for good reason—it ignores the profound wisdom and necessity of darkness, including the need to turn inward, get quiet, dig deep, be present, and really reflect.

Technique: Oracle Cards

For one week or month (depending on your own practice and time), pull three cards from an oracle deck each morning or evening. As you pull each card, notice the use of color, linework, symbols, and message within each card. How does the written or symbolic message relate to you and your life right now in this very moment? What are you refusing to notice, pushing down and away, or trying to forget? What parts of yourself are you repressing or trying to hide from the world?

Spend fifteen minutes journaling about the cards and your observations in a notebook. After you've written down your thoughts, read your notes with a different perspective, without any shame or guilt, through the eyes of nonjudgmental compassion. Consider how you can use this insight to either ...

1. Fully accept and integrate these shadow aspects into your being and life in healthy ways. Consider how these qualities may also serve you. Could they also be strengths? Or ...

2. Work on ways to grow beyond them and let them go. Accept and acknowledge the so-called flawed aspects of yourself, and then rewrite your own narrative. Change your internal story, slowly, consciously, so it eventually reflects outwardly.

As you move throughout each day, notice how the message of the cards shows up in your waking life, offering new opportunities for growth and reconnection with the self.

Note that if you don't have an oracle deck already, there are so many amazing decks available on the market. Opt for one with artwork that resonates with you. A quick search online may reveal a few sample cards, or your local esoteric store may have some to check out. Remember, too, that color and symbolism have powerful influences on our consciousness, so choose your deck wisely.

Technique: Spontaneous Play

Gather up old magazines that you have lying around the house or found at a thrift store, along with an empty notebook or blank paper and glue. Next, cut out random images, words, and phrases that represent parts or qualities of yourself that you dislike or turn away from. Don't question or censor yourself during this process or worry about judgment from others. This project is for your eyes only—unless, of course, you want to share it with others, then you do you.

The point is to stay open to spontaneity in this moment. As you piece together the icky, so-called negative parts of yourself, pasting them onto a new page, notice how those parts come together to form something strangely beautiful. Notice the colors, textures, and complexity of the image you are creating. When viewed separately, the individual parts may not seem so ideal, but together, they form a multifaceted self-portrait. You may notice how many of these qualities are interdependent, with each aspect of yourself formed, shaped, and influenced by another. As Walt Whitman once wrote, "I am large, I contain multitudes."[34] Acknowledge that you are infinitely complex, a web of myriad experiences, all of which were once necessary to get you where you are today.

Let's say you're struggling with doubt or the dreaded yet ubiquitous imposter syndrome. Create a silly portrait of a character who represents this fear. Create a story around them, one that pokes fun, brings joy, or tackles the subject in a humorous way. By bringing so-called negative aspects to the forefront and converting them into something less heavy or serious—even laughing them off—we can begin to see them in a new way and use this new understanding for growth. And if fear had an enemy, it would be laughter. Rather than erase the parts of ourselves we don't like, we can find novel ways to incorporate and integrate those qualities into something more playful and joyous.

Technique: Give Your Inner Child a Big Hug

One of my friends always says to me, "You better give that inner child of yours a great big hug," and this little nurturing reminder has made a huge difference in my life. Before any negative self-talk, think to yourself: Would you speak to a child that way? Would you berate or belittle a small child? Would you make them feel bad about themselves or shameful? No!

34. Walt Whitman, "Song of Myself (1892 Version)," Poetry Foundation, accessed June 5, 2021, https://www.poetryfoundation.org/poems/45477/song-of-myself-1892-version.

So don't do that to yourself. We all have an inner little child inside us, and it's okay to talk to them once in a while, to make them feel seen, heard, and safe. Before going to bed each night and confronting the darkness of sleep—or when the rolling, anxious thoughts start coming through—say to your inner child, "You are safe. You are loved. You are a child of the Divine. You are exactly where you need to be at this moment."

Technique: Journaling for Self-Awareness

Try this four-column journaling exercise. Write down a list of words that describe how you see yourself, and then another list about how you think others perceive you. Write a third list on how you'd like to see yourself. Notice if there are any shared qualities between the three columns. Are there aspects you shy away from or qualities that make your stomach turn with embarrassment? Is there anything you're not so proud of? Think about how you can (1) fully accept, integrate, and balance those qualities within yourself or (2) take conscious steps to evolve those qualities into something higher, while eliminating any associated feelings of shame, guilt, or expectations from others.

Now create a fourth column with active, positive affirmations for each negative association. Let's say you see yourself as lazy (and maybe others might, too). In the final column, transform that association into a higher vibration, elevating your consciousness: "I take things slow, with ease and intentionality, giving myself the gift of rest when needed. I am not a product. My worthiness does not depend on any output." Or maybe you see yourself as way too pessimistic or cynical, and your closest friends would probably say the same. If this isn't something serving you any longer, integrate and move beyond it: "I seek balance in all things, finding beauty in the dark as well as the light, knowing that both are part of a necessary whole. I choose to see complexity, rather than stark difference and lack."

PRACTICE:
RAISING CONSCIOUSNESS TO THE SOUL LEVEL

Uncovering your human potential requires self-reflection; it requires a conscious act of turning inward and facing the unknown (or what we commonly call darkness/shadows), and it's not always comfortable. But there's a way to move *through* this discomfort and uncover something much more profound within ourselves—a kind of magic that resides just beyond the darkness. By turning inward and retreating into the unknown, shadowy spaces of the self through meditation, we can illuminate a powerful inner light within us, one that reveals our true soul nature as pure, loving energy.

While meditation can be used for a variety of purposes, like relaxation and mindfulness, it can also be a tool for tapping into our soul consciousness, the nature of which is love, peace, ecstasy, and joy. These are not transient or passing emotions but the essence of our true being. Within this elevated state of consciousness and awareness, one can feel total bliss—potentially accessing sacred knowledge of the soul—and even ask questions regarding past lives or insight into this life.

My first philosophical and spiritual teacher, Dr. John Miller III, taught a six-to-eight-week meditation course at North Texas State University for about fifteen years, leading his students to a higher level of consciousness to the causal level of the "higher mind" (a particular level of vibration between the regular mental plane and the soul planes). Dr. Miller emphasized the power of intentionally raising your awareness and vibrations upward through various levels or vehicles to shift consciousness. "In the Hindu and yoga tradition, the causal body (Western esoteric terminology) is called the *vijnamaya kosha*, the body or vehicle (*kosha*) in which knowledge of past lives is stored," Dr. Miller once wrote in a letter to me.[35] "Note that the KN-, GN-, or JN in the Indo-European languages refers to KNowledge."[36] The soul level has the "same essential

35. John Miller III, correspondence with Amber C. Snider, April 1, 2020.
36. John Miller III, correspondence with Amber C. Snider, April 1, 2020.

nature as Spirit or 'God,'" he added, and it is where deep insights can come through. The following techniques were taught to me by Dr. Miller and will hopefully help awaken and elevate your consciousness to higher levels.

Supplies

Quiet room
Meditation cushion, pillow, yoga mat, or comfortable chair
Blanket

Step 1: Be Present and Aware

Achieving a meditative state may seem like a very simple, easy thing to do, but it's actually quite hard. That's partly because there are so many distractions in our modern world, and we spend much of our waking time consumed by our inner thoughts. "The simplest and most universal meditative technique is 'mindfulness,' being aware as much as you can of what is going on at the moment," Dr. Miller wrote.[37] "*Be Here Now* is the way that Ram Dass put it in the title of his book. Yes, to be present and aware, here and now, is a beautiful way to train your consciousness." Cultivating mindfulness is about becoming aware of your thoughts and feelings, as well as any outside distractions, and doing so without judgment. Nothing is negative or positive; it *just is*. "'Choiceless awareness' is how [the Indian philosopher Jiddu] Krishnamurti characterizes this method," Dr. Miller wrote.[38] But first, simply observe and accept whatever comes up in your awareness, sans judgment.

Step 2: Enter into a Meditative State

Start by getting comfortable in an upright seated position with your legs crossed, ideally in a quiet space. Sitting upright helps move energy

---

37. John Miller III, correspondence with Amber C. Snider, July 30, 2013.

38. John Miller III, correspondence with Amber C. Snider, July 30, 2013; J. Krishnamurti, "Choiceless Awareness," Krishnamurti Foundation America, video, 28:49, accessed January 13, 2024, https://www.kfa.org/teaching/choiceless-awareness-2/.

through the body and up through the top of the head, but if the position is painful or causes too much strain or distraction, by all means, lie down or sit in whichever way is most comfortable for your body. Relax your toes, legs, hips, shoulders, neck, and facial muscles (and unclench that jaw, too). Close your eyes, letting your eyes rest, and notice the darkness behind your eyelids. Notice your breathing, the sounds around you, the sensations in your body.

Step 3: Visualize a White Light

Now, imagine a bright, beautiful, pure light shining down from above and all around you. Let it encompass and envelop your body and move within you. Affirm that you are drawing in pure energy from this light, an energy of pure love and peace. Visualize a bright beam of this pure light entering the top of your head, flowing down through your neck, into your chest, filling up your abdomen, through your arms, down your legs, permeating all your organs, and out your feet. If you feel tension in a certain area (like your neck or chest), spend a bit more time in that area focusing on this healing light. Feel yourself rejuvenated and cleansed by it, carrying with it any impurities, negative energy, or infections out of your body.

Step 4: Become Aware of Your Physical Body

Next, mentally affirm three times, "I am raising the vibrations of my physical body." You might even feel a slight tingling of the skin as you draw in this energy. In between each affirmation, pause and let yourself relax even further. Stay in this state of consciousness for a few minutes.

Step 5: Move into the Emotional Body

Now, shift your awareness from your physical body to your emotional body. Notice any thoughts and emotions that may come up. Silently affirm three times, "I am raising the vibrations of my emotional body," pausing in between each affirmation. With your eyelids closed, feel your eyes move ever so slightly upward as you do this, raising them just a *tiny bit* higher to assist you. On the third affirmation, let your consciousness settle here for several minutes.

To assist with getting to this higher state of vibration, Dr. Miller recommended saying or sounding out the word *kala* (the Greek word for beautiful, although it is a Sanskrit word) in an elongated manner: *kaaaa laaaa*. Say this as many times as you like, until you're ready to go higher. You should begin to feel a sense of peace at this level, a release of sorts, especially in the chest area, and on your exhale. Embrace this release, letting your breath take you deeper and therefore higher.

Step 6: Move into the Mental Body

Now, it's time to move your consciousness to the mental plane. Slowly and silently affirm three times, pausing in between each affirmation, "I am raising the vibrations of my mental body or mind." Feel your consciousness shift upward and raise your eyes a bit higher, as if you were looking at the ceiling across the room. This fixed, slightly upward gaze (about ten feet in front of you) helps center your focus.

Say the word *rama* (a Sanskrit word that represents divine energy, radiance, or the light within) out loud several times, and in the same elongated fashion as before, as many times as you'd like. Stay at this level of consciousness for five minutes or more.

Step 7: Move into the Astral Body

Now, it's time to move your consciousness to the astral plane. Slowly and silently affirm three times, pausing in between each affirmation, "I am raising the vibrations to the astral plane." This is a plane just beyond the mental, where we're connected to the spiritual realms around us. Feel your consciousness shift even higher, becoming aware of your connection with the light, or Source.

Step 8: Move into the Spiritual or Causal Body

Next, relax your eye muscles and let them slowly drift upward, as if you were looking out your forehead or the top of your head. Try to do this without effort or strain, keeping your eyelids closed. Silently affirm, "I am raising the vibrations of my spiritual body."

Allow your consciousness to center itself in this higher state of the soul, one whose nature is pure love, joy, bliss, wisdom, and peace. While keeping this vibration, say or sing or chant "AUM," slowly sounding out each syllable: *aaaah ooooo mmmmm* (the *mm* sound is hummed).

AUM, or om, is regarded by mystics as the sound of our collective solar system. By using this high level of vibratory sound, we can catapult ourselves into the soul level, to even higher states of consciousness, and become aware of our spirit guides and spiritual masters (see chapter 11, "On Death and Dying," for more on this). Stay in this state as long as you wish. If you are at the soul level, you should have no thoughts, but if you do, let each thought gently flow out of your consciousness and return to a state of peace.

Step 9: Coming Out of Meditation

When you're ready to come out of this meditative state, it's very important to lower your vibrations one by one—otherwise, you can feel a bit jolted, disoriented, spaced out, or even dizzy. Just as you moved upward through each plane of consciousness, you must move back down the same way you came up.

To ground and anchor yourself back to the physical plane from which you began, move through each vibration successively: "I am lowering the vibrations of my soul back to the astral plane." Do this three times and sit in this space for a few moments, letting your eyes drop down just a bit. Move through each plane until you get back to the emotional, becoming more and more aware of your feelings and thoughts, lowering your eyes slowly each time. Then become aware of your physical body and sensations, and once you're grounded in the physical plane, wiggle your toes and fingers, move your neck, and gently stretch your body before opening your eyes again.

As you grow in your meditation practice, you may feel your eyes naturally rising to each level of consciousness (astral, mental, spiritual) and access each vibratory state much easier and faster. "Later, after you have practiced and become proficient in meditation, you may be able simply to look upward and hold that position, in order to attain the inner states of connection with the higher levels of consciousness," wrote Dr. Miller.[39]

You may also want to add soft, relaxing classical music to your practice, since it has its own vibratory level, or singing bowls. Be sure to choose your music carefully, if you choose to use intentional sound to accompany your journey.

INTEGRATIONS

Everything is interconnected; everything is conscious. If consciousness is fundamental to reality, integral to the fabric and nature of the universe, and intelligence is manifested in nature, then we must not only consider our place in the larger trajectory of that awareness but respect all of life—down to the smallest particle—as precious, sentient, and interconnected. This awareness of the consciousness of all things has the power to change our everyday life and interactions in profound ways: every sip of water is a ritual, a spiritual exchange; every intake of breath a fusion with new form; every step on the earth a communicative experience.

We would no longer run our taps without regard, mindlessly pollute the earth and sea with plastics, or let corporations wreak global havoc for the profit of a few. Even the way we run businesses, consume and manufacture products, and invent new products will have to change. The way we think of energy itself will have to change. Evolving our consciousness also requires finding collective solutions to the centuries of harmful damage incurred by the incessant plundering and depletion of our natural resources, as well as the way humans have treated each other throughout history.

Within this framework of interconnectivity also lies the possibility for new, interdisciplinary solutions to systemic societal problems: perhaps many issues we're facing in climate change, war, racism, hate, isolation,

39. John Miller III, correspondence with Amber C. Snider, April 3, 2020.

mental health, social inequality, and division can be addressed with a new kind of consciousness. One that recognizes not only the interconnectedness of all things but also an awareness that these problems are energetic and spiritual ones. If we don't address these problems at their spiritual root, starting with ourselves, they'll continue to manifest in the physical world.

The prime mover, or first illuminating step on any spiritual quest, is becoming conscious and aware of the infinite possibilities (and mysteries) of the cosmos and of the soul. The next step is integrating this awareness and knowledge (or gnosis) into our daily lives and interactions. Change, both inner and outer, personal and societal, spiritual and physical, is possible by remaining curious and staying open to novel ideas about our individual and collective potential.

CHAPTER 2

THE ENERGY AROUND YOU

There are all kinds of energetically charged sites around us. Reading this now, you may recall a specific place where you've felt a strong current of energy: maybe it was a house, a hotel, a room, a forest, a plot of land, a bend of the road, a museum. Perhaps it conjured strong emotions or specific visions. Or it left you feeling energized or even drained, but somehow, you felt beyond what was on the surface.

According to the first law of thermodynamics, energy can neither be created nor destroyed, only converted from one form of energy to another. Some places are so weighed down by history and events that a psychic mark is left and can be felt on this physical plane—a lingering energetic mark strong enough for us to pick up psychically, physically, or a combination of both. This is especially true for places where an experience of great grief or trauma has occurred or where there are restless or lingering spirits. This is why psychic self-defense and auric cleansings are so important, especially for sensitive or spiritually inclined folks, empaths, and psychics.

We all have the ability to tap into the other side—almost like tuning in to a radio signal—and touch upon what lies behind the veil of this reality. Whether we want to or not is up to us, but some energetically charged sites have a more profound effect on us than others. For example, you may have a soul connection or affinity to a particular place, or maybe you knew it in a past life. Or perhaps you're more tapped into the spiritual forces there, and depending on your unique spiritual and psychic gifts, your ability to read and feel the energy of a place may be heightened. For others, it could be an elemental connection (earth, air, water, fire) that draws you in.

Throughout my life, I've always lived near the water: the Chesapeake Bay in Maryland, with blue crabs scuttling beneath its green-brown choppy waters; the Potomac and Patuxent Rivers snaking through our cities and towns, holding the murky history of our nation; in Tampa, the Gulf of Mexico stretching out like a blue-green promise, a wish; in New York, the East and Hudson Rivers like sentient moats surrounding an urban castle, separating the city from the outside world—territorial, wide bodies of water that jostle under and over our subway lines. Water has also always been a source of spiritual energy for me. I could feel its absence whenever I traveled inland, searching for the wide expanse of that blue horizon. There'd be a dryness in my limbs, my senses always focused and attuned toward the direction of the sea. There's so much untapped power within the unexplored terrain of the ocean; we've explored more of outer space than we have the seas. Yet each body of water, whether it be the sea, river, or lake, possesses different energies and contains different lessons.

STORY: THE SPIRITS KNOW YOU WHEN YOU COME

Yucatán, 2017

In 2017, I took a backpacking trip around the Yucatán region, traveling by buses and *colectivos* (inexpensive public transport), eventually making my way to the vibrant capital of Mérida. I stopped in Dzibilchaltún, a once-ceremonial capital dating back to 1500 BC that's now an archaeological zone, and the old temples still stand near the ancient city's most vital water source, now called Cenote Xlacah. Here, water lilies gathered in the center of the cool, clear pool, and when I lowered my body down from the rocky edge into the water, a childlike sensation took over, something akin to pure happiness. It was then that I realized there was magic to be found at these sites. I said prayers to the sky, birds, and trees, giving thanks, swishing my hands around the tendrils of the water lilies. It was a playful, mysterious energy, and each water droplet seemed to be laughing under the sun.

Later, my traveling companion heard of a small town called Homún just outside Mérida, and in the morning light, strapped with two turkey sandwiches from Oxxo, we went in search of *cenotes*, the freshwater chambers or sinkholes there. When we arrived in the tiny town, a grinning Maya man named Francisco gave us a lift on his motorbike for $10 USD each and agreed to take us around for the day to show us the cenotes in the area. He had sparkling eyes and a perpetual smile, graced with a few gold teeth, and I loved him right away. Francisco spoke one of the thirty Mayan languages, his Spanish occasionally intermingling with his native tongue.

We eagerly hopped on the back of the wagon and rode through the dusty dirt roads of the town. Green vegetation and palms peeked out all around us, as well as an occasional bodega with vintage Coca-Cola signs. Barefoot laughing children and dogs crisscrossed the road.

The first cenote was a deep blue wall in the earth, wide and feminine, with light pouring in at every angle, softening the depths below. Here, the earth seemed to open up to us. Veiny limbs of trees traversed the walls, dipping their tips ever so lightly into the water's surface, and a single spotlight of sun in the center. There was a lightness there that felt like a young mother's embrace—reproachful when she wanted, but inviting, smiling. But the next cenote was entirely and energetically different. At the second cenote, a mural erected at the cave's entrance contained a warning, a prophecy: "When all the water on Earth is gone and dried up, this cenote will be the last place to find water." Here, I noticed Francisco, raised with both Indigenous spiritual traditions and Catholicism, made the sign of the cross when approaching, a heady mix of superstition coupled with respect for the land and its history.

This site was tucked deep into the belly of the earth and shrouded by trees. It took several staircases to reach the underground water. A dark, moist air clung to the cave walls, and my breath pattern changed as we went deeper. When the soles of my feet touched the bottom of the stairs, suddenly, a masculine energy enclosed around me. At the water's edge, no natural light touched the surface or the surrounding stone: the sun could not, or would not, enter here. Artificial lights were placed around the cave, revealing swimming ropes under the water.

It was then that I felt a strange, very different calling. I placed my feet on an underwater rope that stretched toward the very back of the cave, and my hips began to sway in wide circles as I walked across. Something was pulling me to the other side; I felt a kind of seductive force, or a kind of seduction *happening*, a dance. An unseen energy sang to me from below and behind, an echo, a masculine force mingling with a siren's sound, causing a trance over my body, beckoning me to the underworld. I began to dance on the rope's edge, feeling my belly rising and falling under the stillness of the water. Something strange was happening.

Later, Francisco told us that each cenote had guardian spirits and *aluxes*, or playful yet mischievous spirits sometimes considered guardians of the Maya lands and entrances into the underworld. This particular cenote was guarded by a "dark horse." And he was right: there was indeed a masculine force here, tempting, alluring, provocative, nearly dangerous. If you listen, if you open yourself up, the spirit world will speak to you. The world is speaking to you all the time, the spirits whispering, but we also must be careful to guard our psychic energies, lest we get pulled in.

Sometimes cenotes welcome you with light and reprieve, as if the spirits there want to share the natural beauty of their home. Other times, there is the palpable heaviness, lingering fragments of the past or unhappy spirits. I could sense danger in this place, a sensation of being sucked into the unknown, and realizing this, I performed my light meditations and auric shields. Before leaving the water, I thanked the spirits and the dark horse guardian for letting us enter, but whatever lay within these waters, it also had to let me go.

Then, something similar happened two years later: While on a travel assignment, again in the Yucatán Peninsula, our press group visited a series of cenotes. Near the entrance of one cave was an altar, filled with trinkets and gifts for the aluxes, and I knew, like the many times before, that respect had to be paid before entering. However, our group had already geared up and moved on farther into the cave. I didn't want to draw attention to myself from others, or be labeled as weird or strange for praying and asking permission from invisible forces, so I did nothing. Looking back, I learned a new lesson: do not let the judgment of the living (or fear of their judgment) stop you from paying respects to the spirit world. The spirits know when you come, and they know if you know better—and I knew better.

As I went into the first cave, deep inside the earth, we swam through the various black pools that continued on in long, craggy stretches with our snorkel gear. Coming up from the water and onto the rocks, I started to feel my throat tightening, like the space around me was closing in. I'm not claustrophobic, but there was a sensation of heaviness there that I had felt before. There were spirits around us, calling for our attention, but I could also sense something dark lurking in the shadows. This time, it was a distinct feeling of death.

Our local guide and instructor seemed to notice the change as we stood on the rock together. Looking into my eyes, he asked rather directly, "You feel something here, don't you?" My eyes widened, because I knew he wasn't talking about the swimming or the physical activity. "Yes. Something horrible happened here. What was it?" I asked plainly. And also, how did this man know?

He nodded and pointed to a shadowy place on the right side of the cave. "It happened recently. Normally, this area is closed off at night. People are not allowed to come once the sun falls. But a priest, a shaman, came with a woman one night. We don't really know why, perhaps to perform a ritual, but they never made it out of the cave." I thought that perhaps he was trying to scare me, but there was a seriousness in his eyes, a sadness. What I was sensing was very real.

"Why didn't they make it out?"

"We don't really know," he said. "They were found in that pool over there. There were scratches on the walls and their fingernails were damaged like they were trying to get out. We think they drowned, but it doesn't make sense... Their faces were distorted. We think something frightened them."

I wondered at the tale and the feeling of death in that place. Still, the group ventured deeper and I had to follow, but the unease kept growing. I was there for a work assignment, I reminded myself. I had to keep it together.

I broke out the main tool in my psychic arsenal: the light meditation I had learned from Dr. Miller so many years ago. I performed the ritual silently in the cave; however, the light seemed to be weaker in that space, faint, as if the place were sucking it all up. I found it difficult to focus on the ball of light, as I silently called to the Great Goddess for protection. Although all water eventually makes its way back to the ocean, and all water is her territory, there were other forces at work here—it seemed a world away, an echo in the dark.

After what seemed like an eternity, we made it out of the series of caves, and I was relieved when lunch came around. We walked through the trees to the hut where an array of food was waiting, but I noticed things kept dropping off me—earrings and shiny pins that were once securely stuck to my backpack kept falling off onto the dust of the ground. I remembered something from years earlier about these sacred sites: the spirits, or aluxes, like shiny things.

While the others ate, I quietly slipped away from the table and walked to the altar near the cave's entrance. I placed the pin on the table and bowed my head, apologizing for entering without permission, for knowing better. I asked the spirits to leave me be, and I prayed for the man and woman who had died there. I asked for peace for every person who enters and every spirit who resides there. And I also gave thanks for allowing me to enter without harm.

The spirits know you when you come. To dismiss the spirit world doesn't make it go away—it doesn't make it less real. Just as there are electromagnetic waves all around us, powerful forces like gravity keeping us locked to the earth, and invisible particles that sustain life itself, the unseen world is as prevalent and powerful as the physical, material world. It's just that sometimes we have to use a different lens, whether it's a microscope or our inner eye, to see or feel it.

CENOTES: AN ANCIENT EXAMPLE

There are over 7,000 cenotes, first formed over 66 million years ago, in the Yucatán region of modern-day Mexico. At the end of the Cretaceous period, a meteorite crashed into the earth (the same meteor that most likely caused the extinction of the dinosaurs), and its impact formed a network of underground rivers throughout the region, connected by a series of unique caves and porous, limestone tunnels.[40] Some cenotes are open to the sky and easily accessible, while others are semi-open or deep within caves.

Fresh water moves constantly at an ultra-slow place through these underground tunnels, permeating the limestone and eventually connecting to other cenotes, almost like an underground neural network. And like the mind itself, it's a complex system that to this day still isn't fully mapped out. The cenotes' mysteries represent layers of our own subconscious: frightening, moving, necessary, ancient. They are stunning to behold and majestic in their unique forms, but they are also highly energetically charged sites.

The Maya originally used cenotes as both water sources and sacred, ritual sites. They were considered entrances to the underworld, a place known as Xibalba, and although today many become travel destinations,

40. Emiliano Monroy-Ríos, "Chicxulub Crater and Ring of Cenotes," Karst Geochemistry and Hydrogeology, February 7, 2023, https://sites.northwestern.edu/monroyrios/some-maps/chicxulub-and-ring-of-cenotes/.

they are powerful spiritual centers meant to be respected and revered. They cradle the bones of the dead (some sites were used for human sacrifice), as well as artifacts, jewels, and secrets of the earth. Cenotes have a very particular energy and mystical quality, each one profoundly unique.

Cenotes typically have a neighboring guardian tree, and the Maya were able to recognize these water sources by the sight of certain trees. One of the most sacred trees in this region, the ceiba tree, is considered the Tree of Life (or Yaxche, the world tree), and it mirrors the Maya's view of the universe: its roots extend deep into the earth and into the underworld, its trunk and middle represent the earth where we all reside, and its branches hold up the heavens.[41] When water and trees form a symbiotic relationship in nature, there's bound to be new magic there.

As I was told on my travels, each cenote is guarded by a protective spirit, as well as aluxes. In modern times, these sites have become popular tourist attractions, used for swimming or cave exploration, but don't let that fool you into thinking the magical energies and spiritual potency of these places have been lost. The spirits are very much alive there, and not all are friendly or welcoming to outsiders. Be mindful and respectful of the spirits and traditions of the native land when you visit. If there's an altar at the cenotes' entrance and you're with a guide, ask them if it's okay for you to place a token there (preferably something shiny), say a prayer to honor the dead and the aluxes, and request permission from the guardian spirits that dwell there to enter.

These ancient sites have always left a lingering impact on me, and over the years, each time I've visited one, I've had a psychic experience or a strange awakening. For me, cenotes are not only ancient and mysterious but also profoundly spiritual. And I would later learn firsthand that while some have healing qualities (akin to awakening dormant, mystical

41. "Ceiba Tree: Sacred Tree of Life of Maya People and Universal Concept in Ancient Beliefs," Ancient Pages, April 14, 2021, https://www.ancientpages.com/2017/06/12 /ceiba-tree-sacred-tree-of-life-of-maya-people-and-universal-concept-in -ancient-beliefs/.

knowledge), others have a hypnotic, somewhat dangerous quality, with a palpable pull toward death.

DEEP DIVE: PSYCHIC SELF-DEFENSE

No person is an island unto themselves. We regularly interact with other people and often encounter unsavory things along the way—whether it's a raving person on the streets, unnecessary sass from a stranger, toxic energy at work, or an especially heavy conversation with a friend or family member. We're also not immune to negative self-talk or really bad days (you know the kind, when it seems impossible to just get out of bed and put on pants) or days when your energy just feels off. It can also leave a negative imprint or residue, attaching itself and following along like an unwanted, invisible trail.

Traveling, as well, opens us up to new worlds, ideas, expressions, and ways of seeing the world, but all those new places, faces, and sensory experiences can leave us feeling energetically drained and depleted at the end of the day. As life-enriching as it can be, it's a different kind of tiredness that has nothing to do with jet lag. Sometimes it's necessary to shut off that openness and turn inward, to rest and recenter. That's why maintaining a sense of groundedness, especially if you're an intuitive, is essential not only for travel but also for just moving about our daily lives. In order to stay open to new experiences, we have to maintain our psychic equilibrium and spiritual hygiene. Each place we visit contains its own unique energy and power, and spaces and places (as well as our auras) hold on to energy. Sometimes it can be pretty heavy stuff, and we can inadvertently end up carrying that energy from place to place, too. By taking care of our spirit and energy, we leave room for expansion, as well as compassion for and acceptance of others.

Negativity, of course, can also come in the form of what we consume, including the films, music, and media we take in every day. Sometimes watching the news can leave us feeling totally, completely, and utterly drained, especially as we're bombarded with traumatizing images and horrifying statistics. This is why spiritual hygiene and light cleansing are perhaps more important than ever.

Many people, especially highly sensitive folks, have struggled with taking on the energy of others as their own. The pain of others can feel overwhelming, so much so that it's easier to simply turn or run away from it. For high empaths or intuitives, even witnessing someone minorly hurt themselves can cause a sharp pulsing pain, or watching so-called funny videos of people falling headfirst on the pavement can make your body lurch and reel, a dull ache moving through the skull. We've all experienced empathy pains, but this is also true for psychic energy, or residual energy, left over in certain places.

While it's a blessing to feel things intensely—sensitivity and vulnerability are profound gifts—these gifts also must be coupled with an emotional and spiritual resistance. We have to find and develop ways to deal with the onslaught of pain, horror, and chaos in the world, as well as navigate ways to deal with our psychic proclivities and the negative effects of ESP. This is why energy clearing and cleansings are so, so important for everyone—not just energy workers, psychics, empaths, and witches, but also teachers, therapists, parents, restaurant workers, doctors, nurses—essentially anyone who exists in a body.

Just like an unkempt household, the cluttered energy of others can build up around us, blocking us from our higher self, inner voice and intuition, and the positive things that are *meant for us*. Like murky bathwater, we simply can't see all the good amid all the muck. Smoke cleansing, light meditations, grounding in nature, prayer, uncrossing spellwork, ritual baths using sea salt, and intention-setting can assist with clearing out the proverbial cobwebs and removing energy in your life that no longer serves you. Psychic cleansing allows you to reset, refocus, and redistribute your energy appropriately, helping remove negativity from your aura and space while releasing anything (including people, ideas, and things that are no longer serving you) holding you back from your highest potential.

The bottom line is this: you don't have to go to anyone—a witch, psychic, guru, healer—for a spiritual cleansing. You have the power within yourself to perform your own magic, remembering that you are a divine spiritual being with incredible potential. As with all magic, it's about taking back control of your life—and this includes taking control of your spiritual hygiene.

Sometimes it can be a bit uncomfortable to get rid of the things that are no longer serving us (just ask any hoarder). It's much easier to stay stuck, apathetic, lulled into the chaos of others, build defensive walls and fortify them over time, and stay in the same routine. But for the sake of growth and well-being, spiritual cleansing is a good first and necessary step to stepping into a life of abundance and realizing your calling.

Outside of regular spiritual cleansings, what about using your psychic gifts to protect yourself when needed? When it comes to magic, the idea of protection can be a tricky subject. I've had countless people ask about protection spells, sigils, and charms over the years, but the problem is that focusing on protection alone can sometimes block the path for positivity, too.

Here's the thing: if we only focus on protection magic and spellwork, we can inadvertently block lessons that we're supposed to learn, including opportunities for growth and possibilities to acquire new wisdom. It's like telling the world that you're not strong enough to handle what comes your way, signaling you're scared or feeling less-than, if you're constantly concerned with protecting yourself all the time.

Eradicate *that* idea, first. You're strong and magical. You already hold the keys inside to protect yourself—you're well equipped already. So it's better to focus on empowerment and tapping into your inherent strength, with assistance from the spirit world. The goal is not to live in fear—it's to eradicate fear and learn from it.

Still, as we move through the world, inevitably there are times when our physical or psychic/spiritual energy is threatened. Of course we should take literal precautions to protect ourselves from harm. Walk with confidence, stay alert, don't go wandering off down dark alleyways like a supporting character in a B-movie horror flick. But sometimes that's not enough, especially in a moment's notice.

It's important to be on guard as you go through daily life, but we also don't want to stay locked in fear. As a woman living in New York City for nearly twenty years, I know that sometimes walking down the street in broad daylight, getting on the subway, or merely existing in a female body can be risky. The possibility of danger lurks at every corner—grimacing, waiting, watchful—yet choosing to not live in fear is a conscious choice, one we all must embody. Fear may be our constant companion and also a means of survival (it does serve a biological purpose), but it's not good for our spiritual health to dwell in that state.

When the world seems more like a battlefield than a holy site, having novel techniques in your psychic arsenal is paramount. And so far, there has been nothing so immediate, so powerfully effective and transformative, as psychic self-defense—and it really, really works.

When I was young and just coming to terms with my intuitive, empathic, and psychic gifts, protecting my energy became a necessary practice. But until I met my dear friend and philosophy professor Dr. Miller, I had no words or tools to address these tendencies, nor any explanation for the exhaustion I'd feel when I'd come in contact with certain people, places, or objects. Dr. Miller, however, understood all too well: "Protecting your energies by an aura shield is a good idea," he intuitively wrote in an old letter many years ago. "I remember years ago feeling drained of energy when I taught or when I'd go into a crowd. It's like a piece of ice in water: the concentrated energy is dissipated into the lower energy environment. When you go into a crowd, your high energy is unconsciously drained from you by others naturally. An aura shield is a good way to preserve your energy."[42]

Years later, while working as the editor for New York City's oldest witchcraft store, Enchantments, light cleansing came in handy in unusual

42. John Miller III, correspondence with Amber C. Snider, April 5, 2018.

ways. I was hired to create a digital publication for the shop, one that would help others from a variety of spiritual traditions use empowerment magic to manifest their intentions, but I also worked in the shop once a week. I'd hand-carve spell candles, blend sacred oils, mix wood-base incense, and advise customers in their own magical practice. We practiced the principle "Do what thou wilt, but harm none," and although I had been going to the shop as a customer for years, working there was very different. As you can imagine, you come into contact with all kinds of folks and energies at a witchcraft shop—customers seeking magical remedies; sharing their innermost desires, dreams, and wishes; asking for advice—and sometimes it can be hard to separate yourself emotionally from the needs and feelings of others. There were some who sought to harm or hurt others through magic, which is an entirely different story, but we'd just have to turn those people away. Others would want us to perform spells on their behalf, to which I'd simply reply, "You have all the magic you need inside you. We just offer the tools."

THE POWER OF
PSYCHIC SELF-DEFENSE TECHNIQUES IN DAILY LIFE

Riding the subway is a daily part of life in New York City. The subway tunnels are the veins and arteries that keep this urban collective flowing, but it's not always a pleasant experience. Over the years, I've experienced some wild things while swiftly snaking my way through these underground tracks and have come across some really unsavory stuff. But most of the time, you'll get where you need to go safely. While headed to work one morning, I noticed a man glaring at me down the aisle of the subway car, his gaze fixated. Now, I'm a generally tough lady and no stranger to odd encounters, but there was something different about this—a sinister energy emanating from this person, even from a distance away.

Something in my gut told me he was about to approach, and sure enough, he got up and sauntered down the aisle and took a seat opposite me, still staring with a deranged look in his eye. As the cardinal rule of the city goes, I minded my own business, looking out at the rolling darkness of the window, passing through graffiti and flickering lights along the tunnels. Typically, I'd just get up, move, or leave the car entirely, but the rush hour train was crowded and there was nowhere else to go.

But I had magic on my side. My spirit guides. My light meditation, which no one—no one—can ever take away. As he hunched his body forward, a sour face twisted in a grimace, he waited for me to visibly react to his stare. I turned to face him directly.

I had already been channeling my psychic self-defense techniques since I first noticed him. By the time the man sat down across from me, light poured from above and throughout me, and my body became hot, bursting with energy. All the while, I silently prayed to my ancestors, spirit guides, and the Great Goddess for her protection. Then, I turned to face him. When my eyes met his, they, too, burned with fire. But I had another secret, another lesson tucked in my psychic satchel. I visualized a protective sigil at my forehead, outlined in light, and whispered the following words: "I send you away in love."

As soon as these words came out, inaudible to anyone else, the man bolted up immediately and nearly ran toward the other side of the car. It was as if something had terrified *him*, and he scrambled to get away. So believe you me, it's effective, but it takes time to channel the energy quickly. This is why daily practice, even for a few minutes a day, works wonders. The man was clearly tormented, spiritually, mentally, emotionally. He had his demons, perhaps literally or metaphorically, but despite knowing he wanted to hurt me, a sensation so strong every cell in my body could feel it, I chose to send him away with love.

When you work in the spiritual arts and as your psychic gifts become stronger, it's similar to turning on a light bulb. But not just for you: others can see it, too, others beyond and behind the veil, all different spirits, and not just the ones you want to keep as allies. The spirit world can more easily recognize you and become aware of your presence as you move through the world, which is why psychic self-defense is so important for many of us, especially witches, healers, psychics, and sensitive folks.

Negative spirits (including some people) prey on fear, on weakness. Fear gives them power. Do not give power to those who wish you ill. Know that you have the power within you to perform your own magic, to call upon that deep divine knowing in your depths, and stand strong in that pure energy. We are children of Mother Earth, of the cosmos, of the First Creator. We have more magic pulsing through our veins than we can possibly conceive of.

Know that you have the power to perform your own magic, anytime, anywhere, with the greatest of all tools: yourself.

WORKING WITH AURIC SHIELDS AND LIGHT CLEANSINGS

Here are some of the most instrumental, essential, and transformative aura cleansing and psychic shield techniques I've learned in my journey.

Technique: Light Meditation, to Both Cleanse and Protect Your Aura and Spiritual Energy

Focus on a bright ball of pure light about six to seven feet above your crown chakra, which is located at the top of your head and the space just above and beyond it. As you focus, let the energy of this light rain down on you, filling your body, and eventually radiating outward to your aura and beyond. This light meditation helps strengthen your psychic shield over time, as well as address spiritual fatigue—and the best part is you can do it discreetly anywhere, anytime. You may notice an immediate difference, a shift, in your body and mind, as your body begins to radiate and vibrate with that light.

Technique: To Repel Unwanted Energies

Visualize yourself encased in pure light. Then add a rapidly spinning disc of radiant light in front of you, spinning away any unwanted energy, as a shield. This also helps protect you from others drawing upon your energy (so-called psychic vampires) and can be used as a protective measure.

Technique: Shielding with Stones

If you're feeling psychically or spiritually drained, wear or carry stones of obsidian, onyx, or amber. These stones absorb negative energy as well as repel negative forces. Raw obsidian works especially well as a cleansing stone that also repels negative forces, while amber can reflect negative energy away from you, while also having a calming, healing effect. It's best to cleanse and psychically charge your stones before wearing them for a long time by covering them in a bed of sea salt (don't put amber in sea salt though, as it can damage it), setting them in direct sunlight or moonlight, or wafting them in sacred smoke (e.g., palo santo, incense, copal, resins, etc.).

Technique: Meditate on the Mystical Power of Three

The number three is a profoundly spiritual number in numerology, representing the divine Trinity, the Triple Goddess, and the mind-body-spirit connection, as well as art and creativity in numerology. Consider the form of a triangle, how it represents this combination of mind-body-spirit as well as a unity between them. It's also one of the strongest shapes in nature. Now add another triangle, in the opposite direction, and notice how the two create a six-sided star. Now draw a circle around the star, connecting each point, noticing how it forms a circle, representing the unity of all things.

Technique: Conduct a Simple Earth Ritual

Connecting with the earth and its rhythms in nature is one of the best ways to ground and protect our energies, release what no longer serves us, and tap into the energies around us. You can close your eyes and place your feet on the earth—anytime, anywhere, even if it's not in the actual dirt or grass—and respectfully petition the Great Mother. Silently pray or speak aloud, "Mother Earth, Great Gaia, thank you for your abundance, thank you for sustaining me. I ask that you take this burden (insert your request) from me and steady me." Wait to feel a response in your spirit—ask and you shall receive—to connect and release. Once you're tapped in and connected to the earth, you may feel a sense of being held. Visualize whatever's burdening you—your woes, grief, troubles—as a ball or stream of energy moving from the top of your head, down your body, and out through the soles and toes of your feet, releasing back into the earth like lightning.

We can also use this to restore and replenish our strength. Imagine renewed energy flowing up back from the earth, into the soles of your feet, while praying: "Fill me up with your life-sustaining energy. Help rejuvenate my spirit, ease my mind, and give me strength to continue." Stand for several minutes in this meditation and allow a sense of peace to wash over you. When you're ready, place your hands on the earth's surface and say thank you three times.

Technique: Light and Fire

Sometimes you may find that a bit of extra umph is required after establishing your auric shield. I found a helpful strategy in the book *A Practical Guide to Psychic Self-Defense: Strengthen Your Aura* by Melita Denning and Osborne Phillips. They describe a light visualization very similar to Dr. Miller's, but they called it "The Tower of Light."[43] In this method, however, I found a defensive strategy when one needs extra protection or feels threatened.

Denning and Phillips suggest adding a bright blue light just outside the white light for psychic protection or, in dire cases, a ring of fire outside of that.[44] Think of it like a cellular membrane: nothing can penetrate it, nothing can go through it, except the energy you choose to send out. To me, this blue light is like a warm security blanket, a barrier, and an extra shield. All sensitive people can benefit from it, including children who have psychic tendencies or experience sensory overload. But the ring of fire is like a warning, a protective repellant force to push away

43. Melita Denning and Osborne Phillips, *Practical Guide to Psychic Self-Defense: Strengthen Your Aura* (St. Paul, MN: Llewellyn Publications, 2002), 45–46.

44. Denning and Phillips, *Practical Guide to Psychic Self-Defense*, 46–49.

unwanted energies, only to be used in dire cases of extreme protection. Unsurprisingly, it's very effective.

Technique: Power Sigils

We should all have a sacred symbol that we keep a secret, one that we give power to. For some, it may be a cross, an equilateral cross, a star, a pentagram, a triangle, or a sigil of your own making. Or you can simply visualize a spinning vortex, moving outward and spinning away from you. Visualize a sacred, protective symbol at the center of your forehead, one of your unique choosing, and take time to imbue it with your personal power before you actually need it.[45] If you feel seriously threatened or need to protect yourself, psychically throw and direct that symbol as a warning to get away and get away fast. I recommend coupling this psychic defense with a positive affirmation, not one of harm: "I send you away in love" or "Go forth and be well." I also recommend saying a silent prayer for that person, asking the universe/their higher spirit/spirit guides/God/Goddess to be with them and come to their aid.

This technique, especially coupled with the light technique, also works if you suffer from bad nightmares or night terrors. The more you practice the light technique and imbue your protective sigil with spiritual power, the easier it is to recall, even in dreams.

PRACTICE:
SMOKE CLEANSING

Sacred smoke, or smoke cleansing, has been used for centuries in nearly every culture and world religion, from the Celts to the Hindus, Minoans to Egyptians, and Catholics to Indigenous Americans. Smudging, however, is specifically associated with the ceremonious rituals of some Native North American peoples, so it's important to not only be mindful of the terms we use, but also respect and pay homage to the wisdom of these lineages, as well as the energy of individual plants and herbs. White

---

45. Denning and Phillips, *Practical Guide to Psychic Self-Defense*, 70.

sage, for instance, has been overharvested in recent years, to the point of ecological damage and detriment, but there are plenty of other herbs and plants we can and should use with mindfulness.[46] Everyone has their own practice, and if done with pure, conscious intention, smoke cleansing can be a powerful healing and cleansing tool to enhance your spiritual life.

You don't need to perform a smoke cleansing ritual every day, but I recommend at least once a week to clear out negative energy and welcome in the new. I don't dust and vacuum my apartment every day, so I'm not going to focus on clearing the spiritual energy everyday either. Everyone is different and we live in a busy world filled with distractions, so do what works best for you. But if, let's say, your job is incredibly intense or you regularly deal with heavy emotions or come into contact with a lot of stress or trauma on a daily basis, regular spiritual cleansings are wise.

Before starting, I must note a quick precaution. Some people are very sensitive to both smoke and scents. As an alternative, you can create a sacred water and oil blend by adding a few drops (six to seven) of essential oils mixed with witch hazel and water in a spray bottle and mist the room. You can also mix in cleansing herbs like rue, rosemary, and basil. Or you can psychically charge a spray bottle mixed with lemon and vinegar with specific intention, or simply use Florida, orange, holy, or rose water instead. It's your magic, so use whatever works for you in your practice.

Supplies

Incense, resin, or herbs of your choice

Essential oils of your choice

Firesafe bowl (small cast-iron cauldron, metal bowl, etc.)

46. Hannah Peedikayil, "Ecological Damage on White Sage," California State University, Long Beach, April 28, 2022, https://www.csulb.edu/college-of-business/legal-resource -center/article/ecological-damage-white-sage.

Step 1

Choose the kind of herb, incense, resin, or sacred wood you'd like to burn. Palo santo, rosemary, cedar, frankincense, myrrh, copal, calamus root, cinnamon, sandalwood, kyphi, and amber incenses are all good choices for smoke cleansing rituals. Try to learn more about each plant, resin, or herb you work with, to respect not only their energy and life but also the various cultures that hold them as sacred. This includes understanding the regions from which they originate, and even the climates in which they thrive, to help you better connect to that plant, wood, or resin's energy.

Step 2

You can also create your own incense blend using a self-igniting wood base, essential oils, and/or dried herbs or roots and add it to a small cauldron or firesafe bowl. Incense sticks and cones also work, but use what you have on hand. Sometimes you already have all the ingredients you need right in your kitchen pantry.

Step 3

Next, if possible, open any and all windows in your home. While walking through each room, speak the following words aloud, using your most confident and assertive voice: "I command any and all negative entities to leave this space. I am a child of God/Goddess (insert the language or practice that works for you here), and I command any negative spirits or energy that does not serve my highest good to leave this space." Sweep the smoke around the room and then out toward the window, flicking it as you go.

Step 4

Then, transform the energy of your space by invoking your spiritual allies and stating your intention aloud: "I call upon (insert the language that works for you here: e.g., God/Goddess, ancestors, spirit guides, the elements, the universe) to assist me in filling this space with divine light,

joy, and positive energy. May this be a sacred space free from any negativity or ill will. May this be a sacred space for creativity, relaxation, and
peace." Next, visualize a ball of pure light three to six feet from the top
of your head. Try to see the ball's radiating light extend outward, filling
every corner and crevice of the room, cleansing the space.

Step 5

When you're done, seal in the goodness you've manifested with an affir-
mative, confident ending: "And so mote it be," "Amen," or "And it shall
be." Say thank you three times afterward to the kind spirits and allies
who've assisted in the ritual.

INTEGRATIONS

When we get overstimulated or let fear steer us, we can also use quiet,
nature-based meditations to bring our energies back to center. Visualize
a clear, bubbling stream hidden within a lush forest. Notice the sounds
of the forest, the babbling of the water, the breeze through the leaves, the
whispers of nature surrounding you. Reach down and graze your fingertips in the water, noticing how it moves freely, flowing over mossy rocks,
dark twigs, floating leaves, effortlessly churning forward. Consider how
the stream doesn't question where it's going; it simply moves, touching
the life around it, nourishing the life within it. The water gives its oxygen
to the fish, knowing it will be replenished; the water permeates the dirt
beneath it, picking up sediment below, and carries the seeds of life within
itself. The stream doesn't stop to question its destination or purpose or
what it can no longer carry. It doesn't try to control—it just is.

Consider how tiny, nearly invisible water droplets move from the
stream, rising to touch the sky, forming the clouds, turning into rain to
begin a new journey, in another destination back on land. Its transformation and evolution are natural, purposeful, and necessary; its cycle
is endless and eternal. In this visualization, focus on letting go of anything you cannot control, anything holding you back from your higher
calling, anything draining your sacred life force. Your concerns, worries,

and doubts are mere gray wisps of energy inside and around you—so let them go, watching them move away with the wind. As you do so, imagine bright sun rays coming out from beyond the thick branches of the forest, bathing you in a cleansing light. It's a restorative light, one that penetrates your skin and moves within your organs, your heart, your aura. Now visualize yourself entering the pure water of the stream, cleansing you, humming its secrets.

Consider your own life, how you, too, are part of a vast ecosystem, both giving energy and taking energy, transforming your environment, and along with it, evolving as Spirit. Consider the flow of your life, your own journey that led you to this very moment. Each exchange, each moment, each transition, each memory a tiny droplet containing part of the whole.

Know thyself, whisper the ancient ones. Be still like water. Become the stream. Let your thoughts flow with it, moving freely and not getting attached to them. You're exactly where you're meant to be.

CHAPTER 3
NATURE SPEAKS IF YOU LISTEN

Nature is constantly speaking to us, giving us cues and insights, revealing itself in nuance and whispers. We all have an innate ability to understand the language of nature since we, too, are a part of it. It begins with a sense of curiosity, which is also innate, and one of our greatest gifts as a species. And if curiosity is cultivated and nurtured long after childhood, we can enhance our abilities to communicate with nature.

The world is full of perplexing mysteries, and the path toward realizing our spiritual potential is riddled with all sorts of difficult existential questions, ones that we have no guarantee or assurance of ever being answered. By remaining curious and staying open to wonder and possibility, we take a first step toward unlocking sacred enigmas of our universe.

Every quest into the unknown, every question, begins with curiosity. And curiosity and questioning go hand in hand. Think of a small child: As soon as complex language begins to form, questions soon follow. Why is the sky blue? Why do I have to go to bed? Why do I have to eat vegetables? Why does lightning happen when it rains? We want to rationalize the mystifying forces around us. We want to label objects and give meaning to experience.

As we grow and make new observations about the physical world, new questions begin to emerge. Even the discovery of gravity started out as a curious observation and question: An apple falls from a tree, but *why* does it fall to the ground? It's a cyclical process, with each new discovery opening up yet another set or series of questions to examine. And then, the process begins all over again. As we evolve as a species, our notions of reality will also continue to evolve and change over time.

In fact, curiosity is the first step toward *any* human achievement: it's at the helm of any great artistic, scientific, or spiritual discovery and the heart of all acquired knowledge. It requires a kind of humble open-mindedness, demanding that we seek the truth in unusual places and continuously ask questions, even if the answers aren't readily available.

Just because the natural world doesn't communicate in the same way as we do, through linear language, doesn't mean it's not trying to tell us things all the time. Remaining open to the lessons of nature, as well as spirit messages, is dependent on our sense of curiosity.

STORY: NATURE KNOWS WHEN YOU COME
Oregon, 2022

One of the most magical road trips in the United States can be found where the "ocean meets the forest" along the Pacific Coast Scenic Byway, Highway 101. Each scenic stop and curve along the coast of Oregon reveals a terrain with wild, elemental beauty along an impossibly cragged shoreline.

For a noise-weary New Yorker, it was a surprisingly immersive, soul-restoring experience; its moody, ethereal vistas changed as I progressed down the coast, morphing from fierce fog and wind within temperate rainforests to long stretches of arid sand dunes and towering coastal pines and flat coastline. The only constant in this stretch of land was the Pacific Ocean, its hushed roar the loudest sound for miles.

Starting in the northern coastal town of Astoria, I traveled from town to town down the coast, stopping off for solo hikes in state parks and enclaves off the PCH. I'd stare out at the thrashing sea, at the waves crashing down onto the jagged rocks, long eroded by wind and rain and salt, and the giant redwood trees along the southern shores. Each stop took my breath away, and although I was on a tight itinerary, with each lunch and meeting timed and mapped out to the hour, I'd spend nearly all my free time, every second I could, standing among the trees and looking out at the foggy expanse, listening to the rustle under my feet, and hearing the calling of the crows. In the redwoods, standing among these giants, these impossibly beautiful beings, I felt my own smallness, my own fleeting mortality. I could almost hear their quiet, reassuring whispers running underfoot, their indifference to human concerns. But most of all, I could feel their magic.

Soon, after several days on the road, I came to a small town near the southern end of the Oregon coast just as the sun was beginning its descent toward the ocean, curving along the sky in a long arc. I spent a restless night in a cabin in the woods, and when the sun peeked through the curtains in the early morning, I quietly gathered my things and slipped out back to the road. I had an ocean kayaking experience scheduled in town, but the wind blew hard over the grass and cliffs—a tempestuous, blustery, warning wind. I wasn't an experienced kayaker and debated whether it was safe. I checked in with the instructor and he said it'd definitely be a rough one, but we'd still make the trek out. At any moment a quick swell of the ocean could prove disastrous, so we rode in tandem, pushing the kayak down to the shoreline.

"It's going to be tough, but we just have to get beyond that jetty and then we can stay close to the cliffs. You ready?" the instructor asked. I was not ready. I barely got any sleep in the cabin in the woods, yet I knew the water would be cathartic and my body yearned for its cleansing force. We paddled out into the choppy swells, and I prayed to the Ocean Goddess: "Thank you, thank you, thank you," I murmured with each oar stroke. "Mother Goddess, She who goes by many names, may you reveal your wonders on this day. May you bless us on today's journey. I come as your child."

The early morning sunlight glittered over the white-tipped waves against a backdrop of craggy cliffs in the south and along the coast. With each stroke, I felt myself becoming more in tune with the water's rhythm, connecting to its energy. As we rounded the jetty, the water stilled, becoming more serene, a wide expanse of blue. The wind whipped around us, yet there was a quietness in the air, the faint cawing of seabirds nestled in the rocky coves. And then, from the stillness, a single white plume of air sprouted up near the kayak.

A gray whale emerged, its rounded back dotted with barnacles. His streamlined, rippled back moved across the water before slowly slipping back into the sea. Elegant, pure, magnificent. We both sat in awe at the sudden sight of the creature. "This is the first whale I've seen all year," he said quietly. "Wow, this is incredible." It was a gift. A beautiful, dazzling gift of nature.

In that moment, seeing this whale reveal itself in the cold waters of Oregon, I was overwhelmed with a sense of awe. I realized just how fleeting true beauty really is. It isn't something you can hold on to— you can't grip it tight in your hands, you can't buy it or hoard it away with your treasures. Natural beauty is something that cannot be captured. It's temporal, somewhat frightening, and sublime. To witness it, to immerse yourself in it, stirs something deep within us, something impossibly difficult to describe in language, whether it's experiencing nature in its purest form or contemplating a piece of music or painting.

The experience with the whale mirrored a larger journey. As I let the rhythm of the sea take over, I was reminded of a lesson that I'd keep returning to over and over in my life until I learned it fully: To remain curious at every step, and to learn to surrender. To release the illusion of control. The lesson of letting go is a lifelong journey, one whose teachings I'd have to resubmit to time and time again. Just as heartache can bring along this sharp, stinging, sometimes unwelcomed lesson, an encounter with beauty can do the same.

For so long, I had been holding on to the idea that I could control the flow of my life. And while it's true that our decisions and choices shape our existence, that they define and outline the path we eventually must walk, there's also an element of unpredictability that we must submit to. And there's beauty in the chaos—there's beauty in the unknown. I simply had to stay present and immersed in the moment. However bewildering, beautiful, or untraditional our life path may be, I knew in my bones there were larger forces guiding me along.

Slowly rounding the bends of the jagged coves, the gray whale revealed himself over and over again, diving back down to the ocean floor for krill. When he left the safety of the coves and continued on out to sea, I heard the whispering of the Ocean Goddess: "I hold many mysteries. I contain it all. Listen, learn, be still. And keep going."

DEEP DIVE: MESSAGES FROM THE NATURAL WORLD

Nature contains hidden lessons and messages for us, as long as we stay open to its meanings. Quiet yourself and pay attention. Listen and watch for signs and messages in nature, even in the form of symbolic messages. Consider how these signs may reflect a symbolic aspect of yourself or represent a quality you need to remember or cultivate from within. As curious, creative beings, we too must open ourselves up to the language of the universe, the language of nature, to the gifts Mother Earth tries to reveal.

Just as I knew on the kayak trip that I couldn't control the flow of the waves around me, the thrashing wind, or the outcome of this singular road trip, I knew I couldn't rely on the mind alone, or intellect, to take me where I wanted to go. We also need our intuition, our inner voice, our emotions—our full presence—as well as the guidance and wisdom of the unseen forces all around us.

Gray whales, for instance, are incredibly ancient beings that have been on the planet for over 2.5 million years.[47] It is thought that they are great recordkeepers of the earth, and on a spiritual level, they represent awakening, creativity, and reliance on inner sight and intuition for guidance. They are curious, intelligent beings, representing the power of communication, psychic callings, and intuition, even over great distances. Their underwater sounds consist of a complex system of bursts, groans, rumbles, and conga sounds, allowing communication across great distances.[48] They are travelers and make one of the longest yearly migrations of any mammal, traveling about ten thousand miles round trip in search of food and sanctuaries in which to give birth and nurse their young.[49] They're seekers, always moving, searching. Just like that gray whale, we, too, must remain in motion, never settling for one way of thinking or getting ensnared in any one dogma.

Nature is always communicating with us, revealing its mysteries in ways that go beyond traditional language; we've yet to decipher the ancient, primal language of the creatures of the sea, but perhaps one day we will. Like whales, trees are also some of the most ancient beings on the planet, containing their own wisdom and sacred life force. In nearly every culture and spiritual tradition there's a story (or several) about the power of trees. In pagan traditions, nature is considered magical, divine, and interconnected, and the belief in animism is common—that is, that all of nature not only is conscious but also has a spirit.

47. Remy Melina, "Gray Whales Adapted to Survive Past Climate Changes," Livescience .com, July 6, 2011, https://www.livescience.com/14931-gray-whales-adapt-habits -survive.html.

48. "Gray Whale," Discovery of Sound in the Sea, University of Rhode Island, accessed June 7, 2024, https://dosits.org/galleries/audio-gallery/marine-mammals/baleen -whales/gray-whale/.

49. "Gray Whale," NOAA Fisheries, last modified April 13, 2023, https://www.fisheries .noaa.gov/species/gray-whale.

The Lessons of Trees

Trees are revered in many world religions, including Buddhism, Hinduism, Judaism, and more. In the Shinto religion of Japan, it's believed that each tree has a spirit known as *kodama*, and it's possible to anger these spirits by cutting them down.[50] In the esoteric Jewish mystic tradition known as Qabala, the Tree of Life represents all of creation, both material and spiritual, and also serves as a map of the various planes of reality. In the Celtic traditions, trees were not only the gateway between worlds but also ancestors of the people, and the Tree of Life represented the divine connection between heaven and earth. The Maya believe in a Tree of Life, a ceiba tree known as Yaxche, which serves as a channel for souls and gods to travel between the underworld, heavens, and middle world.[51]

The lore of trees goes back thousands of years, connecting cultures across the planet, and nearly all ancient peoples considered trees both holy and wise, givers of knowledge and prophecy, sources of healing and health, connectors of worlds. From the Native American tribes in the Pacific Northwest to the Druids in the forests of Wales, each culture gave special importance to various species, whether it's the majestic red cedar or the mighty oak.

In their stoic silence and slow reach for the heavens, trees have endured millennia. They hold the secrets of the earth and are the vital keys to the survival of our planet. Without trees, human life on this planet would cease entirely, and yet trees also symbolize our experience and existence in this world: all trees mirror both our physical reality and our spiritual reality.

For instance, do you ever notice how the shape and design of tree roots also resemble the design of the human brain? Think of the structure of a tree: its trunk, bark, branches, leaves, and roots. The real power

---

50. Glen Moore and Cassandra Atherton, "Eternal Forests: The Veneration of Old Trees in Japan," Arnold Arboretum, Harvard University, May 18, 2020, https://arboretum .harvard.edu/stories/eternal-forests-the-veneration-of-old-trees-in-japan/.

51. Itzel Almaguer, "Yaxche: The Tree of Life," Historical Mexico, Sam Huston State University, accessed June 4, 2024, https://historicalmx.org/items/show/141.

source for trees—their ability to grow and flourish—isn't found in their outward appearance, but rather in what is hidden. The roots, which burrow deep beneath the surface of the soil, allow the tree to thrive and exist above the surface, anchoring and securing it to the earth. It's the roots that allow safe keeping during storms and high winds.

But even more so, there's an interdependency at work: With the help of mycelium (microscopic, thread-like fungal networks connected to a tree's root system), these roots compose an intricate underground web with other trees, communicating and sustaining each other beneath the surface of the soil. The symbiotic relationship between mycelium and tree roots shows that a vast, previously unknown and unexplored network exists all around us—right under our feet. Like this relatively new discovery, I believe we'll also find a similar basis for telepathic communication, ESP, and psychic phenomena. Perhaps we also have a larger "mycorrhizal network" around us that allows for direct thought transfer and energy exchanges. It may seem far-fetched, but the natural world perhaps already functions this way.

Our roots, too, are hidden. They are the invisible parts of ourselves: our inner thoughts, our subconscious, and the sacred aspects that form who we are. They are our soul ties, deeply interwoven connections with others, making up our genealogies, relationships, friendships, and communities. They are the unseen bonds that bind us all together, as an interdependent network to ensure survival.

Time, however, looks different for most trees: while they endure a rebirth cycle every year, our process of physical renewal manifests differently. Each season calls for a different purpose in the rebirth cycle: retreating inward during winter (soul restoration), blossoming new buds in the spring (new beginnings, creative work, possibility), basking in the fecundity of the sun in the summer (reaping the rewards of the year's work, gathering sustenance), and preparing for hibernation by shedding leaves (letting go of what no longer serves you, self-reflection and interiority, preparing for winter), just to repeat the cycle again. Tree rings depict the passage of time and contain a hidden message: *time is not lin-*

ear, but circular. We see this mirrored in the seasons, in the cyclical process of nature, and in the death and rebirth cycle.

In reality, time is tenuous, stretching and slowing down, and in some parts of the universe, like in a black hole, it can break down completely. Objects with large mass can warp time, creating curvature in space. Just because we feel time as moving forward and see its effects, that doesn't mean it exists the way we perceive it. Our notion of time hurdling forward is an economical construction, dictating how we spend our time and efforts in service of so-called productivity. Chanda Prescod-Weinstein, a theoretical physicist at the University of New Hampshire, says that time is entirely a social construct. "A lot of us grow up being fed this idea of time as absolute," Prescod-Weinstein told NPR in a 2023 interview.[52] "The management of what counts as correct time and what time it is in any given place is deeply related to authority," she continued.

Consciousness of Trees

In the 1970s, mycologist Paul Stamets began studying fungi and found that there were "startling similarities between the precursor to the internet, the US defense department's ARPANET, and these fungal networks. Yet, it took decades of research to uncover the sheer breadth of the phenomenon."[53] Scientists have since nicknamed mycelium the "Wood Wide Web."[54] Essentially, trees are communicating with each other. But it's only recently in our history that scientists began examining this phenomenon of communication, and there's still a lot to be answered. For instance, is it possible to decipher this communication? Is it language? And if so, could

---

52. Geoff Brumfiel, "Researchers Say Time Is an Illusion. So Why Are We All Obsessed with It?" NPR, December 16, 2022, https://www.npr.org/2022/12/16/1139780043/what -is-time-physics-atomic-clocks-society.

53. Philip Perry, "Plants and Trees Communicate through an Unseen Web," Big Think, April 25, 2016, https://bigthink.com/surprising-science/plants-and-trees-communicate -help-each-other-and-even-poison-enemies-through-an-unseen-web/.

54. "How Trees Secretly Talk to Each Other," BBC News, video, 1:47, June 29, 2018, https:// www.bbc.com/news/av/science-environment-44643177.

that language perhaps be more evolved, advanced, and sophisticated than our own?

German forester Peter Wohlleben describes tree communication in his 2015 book entitled *The Hidden Life of Trees: What They Feel, How They Communicate*. In an interview with *Smithsonian Magazine*, Wohlleben said, "All the trees here, and in every forest that is not too damaged, are connected to each other through underground fungal networks. Trees share water and nutrients through the networks, and also use them to communicate. They send distress signals about drought and disease, for example, or insect attacks, and other trees alter their behavior when they receive these messages."[55] In order to communicate through the mycorrhizal networks, "trees send chemical, hormonal and slow-pulsing electrical signals, which scientists are just beginning to decipher."

Trees thrive in communities; they are social and interdependent, and in fact, the entire ecosystem of the forest is dependent on them. Deep underground, mycorrhizal networks (a.k.a. symbiotic fungal networks made up of mycelium) send signals, resources, information, and nutrients to help other trees—a phenomenon possible through a symbiotic relationship between fungi and the tree roots.[56] Today, scientists know that trees release pheromones into the air to warn of danger and sustain each other by pumping nutrients to other trees, even long after a fellow tree has died.

Does this mean trees are conscious? While researchers agree that trees are *communicating*, they're hesitant to call that consciousness. But just because we can't decipher the language of nature's communication, especially since it's different from ours, doesn't mean the natural world isn't sentient. The deeper we go into integrating our connection between the spiritual and physical world, learning from the consciousness of nature, the closer we'll be to understanding our place in the universe and the dormant possibilities of our own spirit.

---

55. Richard Grant, "Do Trees Talk to Each Other?" *Smithsonian Magazine*, March 2018, https://www.smithsonianmag.com/science-nature/the-whispering-trees-180968084/.
56. Grant, "Do Trees Talk to Each Other?"

WORKING WITH THE
METAPHYSICAL LESSONS OF TREES

Here, we can use the lessons of trees as a call to get curious about our own place in the world. What do their structures and metaphysical properties have to teach us about our own awakening and spiritual pathways?

Technique: Forking Pathways

Consider how our outward presence in the world is similar to a tree trunk grounded in the earth. Forking out in multiple directions are the ever-reaching branches, representing our lived experiences, choices, decisions, and various life paths. Our starts and stops, beginnings and setbacks, our relationships and encounters, depicting both variations of possibility and the outward effects (growth) of all these choices. On a higher level, the branches also represent the many paths of our incarnations throughout time, all the experiences we've had and are *possibly having* at this exact moment in time, and maybe even in alternative dimensions.

Use this idea of branches as a meditative visualization for all the roads that have led you here to this very moment. Consider how each moment is connected. Each branch is a lesson, a memory, an amalgamation of countless moments, a significant part of the whole. Consider how different branches may need to be healed, shifted, or maybe even cut off or pruned. Was there a turning point (or forking branch) in your life that made you feel less than or unworthy? A time that caused anguish or suffering, or a part of your past that you want to heal? You can psychically cut off that branch in order to expand and branch out in other ways, or you can send it healing energy. Alternatively, rather than try to cut it out entirely, consider the fruit that branch has borne and how these moments were perhaps a necessary part of your personal evolution, leading to the beautifully unique structure and being that you are today.

Technique: Channel Healing Energy to Others

Connectivity with others and community is vital for our survival, as well as for trees. Consider how the mycorrhizal network allows trees to send each other nutrients in times of stress or danger and also to communicate. I believe we have the ability to "reach out," like this mycorrhizal network, and send signals to each other through a similar yet invisible psychic network. The more we learn about mycelium, I think we'll encounter a far deeper network of connectivity that also exists all around us. When loved ones are in pain or in need of support, you, too, can psychically send them healing energy, whether that's in the form of prayers, energy channeling, or light. Imagine the world around you is made up of an invisible network that you can tap into and send energy through to anyone at any moment. It works—and don't be surprised if they pick up the phone to call and say they were "just thinking about you."

Technique: Consider the Sum of the Whole

When you go into nature, consider the branches of the tree as forking paths representing all your decisions and choices and pathways that have created the total sum of your life, each moment leading you to where you are today. Consider how different your own life structure would be if any one of the decisions or moments were different. Visualize the totality of your life as the tree: each branch as a necessary part of the whole, rooted in the earth, and at any point, you can grow new branches, new possibilities, within your life. Now, focus on one part of the tree—a branch, a forking path, a limb—and consider what new leaves you'd like to grow there, what new fruits you'd like to bear.

Technique: Keep Reaching

Constantly reaching for the sun, the ultimate source of energy that sustains all living things on the planet, are the tree's leaves. Like our very own fingertips, they're symbolic of our own search for our purpose. They represent our potential, our higher callings, our spiritual growth. As the tree evolves and transitions with each season, during the autumn when the leaves dry up and fall away, its nutrients retreat inward. We, too, need to take time to go inward, to restore and begin anew. Still, throughout every season, the tree keeps stretching outward toward the sun, reaching for something higher than itself. Honor the seasons of your body, of your own cycles, and know you are never stuck, just perhaps waiting to sprout new leaves.

Technique: Reconsider Our Notions of Time

Time is an illusion, a construct. The past and future could very much be playing out simultaneously for all we really know. The urgent question, though, one that requires a self-reflective answer, is how we choose to spend and manage our time on Earth now—in this very moment, in the present. Will we let moments slip away like sand in an open palm? Or will we use time to cultivate and nurture our unique gifts and share those gifts with others? Embrace change, knowing there is a seasonal flux to all things and that nothing is static or permanent. As a healing exercise, mentally take yourself back in time, to a moment of despair, anguish, or confusion. Sit with your former self and tell them they're just fine. Tell your former self that everything will work out exactly the way it should. Tell them to keep going.

Technique: Get Rooted

What makes you feel safe and stable in an increasingly chaotic world? Some of us thrive as transient people, moving freely across the earth, while others need a specific home base and strict routine to feel centered. Whichever type you may be, getting rooted doesn't mean staying in one place or getting stuck but figuring out what makes you feel nurtured and safe, which environments you thrive in, which metaphorical climates you need to be in to realize your full power and potential. Create a list of must-haves to feel rooted and consciously work each day to build aspects of this in your life. Start small: "I need quiet mornings" or "I need to be around family more" or "I need more financial security to feel rooted." However insignificant anything on your list may seem, it's all part of your current, they're part of your current truth—so work toward incorporating them a little more in your life, each day, week, and month. Turn off your phone in the morning while you have your coffee, maybe drawing a bath instead of taking a shower before work. Or schedule family trips throughout the year in advance, even if it means using your vacation time to do so. Start putting money in a high-yield savings account to build more financial security. Start small, but pay attention to what makes you feel rooted, nurtured, and more secure.

PRACTICE:
APPLICATIONS FOR CULTIVATING
CURIOSITY AND OBSERVATION

Listening to the cues and clues of nature begins with recultivating our sense of curiosity. We're each born with a strong sense of curiosity, but somehow over the years, the world just seems to beat it out of us. We instead put up blinders and no longer become enraptured with the miracle of the mundane. We no longer notice the wonder of nature. Yet curiosity is a forward-propelling spark, one that allows for soul growth and new ways of thinking to emerge, helping us envision a better, more beautiful world and opening us up to new possibilities. It also can enhance your natural psychic gifts and help you listen to the call of nature.

Perhaps you'll notice an intimate moment between friends at a coffee shop, a feeling of pleasure in the sensation of a new fabric, a beautiful mosaic on an abandoned building, a quizzical pattern, the dusty pollen on a bee's legs as it moves from flower to flower. Noticing details about the natural world not only helps cultivate an awareness of one's exterior experience but also helps us become more in tune with and aware of our interior experience, too.

Supplies
Notebook (I personally love the Traveler's notebook from Japan, but a small composition notebook works just as well as any other.)
Pen

Step 1: Keep a Notebook

One simple way to cultivate curiosity is by keeping a notebook. It can be any size, brand, or type—although I'm partial to ones with refillable pages. We're so confined to and dependent on our phones that there's something freeing, and also inherently creative, about writing with pen and paper. Joan Didion once wrote in her famous essay "On Keeping a Notebook" that what is written inside the pages of a journal isn't for the world *out there*; it's meant for you and you alone.[57] It's about keeping a record of one's life, documenting fragments in time, in order to remember who you are and who you've been in order to inform who you'll become.

Step 2: Organize Your Notebook for Daily Life

The bullet journal method, as outlined by author Ryder Carroll, is a great way to organize a single notebook so everything lives in one place, rather than having separate ones for different purposes.[58] Organization can really help with creative flow, and the notebook functions like keeping a log, a record, of your daily life, whether it's a mix of your to-do lists, general observations, and daily journaling or it's rituals, dreams, mantras, and spellwork. Because of this, my notebook never leaves my side and is worth more to me than any bag or wallet with credit cards because all my observations, ideas, musings, loves, and lists are contained within its pages.

Step 3: Ditch the Phone and Take a Notebook

Take your notebook with you whenever you leave the house. Whenever possible, look for inspiration in the mundane. Go to a café and write down overheard conversations, record observations of the natural world,

57. Joan Didion, "On Keeping a Notebook," in *Slouching towards Bethlehem* (New York: Farrar, Straus, and Giroux, 1968; repr., New York: Picador Modern Classics, 2017), 203–5.

58. Ryder Carroll, *The Bullet Journal Method: Track Your Past, Order Your Present, Plan Your Future* (New York: Penguin, 2018).

draw pictures of tiny herbs and plants as you find them, or jot down incantations, mantras, recipes, prayers, and recipes. Stay open to writing down messages from that quiet, powerful voice inside you, which is your higher self, always ready and open to guide you if you take the time to listen.

INTEGRATIONS

Contrary to the cliché, curiosity never killed any cats (at least none that I've heard of). Each day there's something more to learn, something more to know. Most of us go about our daily, mundane tasks without thinking, without questioning them. For instance, when you're doing your dishes, stop to think about how the water arrived at your tap. Where does it come from exactly? How is that water processed and filtered? What about the wooden table where you eat breakfast? Where did the wood come from? Which kind of tree? Who created it? Consider your drinking glass, how it was shaped and molded by fire. Notice all the sacred elements that go into the products you use regularly, all the people who helped craft it, the necessary interconnectivity between each object, person, and action that made it come to life.

Stay curious about the world around you, even in the most mundane moments. Start with a question, however simple, and go out in search of the answer, I tell my students. Follow your curiosity and pay attention to what moves you.

CHAPTER 4

A CALLING FROM SPIRIT

Every place in the world, whether it's a house, school, landmark, restaurant, field, or highway, has its own unique energy, as noted in chapter 2, "The Energy Around You." Spaces harbor and hold energy over time—some are portals and some are more powerful or stronger than others. The more time you spend in a place (or the more sensitive or tuned in to its energies you are), the more likely you can tap into the spirits of place there. Eventually, the spirit world reveals itself in many ways throughout our lives. It can happen suddenly or subtly—a memory of a grandmother, a whisper, a whale that appears out of nowhere, a spirit animal crossing your path, or a direct whispering of Spirit coming through like a soft breeze or a gentle ocean wave.

We each have spirit guides that are meant to help us along our paths. Sometimes we have several guides who show up at different times of our life and intervene when presented with a direct request, prayer, or petition; sometimes they're energies as old as the earth itself, spirits who've been with you since before birth. They help us navigate the lines and thruways between what is seen and unseen.

And just like a radio signal, you have to make sure you're tapped into the right channel, to a higher frequency, and not a lower one. We each also have the ability to see beyond the veil of reality, to connect with the deeper spiritual currents around us, to hear the call of the spirit world. And you don't have to be a natural psychic to notice spirit messages, if you pay attention to their call. Sometimes, deities and ancient spirits of the earth, like the Goddess, will speak to us in novel ways. For many people, including myself, the spirits speak through the waters.

STORY: THE STREETS WERE PAVED WITH BONES
Cuba, 2017

Arriving in the colonial city of Trinidad in Cuba, with its notoriously preserved eighteenth- and nineteenth-century architecture, I was struck by something rather odd. After hours of driving from Havana, I stepped out onto the gnarled, beautiful, cobblestoned streets in the small town and felt a surge of memory, something indescribable that sticks with me even as I write this.

Despite its UNESCO World Heritage designation, I knew very little of the town before arriving. Sure, everyone has heard of the pulsing, vibrant energy of Havana, but Trinidad? It seemed like a forgotten place—typically mixed up in casual conversation with the other Caribbean nation. It was a place stuck in time, and very little had been updated over the last several hundred years, save for new coats of paint and minor government-funded restorations.

I went to Cuba with five others and we toured the island country in a 1960s blue van for ten days, staying in *casas particulares*, or local homes similar to Airbnbs run by individual hosts or families. These were a big deal for the local economy, only possible after the death of Fidel Castro. His brother, Raúl, succeeded him, and as the new president of the Communist Party, he was a bit more lenient with small, private businesses. Many Cubans, in fact, made more money opening their homes to guests and tourists than at their regular jobs as doctors, engineers, or professors. Since the average monthly salary was equivalent to about $30 USD, these private home stays allowed for both extra income and rare glimpses into the "outside world" as offered by the revolving door of travelers.

Placing my feet on the pavement of this ancient city, I was transported, as if something else was brewing just beneath its facade. I put the feeling of unease out of my mind as I entered the home of Elvis and Anna. Both professional engineers with multiple university degrees under their belt, they were welcoming and kind, if not a bit aloof in their demeanor. I sat in the open courtyard in the center of the house, smoking cigarettes and reading the local Cuban newspaper (a treat for an American journalist), while Elvis sat smoking his cigar. Between my baby Spanish and his fragmented English, we managed a few laughs and shared a few secrets in hushed tones. He had been a stark supporter of Fidel and the Revolution, but now in his old age, he was beginning to doubt it all. He explained how this "new business" of opening his casa particular brought in more income than he'd ever made throughout his life.

Despite the shifting political tides and renewed hope, there remained in the town a sense of secrecy and sadness. This feeling permeated the air itself and burrowed inside the chest like a dull, humming weight. On the afternoon of our arrival, I asked Elvis for a good spot for dinner. "People seem to love this one restaurant up on the hill. It's great food. But," he added with a touch of hesitation, "it's a bit strange. You'll see when you get there." I didn't know what he meant by those words, but "strange"? Sure, I'm down. Since it was recommended by the first local we met in this new city, we gathered our small group together and went up the cobblestone hill in search of it.

As I walked into the restaurant, a feeling of dread and suffocation came over me. It resonated in the walls and had little to do with the tropical heat. On the surface, the restaurant seemed lively, bustling with activity. I was surrounded by new friends and the prospect of a really good meal. What could possibly be bad about the place?

After looking at the menu (a bit lightheaded now), I finally took a long look around the dining room and felt a full shudder go through my body. "What exactly is that on the walls?" I asked our tour guide, a bubbly, free-spirited woman who made it her life's goal to show people the *real* Cuba—the Cuba that had been long blocked off for an entire generation of Americans. "Apparently, those are torture devices," she said. "They were used on the slaves brought here years ago. Trinidad was a major port city."

My brief research from weeks prior came flooding back. Trinidad was one of the biggest port cities in the Caribbean, known for its sugar cane and tobacco plantations, and that meant it was also the site of unfathomable atrocities during the transatlantic slave trade. Their main import? Human beings.

I sat staring dumbfoundedly down at the menu. Why would these items be on full display, as if they were trophies? Shouldn't they be stored away, covered up, or at the very least set behind glass in a museum somewhere as a reminder that history should not and would not repeat itself? Not mere relics or tchotchkes used as décor in an eating establishment in the year 2017?

I thought of the whitewashing of history in my own country and how in the United States we paint over (both literally and figuratively) the ugly, gruesome, terrifying parts of our past. But here in Cuba, that history is propped up as a reminder, as if to say, "Yes, pain, horrible pain, is also part of our story." I hurriedly ate the remnants of my meal and breathed a sigh of relief when the check came. I left the table in a hurry, eager for the fresh air, and walked ahead of the group.

The restaurant was perched on top of a hill deeply lined with cobblestones, and as I began walking back down, I had a vision. It came clear as day and was connected with the same feeling I had when I stepped out from the van for the first time hours before. I saw the street underneath me clearly, but I saw it was paved with bones. Actual human bones stretching down the length of the road. And then in an instant, the vision was gone. *The streets were paved with bones.*

I decided to keep my vision to myself. I didn't want to scare away my new traveling companions with psychic visions after all, and despite the bizarre choice of so-called décor in the restaurant, we *had* had a good meal. We were having a great time on the road trip overall. No need to ruin it with an intuitive, wacky vision, for God's sake. I just wanted to get back to the house and rest it off, hoping to put the vision out of my mind.

The next day, we embarked on an architectural tour around the city, led by a local man named Tom. Tom had lived in the town his entire life and only spoke Spanish. We stood on the street corner with him under the blazing midmorning sun, and he began the walking tour of his hometown with a statement that nearly made my knees buckle from under me.

"They say this town is cursed, that it is haunted. They say the city streets are paved with the bones of slaves under these cobbled stones."

Because Spanish isn't my first language, it took a second or two for his words to sink in. I turned to a fellow traveling companion who worked as a translator back in the US and asked her, "What did he just say?"

"He said…" She repeated it verbatim. I had understood him correctly.

The haunted feeling wasn't just me after all: the town of Trinidad ached, groaned even, with the weight of its history. And it was powerful. Powerful enough for me to feel it. Powerful enough to speak to me, to speak through me. It was a vision of the lives claimed by the insidious slave trade. The horror of greed and bloodshed, the horror of humanity. As if to say, "Look what happened here. Here's where their bones lie, deep within the earth. Look what mankind has done."

I walked under the August heat with a headache, self-conscious, groaning like Walt Whitman in Ginsberg's supermarket. Pig heads, bloody and blank eyed, hung on spikes outside shops. Dust circled in the air. Paint pigment glowed like neon in the sun. Something had brought me here. Something wanted me to come to this town. Something that I didn't understand until much later. The city wasn't done with its stories yet. It had something else to show me, too. It wanted its story to be told.

————

Near the Plaza Mayor, the architectural tour was nearly complete. When we stopped to explore a small outdoor market filled with trinkets, I noticed a soft blue and white house off the road and felt inextricably drawn to its open doors and dim interior. I asked my companion, "Can we go inside there?"

I didn't realize it before I walked in, but it was the Casa Templo de Santería Yemayá, dedicated to the Great Ocean Mother herself. In the Afro-Caribbean religion of Santería (or Lucumí), Yemayá is a powerful orisha associated with fertility, witchcraft, the moon, self-love, and healing (among other qualities). Her name, which translates from the Yoruba language to "the mother of the fish," has a variety of spellings and pronunciations depending on where she is celebrated and honored in the world, including Yemòja, Yemònja, and Iemanja. As one of the oldest and widely known orishas (powerful, primordial spiritual entities associated with the elements), Yemayá is known for her nurturing love, emotional healing, and protective energies. Her domain is not only the ocean but all water. Wherever there is water, there is Yemayá.

Cuba, like the majority of Latin America, was colonized by Catholic Spaniards, and anything that deviated from the grip of the Roman Catholic Church was outlawed. Like many religious or spiritual practices outside the dominant norm, Afro-Caribbean traditions (originally brought across the Atlantic by enslaved West Africans in the sixteenth century) had to be practiced in secret. These sacred, oral traditions and spiritual practices were syncretized with the established iconography of the Catholic Church, and over time, Yemayá's iconography merged with that of the Virgin Mary. Images of the Queen Mother of the Ocean, with her radiant dark skin rising from the ocean and shining under the moon, began to merge with Roman Catholic iconography of Our Lady of Regla. Both regal Mothers, queenly in blue and white dress, nurturing, protective, maternal, and holy.

This pushback on the old religions prevailed until fairly recent times, especially under the antireligion communist regime. It wasn't until 1990 that the Cuban government lifted their ban on Santeriá and house-churches, allowing for a semblance of religious tolerance. After that, the Afro-Cuban religion grew rapidly, and a year later the government officially recognized the Yoruba Cultural Center in Havana, which now has approximately 40,000 members (although that number does not account for the thousands of practitioners around the island and now the world).

As I walked into the temple, a singular doll with a jet-black face and red lips was positioned in the center of the room. It was dressed in all white and surrounded by images of fish, the moon, and the sea, and I knew then that it was the orisha Yemayá who'd brought me to Cuba. She was the reason I was there. She was the one who granted me the vision, as if to say, "Look what happened to my children. Here's where their bones lie, deep within the earth. Look what humanity has done." It was a vision of the same people who'd brought her stories over the Atlantic, the thousands, if not millions, of lives claimed by the slave trade.

Yes, I was an outsider, a foreigner, and not initiated in Lucumí, but like any spirit, goddess, or deity, Yemayá's energy wasn't limited or restricted. As Mother to All, her spirit transcends the labels and divisive illusions we tack onto things in order to make sense of the world. Yemayá is an orisha without borders or boundaries, yet she quietly showed me, a sound rising louder than the roar of the ocean: "Look at what they've done to my children." A mother's tears. The unseen world, the current of Spirit, connects us all.

Santería involves long-standing traditions and practices that must be properly observed and respected, yet anyone can embrace Yemayá in their individual practice. Sometimes, the spirit world wants us to bear witness, to use our psychic and intuitive gifts in unexpected ways.

The Great Mother Goddess has many, many names, forms, and faces across world cultures and defies any boundaries placed upon her. Various aspects of the Goddess figure appeared to me at different stages of my life, all with their own lessons to reveal. Some may consider the Goddess figure an archetype, an energy, or a literal being, but to me, they're all reflections of the one.

I first encountered Yemayá when I was a young witch in New York City many years ago and, later, at Enchantments. I've seen her work miracles for others, especially for those petitioning for help in conceiving a child or mending a broken heart. Some women who've never encountered Yemayá before in their lives seem to know her immediately once they learn of her and speak her name. And with all the spell candles I've carved for others, I've had more people come back with tears in their eyes, moved by the powerful transformations of their life, after invoking her, filled with a sense of compassion and reverence. I believe that if you ask for assistance, with a pure spirit and respect, the Great Mother comes to all those in need.

After visiting her temple in Cuba, I saw Yemayá everywhere: in the laughter of the people, in the Malecón in Havana, in the dew of the forest trees in Viñales, hiding behind the hopeful smiles around the family dinner tables. I didn't know back then that Yemayá's nurturing presence would take me to unknown places and faraway lands, guide me through major decisions in my life, ending some and starting others. I didn't know then that she would be there in times of need, quietly confronting and comforting me when I needed to remember my own power, my inner strength. I encountered her as an energy, as a force, as if she came from inside of me, like someone whom I've known since birth or perhaps even before birth. It was as if she tapped me on the shoulder and said, "Hey, remember me?"

When you hear the call of the spirits, sometimes you're asked to do more than just bear witness—sometimes it requires action, however small. A few years later, I went to Coney Island for the Fourth of July, the Cyclone, bustling boardwalk, and historical Parachute Jump looming in the background. I've always loved the unique kitschiness and nostalgia of Coney Island, its self-aware ridiculousness. The fact that it's still technically New York City, although it seemed a place unto itself entirely, is a comical anomaly that I revel in, but during public holidays the beach gets kind of wild. I spread out my blanket on the beach, as thousands of people nestled around me, cracking open beers, dancing on the sand, playing music, and waiting for the fireworks show to start. Everyone carved out a place for themselves, tiny microcosms of families and friend circles, and I marveled at it all in vague amusement.

Like most firework shows, it was unremarkable, but something shocking happened when it was over. After the fireworks ended, everyone simply got up and left—leaving all their belongings behind on the beach. Entire blankets, beach chairs, piles of canned beer, red plastic cups, leftover cutlery, all strewn in the same places their bodies once were, a mass exodus that nearly frightened me.

"How could everyone just leave their things like that on the beach?" I asked my companion, looking around at the near-empty beach littered with human profanity. "We are monsters," I thought. It looked like a postapocalyptic scene. Piles upon piles, heaps of trash, dotted nearly every few feet along the sand. To this day, I've never seen anything like it. My confusion slowly turned into anger at the piles of garbage on the beach. I walked to the edge of the water, where the waves were slowly rolling in, and looked up at the dark sky. Anger rose in my chest, and I waded out into the water, under the full embrace of the moon, and began to pray: "Yemayá, I'm so sorry. I'm sorry this has happened to your shores, that your waters will take this all in. Please forgive us all. What should I do?" Tears formed and rolled down my face like hot beads, and I felt her presence.

"Do what you can," I heard her whisper. "Take what you can."

However minute and insignificant, I knew what I had to do. I turned back to the beach and began gathering up the trash along the immediate shoreline, and it quickly turned into huge mounds. There was no way to get it all, even a small percentage of it, but a few pass-ersby handed me plastic bags to load the empty cans and bottles, and I worked for an hour or more in the night. Finally, I prayed to Yemayá again: "I'm sorry. Forgive us." I walked back to the boardwalk feeling ashamed at the carelessness with which we treat the ocean.

The lessons of the Ocean Goddess are very real. We oftentimes forget just how sacred water is, how our bodies, livelihoods, and well-being are directly connected to and dependent on this element. If we do not honor, revere, and reflect on its power, we're not only turning a blind eye to its endangerment but also neglecting our spiritual connection with water. By disregarding the lessons of the Ocean Mother, we're neglecting something sacred within us, too: when we pollute the water, we pollute ourselves. As within, so without. As above, so below.

DEEP DIVE: WATER AS A CONDUIT AND CHANNEL

The ocean is the birthplace of all life on this planet. It is our original womb, and although it makes up the majority of the planet and our bodies, we know more about the vast expanse of outer space than we do the ocean. Like our human potential and spiritual gifts, we've yet to fully explore the mysterious magic and untapped potential within its depths. And yet there are infinite lessons to be learned there.

We go to the sea to contemplate life's mysteries, to conjure a sense of peace, to acquire sustenance. Like space and the grand cosmos around us, the ocean is a reflection—a vast mirror—of our nature. On one level, the ocean reflects our life blood, our first beginning, our primordial beginning. On another level, it represents our subconscious, our emotional and mental planes, our untapped depths. On another, it represents our evolution and survival—without it, everything would cease.

As fecund and fertile as the ocean may be, churning out and harboring life, it has a twofold lesson for us. The ocean is both a life-giver and a life-destroyer: it creates life and can also take it away. Consider how salt water cleanses wounds, and yet it can wipe out entire towns in a single wave. We each hold these opposing powers within us. Some moments in life call for calm and reflection, periods of peace and nurturing, while others call for surrendering to abrupt change, giving way to grief and relinquishing control; other times, these lessons require invoking our raw power, tearing down walls, raging against faulty foundations, and building anew. Learning what to let go of or what to hold sacred is a continuous, circular lesson, one that we will confront over and over throughout our lives.

Still, the ocean reflects this unmitigated, all-encompassing power within us. It also reminds us of our own beautiful fragility, like standing at the bottom of a mountain and feeling impossibly small in the expanse of such wonder. Like trees, and all of nature, the ocean mirrors our spiritual life. While its depths contain countless mysteries, the ocean's surface is in constant motion and flux. Change is the only constant in this life, as with the sea.

Consider, also, the human body: the blood pulsing through your veins, carrying nutrients and cells to sustain every breath and heartbeat in this very moment is 90 percent water. We're made of this miraculous element, over 60 percent of our bodies, and it's an integral part of our everyday lives. Consider water's long, strange journey from space millions of years ago, crashing into our planet as cosmic ice chunks and burying itself in the earth, only to emerge much later as the ocean.

Many of us don't consider the incredible impact of this circular journey from the cosmos, nor water's cyclical journey everyday across the earth, its presence as clouds, tap water, bathwater, and snow. Whether we're drinking a glass of water or using it to bathe, we tend to forget how sacred it really is, assuming it will always be around.

We are no match for its fertile, forceful, awe-inspiring power, but like all life, water deserves the highest respect. It permeates nearly every corner of the planet, manifesting in new forms, always in constant flux and flow.

Think of the amniotic fluid that once supported us in the womb. Sacred water was present around us before we were born, protecting us, ensuring our growth. What we've done to water, in terms of pollution and neglect, has a correlation to our spiritual health. The more we think of it as merely a resource to use up for our benefit, the more disconnected we'll become with our higher essence. Not only are we putting our physical existence and future livelihood in danger, but deep down, we're unknowingly severing our connection with our First Mother, our primordial start, our original womb. We must remember where we came from, in order to know where we're going. Do we really need a cataclysmic climate crisis to remind us of the things we've always known?

Water is a link between worlds; it's the thread that binds us together. Nearly every culture across the globe has rituals, myths, and deities connected to the element of water. Belief in water spirits, entities, energies, and sacred water sites has persisted throughout millennia, most of which has been passed down in oral traditions or sublimated into sacred statues, symbols, rituals, and the written word. The Ocean Goddess, a Mother Goddess and deeply feminine source, one whose fecundity engenders an endless variety of new life, is often seen as the Great Womb. We see this in spiritual traditions throughout history: the creative, nourishing, loving, yet wrathful and vengeful energy of the Ocean Mother shows up cross-culturally in many forms, going by many names, but her essence remains the same.

Esoterically, and in contemporary witchcraft, water is also placed in the west. When one is invoking and working with the elements, water is symbolically placed in this cardinal direction, a place of frontiers and sunsets, memory and emotion. We can use water as an element to hear the call of spirits, to tap into the language of our ancestors, spirit guides, and ancient earth spirits. Since water connects us all, it's also a conduit for the spirit world.

And each body of water, whether it's a freshwater stream, a churning waterfall, a tepid puddle, a vast blue lake, a blue-green saltwater expanse, or a deep well, has its own distinct energy and presence. As you approach each body of water, stay open to the distinct energies you encounter and insights you receive. Tune in to the energy there, like a radio dial in your mind, staying open to what it wants to share.

WORKING WITH WATER

Water is often connected to our emotions, memory, and subconscious, and like the element of earth, it can be a conduit to access insights from Spirit. The following are techniques for working with the sacred element of water as a tool for purification, insight, transformation, and release.

Technique: Water as Purification

In many world religions, water is seen as a tool or vessel for purification. In Catholicism, for instance, holy water is water that has been blessed by a priest, but we also have the power to sanctify and bless water using our own sacred energies. Whether you're using spring water, filtered tap water, ocean water, or rainwater, focus your intention on the glass and psychically send the water pure loving energy. Focus on showering the water (pun intended) in a clarifying, cleansing light. Next, focus on imbuing the water with a higher vibratory intention. This could be the essence of love, joy, beauty, happiness, and so on. Here you can do the light meditation as outlined in chapter 2, and then rub your hands briskly together to gather energy between your palms and hover them above the glass, sending this purifying energy from your hands into the cup. You can also say a prayer, perhaps from the book of Psalms, over the water. Bottle it in a glass bottle (not plastic). Use your holy water to cleanse your forehead, wrists, face, and hands before beginning ritual or meditation work, add it to ritual baths, use it to spray the corners and entrances of your home, or add it to a vinegar solution with a few drops of essential oil for a home cleaning solution.

Technique: Water as Insight and Awareness

The act of going to water, whether it's a river stream, mountain lake, ocean, or backyard well, can be a ritual used to help us tap into our intuition, higher calling, and spiritual purpose. Being in close proximity with this element brings us closer to our roots, granting interior illumination, rest, insight, and even prophecy. When you go to the water's edge or take a ritual bath, take time to listen, immerse yourself in the moment, and stay open to what unfolds within and before you. Answers and insights from Spirit can come in the form of a hushed whisper; a hum deep in your belly; a quiet, slow, unveiling of internal *knowing*; or a sudden flood of insight.

Technique: Water as Emotional Release

Like the Earth Mother, the nurturing power of the Ocean Goddess can help us release unwanted emotions, pent-up rage, melancholia, and disappointment. When you get into a bath or submerge yourself in the sea, focus on letting go and releasing that which no longer serves you. Visualize these emotions (that probably center around your chest, neck, and hip areas) moving out through your limbs and flowing into the water to be cleansed and purified, or even letting your tears, like tiny particles of experience, messages of your body, hit the surface to be carried away.

Technique: Water as Physical Release

Many of us store our emotions, especially grief, in the hips and womb area, which is a watery center. In yoga, not only do hip openers help release tension on a physical level, but you may also find yourself releasing intense emotion at the same time. My favorite poses for emotional release, especially unprocessed grief and sadness, are the happy baby pose, pigeon pose, and lizard pose. You may be surprised to find yourself in tears (ideally not from physical pain!) after doing these poses for several minutes.

Technique: Water as a Conduit for Spiritual Knowledge

As an ancient, primordial gift from the cosmos, once showering down as ice chunks billions of years ago, water holds the memory of time itself.

When you're submerged in water, focus on tapping into the memory of the water and its journey throughout time. Focus on its expansion, its cyclical journey, its amorphous qualities, and dormant stories. Ask the water to reveal to you its secrets, to share its stories, to reveal sacred insights.

Technique: Commune with Water Spirits

Since each body of water contains its own spiritual energies, every water site has something to reveal. Take a hiking day trip near a river or natural lake, and with each stream you come across, sit quietly near the bank, empty your mind, and focus on the various psychic cues you may receive. Perhaps there's a childlike quality there, similar to faery beings, or it's a sweeping feminine force, or it's a calming, grounding presence. If it's a negative or heavy feeling in any way, just keep moving, but if it's a playful, loving, or peaceful energy, stay awhile and open yourself to any messages you receive in these moments. You should feel a sense of lightness or rising clarity. You may also notice a simple yet spectacular sight, like the swooping of a particular bird, or other natural signs (gifts) that were meant for you in that moment.

Technique: Pray Near a Natural Body of Water

A spell is a prayer, a prayer is a spell. A prayer is a petition to the universe. To pray is to seek the wisdom of the Creator and the Great Goddess, to start a conversation with the Divine. A prayer can also be a conversation with your higher self or a petition to the spirit world for assistance. Through prayer, we open up a channel, a direct current, to the higher energies around us, and when done with a pure heart and with humility, our prayers are always answered. Ask and you shall receive—if you listen long enough, the answers will come. Maybe they come from inside you—from that deep part of your higher self that always knows what to do, but trust that they will come. And I promise you, one way or another, they always come.

Technique: Rules of the Game

Here are some important tips and rules when you engage water in your spiritual practice.

Know the Spiritual History

All water sites are accessed first by land. Before starting any spiritual work with a body of water, find out the history of the land you're standing on, getting to know the names of estuaries, streams, rivers, or bodies of water connected to it. Look into the local histories, legends, and cultural traditions of the area. Be sure to pay homage to the Indigenous histories of the area, paying respect to the people and spirits of the land. Part of honoring the Divine in us is also honoring and learning from the Divine inherently present in nature, as well as respecting the land and people who've helped cultivate it.

Do your research into deities and spirits before working with them. And before petitioning spirits at a water site, psychically tap into the existing energies of that place first to get a sense of it. What are the land and sea telling you at that moment? Pay attention to your feelings, thoughts, and emotions as you read the energy before you invoke anything.

Respect Cultural Surroundings

Let's face it: we live in a post-post-colonial world, and the concept of private property is enforced in most places. While the earth belongs to all of us, it's not wise to trespass on other people's land without their permission. But higher than that, if you're performing spells or petitioning spirits at a water site, respect the spirits and deities and cultures that are already a part of that area, specifically those of Indigenous peoples. We don't want to use magic to recolonize sacred spaces, but rather *decolonize* them, and that includes not imposing our own traditions in places that have their own unique spiritual energy and history.

Practice Earth Stewardship

Don't bring plastics or non-biodegradable products to sacred sites—and everywhere on earth is sacred—and leave them around as trash. It's a good way to anger the spirits, plus it's just outright bad form. We can and should all try to do better, in the little and big ways we can. As with any spiritual practice (or just being a good human being), if you bring objects to water sites, especially if they didn't come from that specific place, take them back with you.

There are exceptions to this, however, as I know some magical practitioners who regularly leave offerings of flowers, fruits, and sacred foods—everyone's spiritual practices and traditions and beliefs are slightly different—so use your best judgment, trust your instinct and gut, and pay attention to the signs. You'll know what's right at the moment. Do what thou wilt, but harm none.

Look for Symbols and Metaphors

The waters are abundant and rife with symbolism and metaphors that can help us on our spiritual journey. If you keep encountering certain animals while you're near a body of water, consider what message that animal is bringing to you. These messages may be callings from a deity or other spirit.

Here's a simple example: I was recently standing in the river with a woman who was mildly stung by a jellyfish. Frustrated, she said, "This is the second time this month that I've gotten stung. Why does this keep happening to me?"

I asked her if there were, perhaps, lessons to be found in the recurrence of the presence of the jellyfish in her life right now. "Are you struggling—at work or at home—with going with the flow of things and letting go of control? Do you feel like there's a tension between defending yourself (perhaps with biting remarks) and accepting things as they are? Are you struggling to find empowerment in some way?" The jellyfish, flexible and flowing, moves with the currents of the sea, amorphous and never rigid. It seems defenseless, but it's not—with one touch of its ten-drils, it deters predators with a lingering sting.

This comment, in fact, opened up a deeper discussion into her inner life and current struggles; the lesson of the jellyfish was to learn to embrace change and fluidity, to let go of rigid or outworn structures, while also remembering to stand her ground (a.k.a. sting when you have to defend yourself). The world is brimming with symbols and lessons, even in the form of animal encounters, if only we stay open to the signs and consider their lasting imprint.

PRACTICE:
TAPPING INTO SPIRIT AND ACCESSING SPIRIT COMMUNICATION

We all have psychic ability—it may just come easier for some. Like any muscle, it can be trained and built up, but the first step is acknowledging the power of our own intuition and inner sight. We've all had gut feelings before, or the ability to read someone's energy before they've even opened their mouth to reveal themselves. That's our spiritual energy, our life force, our divine gift.

The mind is the filter we use to understand and make sense of the "nature of reality," guiding us along in necessary, fundamental ways, but we need Spirit in order to *live*; it's our invisible essence and true identity. To access the greater, mystical, magical force of the universe and its mysteries, we can access and communicate with the spirit world anytime.

The following technique may help you access spirit communication and divine wisdom, as well as receive messages from your spirit guides or God/Goddess, depending on what is in your practice.

Supplies
½ cup of sea salt (not table salt)
Paper
Pen

Purple (for wisdom or divine guidance) or white candle. For a shorter
ritual, use a small pillar candle (2" × 3" or 2" × 6"), which will burn for
between 5 and 7 hours; for a weeklong ritual, use a pull-out candle,
which will burn for 7 to 10 days.
Tarot or oracle deck

Step 1: Begin the Work
If it's in your practice, time your ritual according to the lunar cycle. Begin
at the new moon, which is a good time for new beginnings and receiving
wisdom.

Step 2: Take a Ritual Bath
Add a half or cup of sea salt to a warm bath. This helps cleanse and purify
your aura and energy before beginning your ritual magic. However, you
don't have to do this every time you relight the candle after that.

Step 3: Focus on a Specific Intention for Your Ritual
Write down a specific intention for your ritual on a piece of paper (something simple, like "I seek wisdom from my higher self" or "I want to
channel the divine energies present within me" or "I'd like to channel
messages from my spirit guides"). Speak your intention aloud and place
the paper underneath the candle.

Step 4: Light the Candle
Focus your intention and light the candle. As it burns, sit with the burning flame for fifteen to thirty minutes each day. Remember not to leave
a candle burning unattended. Light and relight each day until it's completely burned out.

Step 5: Pull a Daily Tarot or Oracle Card
Each day while the candle burns, pull one card from a tarot deck with
the intention of unlocking hidden wisdom and receiving a daily message
from your spirit guides or a close deity. Perhaps it's to reveal something

you've been overlooking, a part of yourself that you've been neglecting, or an aspect of your psyche or daily life that needs attention and intention.

Step 6: Interpret Each Card Accordingly

Even if you aren't an expert at tarot, that's okay. Let your intuition guide you when analyzing the card. Notice the different symbols on the card, the details, the colors, and the suit. As a general tip, wands represent matters of the spirit, magic, and the self or ego; pentacles represent financial matters and effort or labor; swords represent matters of intellect, words, logic, and conflict; cups represent emotion, relationships, and creativity. See how the meaning of the card may apply to your everyday life, and consider what it represents and what Spirit may be trying to tell you through the symbols within the card. If you choose to work with an oracle deck, there's typically a mantra written underneath. Write it down and see how the mantra influences your day and perspective.

Step 7: Stay Open to the Messages You Receive

As the candle burns each day, write down the images and words that come to you. Or try a stream of consciousness writing exercise while focusing on the flame. Don't focus on grammar or making logical sense—no one will read this but you; don't judge or censor yourself. Once the candle is completely burned down, re-read your notes over the week and notice any patterns, nuggets of wisdom, or insights that came to you—or through you—at that time.

INTEGRATIONS

Some people believe that you need to be a skilled psychic to hear the call of the Divine or spirits. That is not the case. We're all a little psychic, and there are many ways we can improve our abilities. Listening to our inner voice, noting our dreams, staying open to the gifts of the natural world, honoring the sensations of our bodies (i.e., our gut instincts), and simply paying attention are enough. Staying open and believing that the universe has your back and wants to communicate with you is a great start for opening these channels. But I've also found that sometimes the spirit world won't directly interfere or intervene unless you ask for it. Acknowledging that there's more at work than what meets the eye and holding an intention of tapping into these higher callings and vibrations are the only real tools you need to train your inherent psychic gifts.

It's also true that some have stronger psychic gifts than others and can tune in to the spirit world more readily, but many, many more have untapped potential, and some may even turn away from this inherent ability. We're here on Earth to use our gifts, all our gifts, however difficult they might be to endure or even tame. If you're given the gift of sight, psychic abilities, or deep intuition, do not turn away from it or shun it. For some, it might be a lifelong process to come to terms with the fact that they are even gifts at all, since it can sometimes feel like a heavy burden to bear. As long as we remain balanced, grounded, and connected to the physical and sensorial planes and we petition with a pure heart, the calling of Spirit can only enhance our life. Remember that it is your birthright and first language.

CHAPTER 5

THE POWER OF MYTH, STORYTELLING, AND RITUAL

Storytelling has been the greatest currency and perhaps the most valuable exchange we've ever made as a species. Stories are the powerfully rich threads that bind us together and weave into the collective tapestry of our social fabric. They reveal the hidden chambers of our subconscious and inner life, while shedding light on what it means to be human.

Stories, in short, teach us how to live. They're like lampposts in the night, guiding us along, sometimes with teachings from those who've walked before us long ago. They contain messages of the past and glimpses of our future. As children, we relished in bedtime stories and became enraptured in fairy tales, begging for just one more story until we could barely keep our eyes open. We craved the adventures, the far-away places, not knowing tiny lessons—like seeds of new life—were also being planted in those moments. At some point, for some reason, we put those stories away in the name of adulthood. We grew up and left those fairytales behind, packing away the breadcrumbs of the forest and forgetting the enchanted gardens. But we really never truly forget them.

Our own personal stories—the ones shared by family, the lessons of survival taught by aunties, parents, and grandparents, even the secret scandals spoken in hushed tones—define us, too. We pass them on, they live within us and emerge in fascinating ways throughout our life. The stories we are told and tell shape our value systems and form the lens through which we view the world. "We tell ourselves stories in order to live," wrote the essayist Joan Didion.[59] We need stories to survive, and we each have a story to tell, but storytelling requires introspection and vulnerability, qualities that are also an essential part of embarking upon any spiritual or magical quest. And magic, like writing, is not a scientific process.

Oral storytelling and rituals have been a part of our human ancestry since the very beginning; they are the vessels in which to share sacred knowledge, transmit culture, and remember history. Myths are not only built into the foundation of our human culture, but they are also the source wells of imagination and inspiration, from which all human achievement flows. "It would not be too much to say that myth is the secret opening through which the inexhaustible energies of the cosmos pour into human cultural manifestation," the great mythologist and scholar Joseph Campbell once wrote.[60] What he calls the "magic ring of myth" gives rise to new ideas in virtually every field—science, philosophy, the arts—and it's through the circularity of the myth that we catch glimmers of truths, truths often obscured by, and yet perceived through, both symbol and metaphor.[61]

Myth simply means story. Stories, like tiny breadcrumbs scattered throughout place and time, mark a path to show us where we've been, where we're going, and who we are. Myths teach us how to live, shedding light on what lies within the inner recesses of the unconscious mind, revealing our true nature, and the death-rebirth cycle. Even a child's fairy tale contains a certain map of wisdom: "The happy ending of the fairy tale, the myth, the divine comedy of the soul, is to be read, not as a

59. Joan Didion, *The White Album* (New York: Farrar, Straus and Giroux, 1979), 11.

60. Joseph Campbell, *The Hero with a Thousand Faces*, commemorative ed. (Princeton: Princeton University Press, 2004), 3.

61. Campbell, *The Hero with a Thousand Faces*, 3.

contradiction, but as a transcendence of the universal tragedy of man," Campbell wrote.[62] Stories are maps, pointing the way toward a kind of transcendence, through a series of trials and errors, battles and endings, however seemingly simple they may appear.

Wisdom can also be conveyed through conscious ritual, or the retelling of myth. We see the power of ritual in so many ways, including organized religion, but we've somehow lost our connection to nature-based rituals along the way. We forget that by reconnecting with the earth, we reconnect with Spirit. We were all once nomadic people roaming the earth, listening to the rhythms and whispers of nature, marking time by the rotations and cycles of each season. Eventually, after we mastered the art of fire, using it to cook our food and protect us from predators, we began settling around that fire to share stories—through language, dance, song. We used the fireside to reconnect with our communities in deeper ways, without the distractions of daily duties; we used the fire to reconnect with Spirit.

Storytelling, as one of the oldest and most pervasive rituals, traverses time, space, and geography. Ritual storytelling is an act of not only remembering but *re-membering*—that is, putting things back together again. So much of our sacred histories, rituals, and mystical practices have been lost to time, cut out and trampled on, condemned by corrupt men to service their own power within patriarchal systems, or in the so-called name and service of God. Just think of all the precious gems of history and wisdom of the ages lost at the Library of Alexandria, the nature-based wisdom found in pagan practices that was subverted and demonized during the Crusades and Inquisition, the attempted destruction of culture and spiritual traditions of enslaved Africans during the transatlantic slave trade, the attempted annihilation of the sacred Jewish traditions during the Holocaust, the repression and near eradication of Indigenous American traditions. The list goes on. Entire languages have been wiped away, women's histories dismantled, Goddess worship and

---

62. Campbell, *The Hero with a Thousand Faces*, 26.

the Divine Feminine subsumed by male-centric religions, the healing powers of the earth (herbs, plants, and medicine) expunged and blotted out by the large pharmaceutical companies.

When individuals or entire power systems seek to erase stories and the sacred, mystical, and cultural power they hold, a literal and psychic silencing occurs. This can result in a kind of collective trauma, the symptoms of which can be seen in divisionist rhetoric, separatism, hate, and the disintegration of our connection to the land. And the latter effect is currently leading to the critical endangerment of the planet itself.

In order to help heal the planet and each other, in order to combat cultural degeneration, we need ritual and storytelling more than ever. We must remain curious about the past and stay open to the stories of others, including our own. Mythologies and folklore hold the key to a deeply embedded yet often hidden truth; they teach us not only how to survive, but how to live well. True healing is possible when the wisdom of our ancestors and of all the ancient ones who've walked before us are consciously integrated back into the social and spiritual fabric.

STORY: THE SACRED MOʻŌLELO

Hawaii, 2020

The Indigenous Hawaiians are no strangers to the attempt at cultural erasure. Starting in 1896, after the overthrow of the Hawaiian Kingdom by the American government, the teaching and learning of the Hawaiian language was banned in schools. This also included *hula*, a sacred dance used as a form of ancestral storytelling. In many ways, this was an intentional effort to eradicate the sacred customs, rituals, and *moʻōlelo* (stories) of the Hawaiian people. It wasn't until the 1970s during the Hawaiian Renaissance, a political and cultural movement led by key figures such as Edith Kanakaʻole, that this law was finally reversed.

When I first met Micah Kamohoalii, a *kumu hula*, community leader, and ancestor of Kanakaʻole, in Hawaii's Waipiʻo Valley in early 2020, he shared intimate stories of this lineage, as well as how storytelling informs ethos and genealogy. "Our stories teach us the laws of the land and remind us how to behave as people. Our stories are a road map. Stories tell us what is righteous, what is sacred," Micah told me. Hawaiian genealogy and storytelling are deeply interwoven, and many origin stories of deities can be traced back to ancestral ties of notable community members, as well as the Hawaiian people as a whole.

Nearly every culture around the world has their own unique myths, legends, and origin stories, all of which are based on oral traditions that bridged the past and present. These stories inform us of who we are, how we should live, and where we come from. But for the Indigenous Hawaiian people, these stories are not myths or legends but living, historical truths that are integrated into their daily lives, ancestry, belief systems, and spiritual practices.

Moʻōlelo, or stories, are an integral part of their social, cultural, and spiritual fabric. "We use the word *moʻōlelo*, or the history of how we became, since the word *myth* kind of implies something is fabricated or a fable," he said. "When we say this land or mountain that we're fighting for is our ancestor, our *kupuna*, we're literally saying it's our ancestor. It's the same grandmother we were born from. The taro plant is not just our staple food; it's our grandparent. These stories lay the foundation for who we are, and they continue on and remind us who we are." In this earth-worshiping society, Micah explained that the elemental forces are considered the body forms and manifestations of the Hawaiian gods.

Micah, an effervescent personality and respected community leader, spent the next couple of days sharing his family's customs and stories with a particular joy that stayed with me long after I left the island. Despite the fact that I was a *haole* (a foreigner), the family welcomed me with open arms, eager to share their unique perspective of the world. After I met with Micah during one of his private hula practices, he invited me to join him the next day for a ritual. I journeyed up the mountainside in the back of their family's pickup truck in the midafternoon, the verdant green expanse of the island stretching out as we rose higher, the horizon coming into focus. We settled on a grassy knoll, and I watched as the family began to dance, calling to the elements and their *kupuna* (ancestors), chanting to the earth and wind. There was an electricity in the air as they performed their sacred hula dances on the mountain slope in unison, recreating their creation stories through sound and movement. As the wind picked up, the elements seemed to respond to their call.

Hula is based on moʻolelo, and it's the physical representation of those stories, passed down and performed so the next generation can keep it going. Hula allows for the flow and transmission of *mana*, or sacred life force, and both the performer and observer can tap into that higher, healing frequency. "You can't live in that space all the time," Micah said, "but we can enter that realm and be able to connect with ancestors, and the winds, and the rains, and the trees."

In our talks, Micah recounted the Hawaiian creation stories, their sacred genealogy, beginning first with the God of the Sky and Heavens, Wākea, and the Earth Mother Goddess, Papahānaumoku. "*Papa* means 'surface of the earth' or things that are flat," he said. "*Hāna* means 'to give birth,' and *moku* means 'island,' which literally means 'Papa who gives birth to the islands.' Wākea, which means 'expanse of the sky,' meets Papa, and they mate." Their first child becomes a celestial deity, named Hoʻohokukalani, which means "the one who makes the stars." Papa and Wākea then give birth to Mauna Kea (the tallest mountain in the world when measured from its base beneath the ocean to its peak), and this sacred mountain is considered an ancestor, a deity, born with the island itself.

Wākea then decides to sleep with Hoʻohokukalani, but since Wākea took his daughter to bed instead of his wife, the child was stillborn and returned back to its grandmother, the earth goddess Papahānaumoku, and was buried in her body. This child eventually grew to become the taro plant, or *kalo*, the sacred food staple of the Hawaiian people. "From that grave, the taro grew," Micah explained. When the God of the Sky and Hoʻohokukalani mated again, they produced a human child, the first human, who was named *Hāloa*, which means "the long breath." But Hāloa was born with a defect: he didn't have magical powers and couldn't control the rains or earth or stars.

"The oldest in the family is considered more sacred because they have more responsibility. It's their job to make sure that the family is fed and the children are taken care of because the parents are working," said Micah. "It's the same thing in our stories—the first child died and became the food to feed all the rest of the siblings that followed." In this sense, the eldest also becomes responsible for passing on the spiritual teachings of the family. Ancestral reverence is built into the fabric of the culture, as Hawaiians know they are part of a larger, interdependent continuum.

Stories and rituals indeed hold tremendous power—and it's these stories that not only have shaped the cultural and spiritual identity of the Hawaiian people but also contain vital lessons for us all on how we can live consciously, treat the earth with respect, and take care of each other. Being with Micah and his family, I couldn't help but think how much better humanity would be if everyone understood even a fraction of these lessons: that the earth is a sacred, conscious, living being.

DEEP DIVE: BEARING WITNESS

Among the most famous sayings from ancient Greece, inscribed on the Temple of Apollo at Delphi, were the words *Know thyself*. In Greece's golden age, a time imbued with architectural, artistic, mathematical, and literary triumphs, *knowing thyself* was a philosophical pinnacle. Yet we can only truly know ourselves through the lens of the other—that is, we need others in order to recognize ourselves and to see ourselves clearly. The macrocosm of society mirrors and projects back the microcosm of the self.

To know oneself requires language—a medium of exchange, a vessel for communication. It requires narrative and reason. It also requires remembrance, continuity, and *re-membering* the past. But when the continuity of language and storytelling is severed, we are left psychically injured, cut off from invaluable, invisible parts of ourselves and the value of our shared histories.

Simply look at the devastating spiritual and physical effects of the erasure of women's histories, BIPOC histories, or any marginalized group of people who've suffered by the hands of those in power. It's been a systemic and systematic erasure, one that has led to silencing, disconnection, and violence. And from that, there's also been a kind of severance—a severance or shattering of identity, voice, and power.

To erase and shatter the collective and individual narrative stories of others, to destroy culture, is the worst kind of evil. It aims to strike down and annihilate humanity itself. The Holocaust, which happened not that long ago, was a vile attempt to not only destroy Jewish bodies but also stamp out their very humanity through the attempted erasure of their culture, stories, and identity.

When the ability to know or share one's story is severed—when our shared mythologies are erased—there you will find trauma and disconnection. And when one does not have the narrative means to *share* their experience (due to subjugation, erasure, censorship, etc.), it becomes an issue of survival. Storytelling is more than just a pastime, it's also a means of survival.

Dr. Dori Laub, a trauma researcher, Holocaust survivor, and former clinical professor in Yale University's Department of Psychiatry, spent years interviewing Holocaust survivors and their children to understand the multifaceted impact of massive trauma.[63] In *Trauma: Explorations in Memory*, Laub writes that survivors of the Holocaust needed to survive so that they could tell their stories, but they also *needed to tell their stories in order to survive*: "There is, in each survivor, an imperative need to tell and thus come to know one's story, unimpeded by ghosts from the past against which one has to protect oneself. One has to know one's buried

---

63. "Dori Laub M.D.," Trauma Research, Yale University, accessed June 4, 2024, https://traumaresearch.yale.edu/dori-laub-md.

truth in order to be able to live one's life."[64] Turns out, storytelling—that is, sharing a coherent narrative of one's experience—is paramount and integral to survival. Storytelling, whether through ritual, writing, dance, or art, is also known to help foster and develop empathy (see chapter 7, "The Healing Power of Art and Color").

For survivors of trauma, according to Laub, *not telling* one's story can serve as a perpetuation of its tyranny: "The events become more and more distorted in their silent retention and pervasively invade and contaminate the survivor's daily life."[65] Our concepts of self are dependent on the stories we tell ourselves and others, but when "one's history is abolished, one's identity ceases to exist as well."[66] And under extreme traumatic conditions, memories can be displaced in the brain.

Think of the brain like a filing cabinet with millions of different folders. Normal, everyday memories are stored in these folders, and they all make up a larger whole—that is, the brain. But traumatic memories lack a traditional folder; there's quite literally no place for them to go in the filing cabinet, so they become disassociated. Since some traumatic memories can't be integrated into the brain's existing schemas, they can become dissociated and removed from conscious awareness.[67]

This phenomenon also extends to society at large, where atrocities of the past are buried under forgotten rubble, washed away, covered up, and hidden. Yet they're still there. We have been in a state of crisis for quite some time, and societal issues were exacerbated in the wake of the global pandemic. We see the symptoms of it through social and political divisions, racial disparities, religious intolerance, violations of human rights, economic iniquities, mental health issues, and gun violence. We

64. Dori Laub, "Truth and Testimony: The Process and the Struggle," in *Trauma: Explorations in Memory,* ed. Cathy Caruth (Baltimore, MA: Johns Hopkins University Press, 1995), 61, 63.

65. Laub, "Truth and Testimony," 64.

66. Laub, "Truth and Testimony," 67.

67. Bessel A. van der Kolk and Onno van der Hart, "The Intrusive Past: The Flexibility of Memory and the Engraving of Trauma," in *Trauma: Explorations in Memory*, ed. Cathy Caruth (Baltimore, MA: Johns Hopkins University Press, 1999), 158–82.

are hurting. We are calling out for answers. We have stopped listening to the earth, stopped listening to our inner voice, and turned away from our inner wisdom and the lessons of the past.

Dr. Wendy Griffin, a professor of women's studies, once wrote that "mythos, then, may be partially understood as a cultural vision of the world, one which 'links the individual self to the larger morphological structure' of society. [But] if not reinforced through the regular performance of religious ritual, myths run the danger of being forgotten or reduced to 'mere' literature or art" and risk losing their "vitality when they fail to reinforce the link between the self and the experience [of the] world."[68] We must then not only create space to remember but also create a revitalized mythos, one that links that past and present and is remembered through ritual. But as we create new standards for living, thinking, and being, there is bound to be tension in the process.

This is where both storytelling and bearing witness come into play: in trauma studies, part of the recovery process is the *reintegration of memory* into normal brain schemas.[69] That is, giving language to memories and stories. By remembering the past and reintegrating ritual and narrative, we can help heal ourselves and others. This is true not just for victims of trauma but also for the planet at large, for every inhabitant.

The reintegration of myth, ritual, spirituality, nature-based practices, and remembering is imperative; it's essential to our intellectual, emotional, psychic growth and our survival as a species. Just as we are "well advised to keep on nodding terms with the people we used to be," as Joan Didion once wrote in her famous essay, we must also keep on nodding terms with the stories of the past—both individual and collective, lest they become ghosts and come "hammering on the mind's door at 4 a.m. of a dark night and demand to know who deserted them, who betrayed them, who is going to make amends."[70]

---

68. Wendy Griffin, "The Embodied Goddess: Feminist Witchcraft and Female Divinity," *Sociology of Religion* 56, no. 1 (1995), 39, https://doi.org/10.2307/3712037.

69. Van der Kolk and van der Hart, "The Intrusive Past," 158–82.

70. Didion, "On Keeping a Notebook," 203–5.

It is through storytelling and the act of remembering (or re-membering, a.k.a. putting things back together again) that one can create a bridge between the past, present, and future. The act of remembering creates a bridge between this world and the next—that is, the physical world and the ethereal—and unites the past, present, and future. While we shouldn't live entirely in the past (or the future), memories and stories have a way of transcending the present, creating continuity between worlds.

In many ways, we are all survivors. Some journeys are more intensely difficult than others, yet everyone has their own unique experience and threshold for pain. There's no hierarchy for pain; there's no singular badge for suffering. There's no way to know what one experience may do to another or how they might react—and what might be traumatic for one person may not result in the same thing for another. We do not know each other's individual experience of the world, and this is why we must show compassion.

One possible solution to such mass suffering is bearing witness to the stories of others. By listening to the stories of others (openly, without judgment), sharing ours, and making space for one another, we are effectively rebuilding a continuity with the past and helping each other re-member who we are. And we need each other for this process of healing. "No man is an island, / Entire of itself; / Every man is a piece of the continent, / A part of the main," wrote the poet John Donne.[71]

But we must also be careful not to be a "false witness," a term used by Robert Jay Lifton, a distinguished American psychiatrist who studies memory and the effects of political violence and war.[72] False witnessing plays into false notions of the past and replays them as truths. It can contribute to collective delusion, where culture is literally shaped by misinterpretations of the past. Women's history, for example, has been plagued by misinterpretations of the past; the weight of the patriarchy has molded

---

71. John Donne, "No Man Is an Island," All Poetry, accessed June 2, 2024, https://all poetry.com/No-man-is-an-island.

72. Cathy Caruth, "An Interview with Robert Jay Lifton," in *Trauma: Explorations in Memory*, ed. Cathy Caruth (Baltimore, MA: Johns Hopkins University Press, 1995), 138–44.

history to its likeness, a deformed delusion, creating a subversion of literal and spiritual truths. We see the proliferation of false witnessing today across social media and news, in the repetition of vacuous images and placeholders for substance. We see it doled out in hateful rhetoric, in the emotional manipulation of the masses, in the clickbait culture that lines corporate pockets.

When bearing witness to others and to ourselves, we must dig deep to perceive truths, but we also must maintain a sense of rationale and healthy barriers. Just as there's always learning to be done, there's always *unlearning* to be done, too.

We must unlearn the tale that we are merely consumers living in a physical body; we must unlearn that we are separate from nature and each other. And just as importantly, we must also listen to our inner voice and innate wisdom for answers. Turning inward—that is, looking into the microcosm of the mind and spirit to see what truth and beauty we can siphon from the depths—is just as valuable as what's going on *out there* in the macrocosm.

WORKING WITH SACRED STORIES TO REENCHANT LIFE

Reintegrating narrative (or stories) within our lives not only helps with trauma but also allows us to fully integrate the connection between the body and spirit

Technique: Star Magic

We all, quite literally, come from the stars. Nearly every element in the human body—our skin, organs, hair—every part of us was once a part of a blazing star. It's wild to really think about, but we all once came from a powerful supernova that occurred many, many eons ago. Interestingly enough, as Micah explained, the Hawaiian people have known this for thousands of years: the Star Goddess gave birth to the first human.

Candle magic can help us remember the eternal fire within us, brimming in our cells, from the stars. Take a white candle (or gold or yellow) made from beeswax or soy, and using a dull knife, carve the symbol of a star in the center. You can also use a pencil to carve out the star, if you're not comfortable using a knife. It can be any star you like, a five-pointed star or a simple burst of rays. Now, draw a symbol of a crown above the star, representing your divine power. As the candle burns, imagine the light of the flame unlocking the same fire within you, one that is pure magic, remembering your original state as once part of a blazing star, imbued with power. Remember that you are both part of the cosmos and one with it, particles that once were spread out across the universe, only to come back together in new ways to form your exact body.

Technique: Harnessing the Power of the Solstices and Equinoxes

Many cultures—the ancient Celts and the Hawaiians, the ancient Greeks and Maya, modern-day pagans and Wiccans—have long acknowledged the power and significance of the solstices and equinoxes. Earth's rotations and tilts within the shifting, constant dance of the cosmos are deeply embedded in our nature as a species—and these pivotal points aren't just markers in time or seasonal changes; they reflect something deeper within our internal or psychic rhythms as well.

In Hawaiian culture, Kāne—the God of Life, fresh water, and sunlight—is celebrated during the summer solstice. His brother Kanaloa—the god of the underworld, deep oceans, and darkness—is celebrated during the winter solstice. In ancient pagan traditions across Europe, specifically Germanic and Celtic, as well as in modern paganism, Midsummer (referred to as Litha in Wicca) is a time when the Sun God and Earth Mother are at their most powerful. It's a time for celebrating the fecundity of the earth and basking in the sun, a time for joy, growth, prosperity. Similarly, Yule, or the winter solstice, the shortest day of the year, is a time for reflection, turning inward, harboring and harnessing the fading light, while awaiting the return of the Sun God. The spring and fall equinoxes are the midway points. Spring is a time for creativity, rebirth, and new possibilities and beginnings; fall is a time for preparation, retreat, and harvesting.

Regardless of our religious backgrounds, we can view these seasonal markers as mirrors of our own internal and interior cycles.

Spring Equinox

This is a good time for starting or planning for a new beginning, allowing your creativity to bubble up and burst forth. What would you like to give birth to this season and year? Make a list of a few things you want to cultivate and bring forth this year, whether it's a creative project, a new job, or a new mindset. Consider how you can break these goals up into achievable parts throughout the year. Use this time to get a little wild and spontaneous, infusing new fertile energy into your intentions.

Summer Solstice

Summer is a time for celebration and harnessing the magical potential present in nature. The summer solstice is also associated with the element of fire and the power of the sun, representing growth and prosperity. Focus on manifesting your highest dreams and goals at this time, taking concrete action to bring them forth into the world. How can you continue to stoke the creative fire you've cultivated within so that it remains abundant throughout the coming months?

Fall Equinox

Fall is a time to surrender and let go of things that no longer serve us, while harvesting the fruits of our labors throughout the spring and summer months. It's a time to honor the past, as well as our ancestors, and find ways to incorporate these lessons into our waking life. Use this time to channel spirit messages from your ancestors and spirit guides, and take stock of the blessings in your life today, many of which have been made possible by and through the ones who've passed before you.

Winter Solstice

Winter is a time for self-reflection, where we begin to plant the seeds that may come into being in the spring months. Consider the lessons of the year and honor the sacred fullness of wisdom that comes in stillness. Remember that the fullness of light will soon return. Focus on nourishing your body with wholesome foods, sharing stories, spending quality time with loved ones, and settling into the comfort of stillness.

Technique: Remember to Stay Connected to Your Source

In Hawaiian, *piko waena* means the "navel" or "belly button," and it has an important significance in the birth-death-rebirth cycle in Hawaiian culture. Micah explained that when a child is born, the umbilical cord is regarded as sacred, since it connects the child to the mother in utero, who is also connected to her mother, and her mother, all the way back to Papa, the original Earth Mother. He described the piko as an "extension cord from one to another," connecting each generation. It retains mana, or the sacred power of life, since it once kept us alive, so in his culture, they don't throw away the dried cord.

"We take it and plug it back into the earth, in a sacred place that's worthy of the cord," he explained. For Micah's family, who comes from Waimea, they go to a lake on top of the mountain and return the piko there, since Mauna Kea is the oldest ancestor. "We do a ceremony and wrap up the small, dried-up piko, put it into the lake, and ask them to continue to feed our children spiritually: 'May this mountain become the home base for the baby and may the deities continue to feed the child through its umbilical cord,'" he said. "The older kapuna, the elders, say 'How is your piko?' And it means 'How are you? How's your piko doing? Are you in alignment? Are you doing things that are correct and *pono*?' We're not just asking how you're doing—we're asking how is your umbilical cord, does it have connection?"

For many of us, our pikos from birth are long gone. But as a spiritual exercise, take yourself back in time and imagine the moment of your birth. That point of agony and joy for the mother ends with a kind of separation: once you emerged into the world, your physical connection to your mother—through the umbilical cord—had to be cut and severed in order for your life to begin. Ask yourself how you, too, can nurture and realign your connection to the Source. How you can honor your connection to the land, your connection with yourself and Spirit. Visualize restoring an invisible cord, extending from your navel, that you can use anytime to tap into and connect with the earth, as well as your innate and sacred power. Within us all lies a divine thread to our source, a map of sorts, to the infinite pathways of divine knowledge. All we have to do is retrace the steps.

Technique: Listen to the Stories of Others with Compassion

Listening to the stories of others with compassion can have a transformative effect on not only the speaker, but also the listener. Remembering (and re-membering) the past through narrative and bearing witness to the stories of others is important not only for history's sake but also for healing and reconnection. Make time to be quiet, to be still, and to actively listen to other stories.

PRACTICE:
RECONNECTION THROUGH RITUAL

Joseph Campbell, one of the world's foremost scholars on mythology, described the hero's journey as both circular and universal. In a sense, we're all the heroes of the story of our lives. And this journey, he identified, regardless of culture, time, or place, has three distinct stages: departure, initiation, and return.

The hero must leave the comfort of their community behind in order to embark upon a quest (departure), which is always, at its core, a spiritual quest. They face trials, tribulations, and tests along the way, encountering roadblocks, setbacks, and battles (initiation). Although it is arduous and difficult, new knowledge is acquired on this journey, which must be brought back to the community (return). Nearly every heroic tale follows this arc, although the specific details of the story vary according to time, place, and culture. At the crux or center of each tale, the hero typically finds that they had the answers within them all along and that their story is a part of a larger or an interconnected whole.

As we grow and develop, we create new labels for things, moving further away from this simple truth of universal consciousness and connection. Like the heroic journey, the spiritual journey also involves battles with the ego, dark nights of the soul, suffering, and existential confusion (initiation), and our motivating force is to get back to a sense of wholeness or oneness with the Source (return).

In order to evolve our consciousness and realize our soul purpose and calling, we must go back and find where our disconnection began (departure), dive into the proverbial wreck (initiation), and reconnect with nature (return) to find unity within a fragmented whole.

The hero's journey of departure, initiation, and return is also a symbolic journey that can be re-created through simple, nature-based rituals. Sometimes language fails us and words aren't enough—this is where ritual and action come into play. "Plato says human language is inadequate to express the ultimate realities directly. Words conceal rather than reveal the inner natures of things," wrote Raymond Moody. "It follows that no human words can do more than indicate—by analogy, through myth, and in other indirect ways—the true character of that which lies beyond the physical realm."[73]

Ritual is one pathway to opening up a connection to Spirit and our higher calling, and it also provides incredible healing and soul enrichment. Everyone's practice and path are different, but here is a basic sea ritual structure that you can personalize and modify as you wish.

Supplies
Small pouch or cloth bag
Paper
Pen
Small white candle (or use a particular color that is connected to the intention of your ritual; see chapter 7 to assist with your color choice)

---

73. Raymond Moody, *Life after Life: The Bestselling Original Investigation That Revealed "Near-Death Experiences"* (New York: HarperCollins, 2015), 115.

Step 1: Departure

Pick a secluded area so you're not distracted by others and take a mindful walk along the water's edge, feeling the soles of your feet connecting with the earth. Notice the abundance of life around you. Each sprig of grass, grain of sand, strand of algae, spiral shell, and even the sea itself contains energy and life. Notice how all these different life forms congregate together, relying upon the elements for sustenance, forming a living consciousness. Collect a few objects on your walk—shells, sea glass, a piece of driftwood—and place them in your pouch, but as you select each one, *ask* the object if it's okay to be taken (you'll know the answer when you ask). Give thanks as you go along.

Step 2: Initiation

Find a place to sit and draw a circle around yourself (in the sand, in the dirt, or psychically by using the forefinger of your dominant hand). Now, set out the objects and ornaments in front of you in the shape of a sacred symbol or sigil, a star, or simply a beautiful array. Place the small white candle in the center of your sigil or design. If you brought other offerings along, place them around you as well, either in the center, along the edges of the circle you've created, or in the cardinal directions represented by the elements. Earth corresponds to the north, fire to the south, water to the west, and air to the east.

Now it's time to call upon the elements (earth, air, fire, water), the cardinal directions or four corners, your ancestors, spirit guides, the Great Mother Goddess, God, or the universe to help guide your ritual. There's no right or wrong way to perform this ritual, so I recommend starting with an intention or incantation that you create for yourself, one that centers around reconnection with Spirit.

Your intention should be a wish, a desire, something that you wish to manifest in your life. It can be anything: "I wish to find peace and stillness. I wish to be fully connected to the land and in tune with its energies. I wish to be reconnected with the divine power that lives within me and is present throughout nature. I wish to honor the ancestors of this land, to all the souls who've gone before me, to the invisible Spirit that dwells in all things. I wish to embody love in all forms."

If it helps, you can write these intentions or petitions on a small piece of paper to help your focus. In fact, writing them down can do more than help you focus, since it's turning an abstract thought into something tangible and material. Try to envision the positive effects of this intention as it permeates throughout and becomes manifest in your waking life—helping not only you but everyone around you. Envision how you will feel, look, walk, act, and speak if this intention becomes reality. Let that image and feeling fill you.

Sit in the sacred space you've created and be present to the sounds, scents, and energies around you. Notice the birds, the wind, the echoing of a faraway car, the fluttering of branches, the rolling ceaseless waves, the trickle of the stream. You may want to get up and dance or move to release stagnant energy, or to summon the energy of your intention within your body.

Step 3: Return

When you're ready, burn the paper in the flame of the candle and say, "So mote it be" or "Amen." If you invoked the four corners, now it's time to close them. Start in reverse, thanking each element for its power and presence, and bid them farewell (for now). Thank and say goodbye to the spirits who attended your ritual, who've offered their wisdom and paid witness to your intention, and erase the circle in the sand or dirt as you go along.

Collect everything you brought with you, but leave the natural shells and native objects. Continue to light the candle at home over the next few days until it's completely burned out. As it burns, pay attention to the signs and inner messages that come to you during this time. Follow up your seaside ritual with a gratitude ritual to give thanks for any new wisdom and insight that may come.

Remember to pay attention to the signs. Notice the details in the mundane. Perhaps it's a certain bird call or the presence of an animal, a repeated number, a certain song, a moment of serendipity, an unexpected piece of news or information, an urge to go to a particular place, a chance encounter, and so on. Stay open to the possibility of magic in the everyday.

INTEGRATIONS

Western society instills ideas of separation, emphasizing individuality at a very young age. Starting at about six months old, when we first begin to recognize ourselves in the mirror, we view ourselves as separate entities (from the mother) for the first time.[74] Twentieth-century French psychoanalyst, cultural theorist, and post-structuralist Jacques Lacan calls this the "mirror stage" in infancy. It's the first time we recognize ourselves as individual beings, thus beginning the formation of the ego. We begin identifying distinctions between the *self* and the *other*—that is, *us* and *them*. These binary constructions are further instilled in us throughout our lives, reinforced in subtle and overt ways. Separation is easier to understand than unity; it's much easier to think in terms of black and white, binaries and polarities, but we know that on a spiritual level these separations are merely illusions.

We're at a pivotal stage in history where we're constantly bombarded with extreme polarities and binary thinking. Whether it's the extreme right or extreme left battling it out on the American political stage, backtracking in women's rights, or the resurfacing of hateful, racist rhetoric that should've been addressed and eradicated long ago, thinking in binary terms or extremes is not only problematic but dangerous.

Luckily, we always find a way, however slow and irregular it may seem, to move forward. According to the eighteenth-century philosopher Hegel, history itself is not linear but dialectic in nature. Hegel remarked that the flow and progress of history occurs through a thesis (one extreme) and its antithesis (opposite extreme) eventually synthesizing to create a *new* thesis—which can be thought of as change, progress, movement, and new

---

74. Nasrullah Mambrol, "Lacan's Concept of Mirror Stage," *Literary Theory and Criticism* (blog), April 18, 2021, https://literariness.org/2016/04/22/lacans-concept-of-mirror-stage/.

ideas—that exists between those extremes. Sometimes history moves backward before it moves forward, but it doesn't mean we're not headed in the right direction.[75]

Still, when we other each other and create an us/them mentality, we're not acknowledging the divine current of connection around and within us. To put it simply, extremism of any kind is just small-mindedness, even if it somehow balances out in the end. The dialectic model also applies to our spiritual progress: it's only with a new thesis, a new synthesis of thought, one that centers around the interconnectedness of all things, that spiritual consciousness can evolve in our human timeline.

75. Julie E. Maybee, "Hegel's Dialectics," Stanford Encyclopedia of Philosophy, last modified October 2, 2020, https://plato.stanford.edu/entries/hegel-dialectics/.

CHAPTER 6

ON THE DIVINE FEMININE

At its etymological root, the word *myth* comes from Greek *mythos*, meaning "story." In this sense, all religious and spiritual texts are myths; they are neither true nor false but stories that contain glimmers of our essence, nature, and clues to our purpose, our *raison d'être*. Humans have always been preoccupied with origin stories in order to make sense of the world, and while science has taken up that search for meaning in its own way, world mythologies also offer a glimpse into our beginnings: all myths contain traces, symbols, and sacred teachings of our origins and nature, whether they're found in Ovid's *Metamorphoses* and the Homeric Hymns, the Popol Vuh, or the Upanishads.

Most ancient peoples across cultures worshiped many gods and goddesses (also known as pantheism), rather than a single, unified god (or monotheism). We see pantheism in the Celtic and Norse traditions of Northern Europe; in the ancient Maya and Aztec peoples of North and Central America; in the pantheon of gods of ancient Egypt, Greece, Rome; and in the Vedic gods of India and East Asia. The gods and goddesses sometimes provide an explanation for natural phenomena like rain and wind, or show why things are the way they are, including the beginnings of the world and how we humans came to be. Many of our world mythologies have trace similarities between them, despite their geographical and cultural separations, but all myths hold one thing in common: they show our human desire, or perhaps need, to label phenomena, put faces on forces and energies, and sublimate what is too big to behold or comprehend through our regular senses.

The idea of the sacred three, or the Divine Trinity, shows up again and again in world religions (as in Christianity's Father, Son, and Holy Spirit), although the concept of the Divine Trinity is most likely of pagan origin, dating back to ancient Sumer, Greece, India, and Babylonia.[76] In contemporary paganism and Goddess-worship traditions, this trinity is often referred to as the Mother, Maiden, and Crone, or the Triple Goddess, and the truth is, her original geographical and historical origins have always been shrouded in mystery, especially with the dismantling of pantheism and matrilineal spiritual traditions with the onset of patriarchal religions and systems. But the Goddess figure was and still is very much revered across cultures, and the Divine Feminine, especially the Female Trinity, is still deeply embedded in our consciousness to this day.

By turning back to her ancient wisdom, we can begin to reintegrate parts of ourselves that yearn for connection with the earth and cosmos, as well as our higher purpose and calling. The Female Trinity—either as Goddess figures, energies, archetypes, levels of consciousness, or all of these things at once—teaches us compassion, surrender, and acceptance, as well as how to harness our innate gifts and live in awe of the natural world.

The Maiden, Mother, and Crone figures (also known as the Female Trinity or Triple Goddess) are an integral part of pagan mystical traditions and show up in spiritual traditions across the planet. In modern-day witchcraft, the Triple Goddess is connected to the phases of the moon (waxing, full, and waning or dark moon) and is a reflection of the life cycle, or the three stages of life. The sacred three, making up the totality of the Divine

---

76. "How Ancient Trinitarian Gods Influenced Adoption of the Trinity," United Church of God, July 22, 2011, https://www.ucg.org/bible-study-tools/booklets/is-god-a -trinity/how-ancient-trinitarian-gods-influenced-adoption-of-the-trinity.

Feminine, are sometimes viewed, depending on the person or spiritual tradition, as archetypes, psychic or emotional states, mystical energies, symbols, deities or spiritual entities, or a combination of all of these.

The most pervasive form of the Divine Feminine is the Great Goddess, who provides nourishment for all life and can be seen cross-culturally, throughout time and space, as the Earth Mother figure. She goes by many names: Gaia or Demeter in ancient Greece, Ceres in ancient Rome, Coatlicue to the Aztecs, Papahānaumoku in Hawaiian moʻolelo, the mother goddess Ninhursag or the earth goddess Ki in ancient Sumer, Ishtar/Inanna in ancient Mesopotamia, Pachamama to the Inca, Danu (Anu) in Celtic culture, Isis in ancient Egypt, Bhumi Devi or Pṛthvī Mātā in Hinduism, and many more. Sometimes the Great Goddess is a combination of several goddess figures, with each goddess representing a specific part or aspect of the whole, or is known cross-culturally as the Ocean Goddess, whose primordial energies continue to nurture all of life.

The Great Goddess provides and nurtures life; she is a vessel and a creator in her Mother and Maiden forms, yet the Crone aspect also has the power to both nurture and destroy life. Still, she is a combination of all these energies, as a life giver and destroyer, containing both parts within herself. For instance, in the Celtic traditions, the Cailleach is a creator goddess, but she sometimes makes herself known in the form of a hag or crone figure. In ancient Greece, we see Persephone as both the goddess of spring and the queen of the underworld.

The Crone figure also has many cross-cultural names: Hecate in ancient Greece and Rome, Baba Yaga in Eastern European traditions, Kali as the life giver and destroyer in Hinduism, Mictecacihuatl ("Lady of the Dead") for the ancient Aztecs, and more. As necessary as she is, the Crone figure can be frightening, for in her we see mirrored back at us the creeping of old age, the tinge and scent of death lurking nearby. She forces us to confront our own inevitable mortality and dwindling time on earth, but as the wise grandmother figure, she forces us to come to terms with the harsh realities of life, showing us what we *need* to know, however difficult it may be to bear. Her presence is marked with awe, mingled with the terrifying; she reminds us to face our fears but is also a visual, prophetic marker for *rebirth and new beginnings*.

STORY: ENCOUNTERING THE SHEELA NA GIG

Ireland, 2013

Ireland is the land of my ancestors, the land of my great-great-grandmothers. It called to me in dreams and visions, but since no known living relative had touched the soil, it remained a mythical place of my family's past. While working on my graduate thesis, I began to feel the slow, creeping approach of burnout and decided to take a spontaneous trip to the Emerald Isle to clear my head. I had very little money, but I scoured the internet for a cheap ticket, reserved what seemed to be the only automatic rental car in the country, and decided to wing it. It was a difficult year and I longed for some kind of physical and creative rejuvenation, some inspiration to keep going, but I also heard, deep down, a spirit calling from afar.

When I touched down on the west side of the island in Shannon, I headed north with no itinerary, nowhere to stay, and a very tight (student) budget. Hostels, I knew, were cheap and surprisingly comfortable compared to those in America, so I'd just find some along the way. This was before smartphones were ubiquitous, and my only armor was a paper map, a prepaid phone, a few Euros, and a tank full of gas. Whatever happened would be all right.

As I rounded each bend of the wild curves of N67, I was amazed at the natural beauty of the island: the green expanse of verdant land abutting the ocean, the angry and white-tipped waves at the rocky edges of the crags below, the serene meadows to the right. The road dangerously hugged the cliffs' edges, winding in sharp turns, and I held my breath for most of that very first drive. With so much natural wonder, it was hard to keep my eyes on the road. Yet I also felt all the women, all the mothers and grandmothers of hundreds of generations that shaped my blood and body, the call of my ancestors buried in the land. It was the beginning of a new awakening.

Soon, Galway, with its bustling shops, cafés, and lively college town atmosphere, came into focus, and I pulled into the first hostel I could find. There I met a young Canadian woman, another solo traveler, with kind eyes and a wide-brimmed gray hat, and we kept each other company that first day. It's interesting how we can form immediate bonds with strangers, connect and share secrets, even knowing afterward you'll probably never see them again. This is perhaps one of the beauties of solo travel—by leaving so much up to chance and fate, you have no choice but to trust the universe. That night we danced together at a lively inn with a roaring fireplace, staving off drunken men with roaming hands, spinning wildly across the floor, a divine feminine energy around us. By the early light of morning, I left the cold, crisp, illuminated streets of Galway and headed south toward the Cliffs of Moher.

On the road, when I neared the tiny town of Doolin, the land came alive once again, ash and elder trees hung over the edge of the road, a grandmother's song. The grass, like a wispy-backed old man, curled and loosened in the February air. There, I borrowed a horse named Airge from a nearby farm, a gentle creature with brilliant white lashes, and climbed up the hills. He touched his nose to my belly before I mounted him, and we rode through the famine ruins. Crumbling rock was scattered in odd places, the silent cries of the dead echoing in the ruins. I heard the Spanish murmurs, "*Abajo Cromwell*," from the faint outlines of spirits over the cliff's edge. It was as if the land waited for others to return. I felt the presence of young Spanish men once trapped on these shores, shipwrecked, hung at the old gallows up the hill, the blood long dried. Only the horses could remember the old wounds; they too could hear the cries and mantras in the wind.

In these lands, walking over the bog in my rubber boots toward the craggy cliffs' edge, I was reminded of the fragility of my own flesh. "Look over me, old souls of Earth. I am here, and so are you." Underneath, down below, seagulls made their home nestled in the jagged rock, black and white wings beating in flashes over the blue. Even a death in the Atlantic wouldn't disturb the bog, the loud, roaring silence of this place.

As it would happen in Cuba and Mexico, I felt as though someone or something had brought me here. Had I once lived out on the Burren? Was I remembering something from long ago, a past life? Or was it the knowing call of my ancestors, old countrymen and women, the energy of the land like a pulsing heart underfoot? I had come to the isle of my grandmother's grandmother, their memories long buried in the soil. The limestone and mossy mounds seemed to breathe, more alive than my own city, the brush whistling underfoot. "Tell me the past," I whispered. "Mother Earth, show me your secrets." My voice sounded clear against the wind. "Breathe life back into me, Mother," I said to the webbed moss, the rocks, the expanse of sea.

That night, sleeping next to the Burren, I had a premonitory dream, one that involved an ex-boyfriend whom I had recently broken up with. In the dream, I found myself back in my old neighborhood in New York City's Washington Heights. He turned his car onto my block but nearly hit me with it in the process, then stopped and stated plainly, completely emotionless, "I got married. I married someone else on your birthday." After several years together, part of me was still grieving the loss of this relationship, so this admission of marriage to someone else in the dream seemed startling. Later that morning, I walked to the Cliffs of Moher, looking across the Atlantic, and said aloud, "I've already let you go. Go on your way and leave me at peace." A few years later, the dream finally made sense. Strangely enough, he ended up marrying someone else on my birthday. Sometimes you know things before you know them. Pay attention to your dreams, pay attention to the signs, pay attention to the whispers of the land, even in waking hours and in sleep.

That evening at the local pub, the fire burned hotly and faint ash fell from the chimney. A man played a flute, another a fiddle, and as I walked in, the local faces scanned me for signs of recognition. I heard whispers as I ordered a pint of beer and saddled up to the bar. "So, what brings you here?" an older man asked.

"Ah, I'm just exploring. I'm a student, a writer, from New York. I've been driving around your beautiful island, sightseeing, taking a quick break from my research work." That seemed to set him at ease, the suspicions of an outsider quelled, a foreign girl traveling on her own, and the music picked up.

A young couple, overhearing the conversation, chimed in. "New York, huh? What're you studying?" the woman asked. I told them my focus and research—women's studies, the female body, trauma, mythologies—and the girl's eyes widened. "Oh! Then you must have heard of the Sheela, yes?"

"The Sheela? No, I don't think so."

"The Sheela Na Gig. Oh, you're in for a real treat then. I think you'd be interested. You see, it's this very old symbol, but no one knows who she is or where she comes from ..."

Naturally, I was intrigued immediately and made a note to seek out the symbol. The Sheela was exactly what I had been looking for, except I didn't know that before I came to the island. Back in New York, I dove into my research, renewed with something else to explore. Meeting that couple in the old Irish pub proved fortuitous. I still didn't understand the Sheela Na Gig—what or who was she?— but I was determined to figure it out.

THE SHEELA NA GIG

The Sheela Na Gig, a strange stone effigy of a female figure, dates back to the twelfth century. She is found in over 100 places across Ireland, as well as throughout the UK, primarily adorning doorways, well sites, and archways of churches. Often grotesque, shriveled, and frightening in appearance, the Sheela Na Gig has one aspect that's particularly unusual: she's often shown holding open a gaping, exaggerated vulva. Irish literary critic Vivian Mercier describes her as having "an ugly, mask-like skull-face, with a huge, scowling mouth; skeletal ribs; huge genitalia held apart with both hands; bent legs."[77]

But even more fascinating, her original purpose is largely up for debate among scholars. Was she a fertility symbol? A Celtic goddess of creation and destruction? A deterrence against sexuality? A gargoyle to ward off evil spirits? Or something more altogether? The origins of this provocative figure are still largely unknown, and like many pagan traditions, her original meaning was buried away in the rubbles of history. Still, there are several clues to her elusive, hidden meanings.

Ancient pagan traditions, symbols, and rituals were often syncretized with the early Christian Church in order to encourage assimilation and conversion. We see this throughout Europe and across the globe, especially in colonized countries within Latin America and the Caribbean, where Indigenous deities, spirits, and orishas were syncretized with the practices and iconography of the Roman Catholic Church. While the original meaning of the Sheela may have been lost due to this forced assimilation, it's surprising, not to mention strange and perplexing, to see such a vagrant display of female sexuality still present in and around Christian churches and castles throughout Ireland and the UK.

It seemed her presence meant much more than a mere discouragement against lust or sexuality, especially female sexuality, in the form of a gargoyle. I began to see the Sheela in a different light: the more I studied her, the more I came to understand her as part of the Female Trinity, as representative of the Mother and the Hag/Crone figure. The Sheela is both a life giver and a life destroyer. Her body gives life and also consumes it, providing an entryway into the world and in between worlds.

For me, the Sheela Na Gig represents the womb-opening of Mother Earth, the place we come from and will one day return to, a place of both creation and destruction. The Sheela's close proximity to water, such as wells, amplifies this symbolic connection to the womb and sea, as a source, as a deep-set power within the earth. She can reach within her

77. Vivian Mercier, "Samuel Beckett and the Sheela-na-gig," *The Kenyon Review* 23, no. 2 (Spring 1961): 305, https://www.jstor.org/stable/4334122.

body and spring forth new life. Not only is she one with creation, but she is the guardian of it.

The womb, with its deep, watery mysteries, is often linked to the symbol of the cave—a portal, where life begins and ends—as well as the sea, a source of deep power set within the earth. To give birth is a terrifying, albeit beautiful, process, and even the womb itself is *still not* fully understood by modern science. A quick look at research, or lack thereof, on women's healthcare shows this. The womb, to this day, is still ripe with mysteries, producing both terror and awe. Like birth, death, too, is a terrifying, albeit beautiful, process, one we must all contend with—we all enter into this unknown, sooner or later.

Yet this visual focus on her womb-center also marks something else: an actual locality in time and space, representing sacred, energetically charged sites or meeting places of antiquity, not just the representative power of Mother Earth. In his *Celtic Mysteries: The Ancient Religion*, John Sharkey writes that "every sacred spot had its guardian spirit who tended it, observing the daily rites with proper ceremony, and could materialize as cat, bird, fish, or whatever form was most pleasing to the goddess— even as a hideous hag or beautiful being, depending on the circumstance or disposition of an intruder or visitor. Such places were womb-openings of the Earth Mother, who was invoked under many different names and aspects."[78]

Like many cultures, the Celts rarely, if at all, transcribed their history into the written word; they conveyed their stories orally. Myths, or storytelling, weren't simply pastimes or novelties to the ancient peoples, but they ensured a continuity between the past and present. The constant metamorphoses of motifs found in Irish tales, coupled with the "easy intermingling of physical and supernatural realms, made the world of the Celtic imagination tangible through thousands of years of story-telling," wrote Sharkey.[79] But through the erasure of myths and the diminishment

78. John Sharkey, *Celtic Mysteries: The Ancient Religion* (New York: Thames and Hudson, 1975), 22–25.

79. Sharkey, *Celtic Mysteries*, 12.

of oral traditions at the tyranny of patriarchal systems, not only were the Sheela Na Gig's true meanings and origins lost, but a kind of severance between cultural and spiritual identity occurred as well. When this continuity with the past is broken, the effect is detrimental: not only do we lose sacred knowledge, but we also lose our connection to the earth itself, to its mysteries, whispers, teachings, and gifts.

When the true meanings of symbols of the Divine Feminine are lost and then reviewed again under a modern, patriarchal lens, a kind of vulgarity and stylized sexuality emerges, one that diminishes, subjugates, and kitschifies, rather than illuminates, respects, and reveres. In turn, the power of the Female Trinity is put away, forgotten, and dismissed.

The Sheela, as a guardian figure, an archetype, the Maiden-Mother-Crone, holds open the doorway between worlds, between birth and death, standing at the crossroads. Her body is a pathway, which cannot be severed from her power. As the Earth Mother, the Great Womb of Life, she's all-encompassing, ancient, and profound. Her continued presence is a lingering, occluded mystery: a memory of our primordial beginnings and our future, hinting at the greater forces beyond us that defy rational understanding.

When we lose her, we lose a part of our essence—our connection to the Great Mother—and with it, the wisdom of our own divine power. The Sheela, standing at the doorway, serves as a reminder of these ancient forces around and within us.

DEEP DIVE: PERSEPHONE, DEMETER, AND HECATE (OR MAIDEN, MOTHER, AND CRONE)

In Greek mythology, the Female Trinity can be seen in the story of Persephone, Demeter, and Hecate. Some of the first written stories associated with these goddesses, as well as the gods, show up in what's generally referred to as the *Homeric Hymns*, although the ancient authors are unknown. These hymns were written in the old epic style sometime between the sixth and eighth centuries BCE, and the "Hymn to Demeter," according to modern scholars, was most likely written between 600 and 650 BCE.[80]

The "Hymn to Demeter" is a tale of a cyclical journey; it tells of the strength of the Mother's love, the persistence of the Maiden, and wisdom of the stern yet helpful Crone figure, as a testament to their unity. It's also one of the first intergenerational tales of women found in Western literature, describing the loss of female autonomy, trauma, and severance from our divine source—serving also as a warning against the violence (both spiritual and physical) of the patriarchy.

The story begins thousands of years ago. One day, while out frolicking in the fields with the daughters of Oceanus, youthful Persephone—also known simply as Kore, the goddess of spring and daughter of Demeter—gets caught in Hades's clutches. As she stoops to admire a sweet flower, the earth cracks open to reveal the god of the underworld's terrifying chariot. He sweeps her up and carries her away, down to his deep domain. There, he forces the innocent maiden to become his wife.

In agony, the girl's mother, Demeter—the goddess of the earth, fertility, barley, and harvest—scours the land for her daughter. She's tormented in her grief, tearing at her hair, crying out for Persephone, refusing even a sip of sweet ambrosia, which is beloved by all the gods. She does not bathe, nor sleep, nor cease in her search for her daughter.

No one heard the cries of the maiden girl when she was abducted, except for two: deep within her own cave, Hecate heard the girl's cries, as did Helios, watching from his position in the sky. Over a week passes, and Hecate, holding her ever-present torches, meets with Demeter to help her in her search.

The two goddesses speed off to speak with Helios—the sun god who drives his chariots across the sky each day—to see if he had seen the girl. Taking pity on the grieving mother, Helios tells the women that Hades has taken the girl, and upon hearing the news, a new rage burns within Demeter's heart. In her wild grief and agony, she refuses to congregate

80. Martin L. West, trans. *Homeric Hymns, Homeric Apocrypha, Lives of Homer* (Cambridge, MA: Harvard University Press, 1998), 8–9.

with the gods of Olympia any longer. So she wanders the earth in rags, disguising herself, and mingling with mortals.

While grieving her lost motherhood, she begins tending to and nursing an infant son of a nobleman in Eleusis, secretly bestowing the child with immortal gifts in the night. But once her divinity is revealed and the women of the house find out who she is, they fear her. And so Demeter flings off her disguise, allowing a bright radiance to emanate from her body, and assumes her full form. She then commands a great temple to be built in her honor, and in return, she will teach the people of Eleusis her secret rites.

Still away from her daughter, Demeter shuns the other gods and begins wasting away in yearning within her newly built temple. During this time, for one year, nothing on the earth will grow—not flowers or crops—and soon the people across the earth begin to starve. Before her daughter was taken, the fields were always full and the earth bountiful, but now a cold, inept darkness creeps over the land.

Soon, the gods of Olympia begin to take notice. As humankind is dying of famine, they are also not getting their aromatic sacrifices of sweet meats made at the temple's altars. So the gods of Olympia plead, one by one, with Demeter to stop her raging grief. But she will not relent. Zeus finally sends his son Hermes, the messenger god, into the underworld to speak with Hades. There, he finds the maiden girl with her husband, now honored as the queen of the underworld.

Yet still she yearns for her mother. The god of the dead, knowing that no one can return to the earth forever after having eaten in the underworld, gives the girl a single pomegranate seed. After she has eaten it, the young bride is permitted to visit her mother. At Demeter's temple, the Maiden, Mother, and Crone are reunited, rushing toward each other with tears of joy. All three women embrace, grasping at each other in relief.

But soon after, it is revealed that the girl has eaten the pomegranate seed and will not be able to stay on Earth for very long. She will have to return to the underworld with her husband for the majority of the year. Having her daughter back, even for part of the year, revives Demeter's spirits, and she brings fertility back to the land again. The crops will thrive in the spring and summer months when she is reunited with her daughter. And when it is time for Persephone to return to the underworld, the earth will grow barren once again. But from that time on, Hecate, the wise woman of the cave and night, is minister and companion to Persephone and a guide and friend to Demeter.[81]

It's important to note that the goddess figures are not restricted to gender per se; they are distinct energies made manifest in the living world. Just as there are both masculine and feminine energies within all of us, they are also made manifest in the material, physical world; they are spectrums that make up the whole.

As with all things, everyone's spiritual path is unique. There is no singular path to the Goddess, nor does she have one name, face, or identity—she may show up in many ways. While there are many Mother Goddess figures across cultures and traditions, look for one that speaks to you personally, but do not get preoccupied with her physical attributes so much as her spiritual ones. Whether you call to Mother Mary or Yemayá, Gaia or Pachamama, remember that the Great Mother Goddess has many names, many faces, many sides, and embodies all of life.

WORKING WITH THE MAIDEN, MOTHER, AND CRONE

The Maiden, Mother, and Crone, distinct yet united, are representative of the cycles of nature, seasons, and the cyclical unity of all things. Yet the Divine Feminine Trinity is not simply representative of the phases of physical life, carrying out an extensive symbol of life and death cyclicality. It also embodies occult knowledge and sacred mysteries. Here is what we can learn from these goddesses as archetypes and energies.

Lessons from the Maiden

The youthful, spritely figure of Persephone is representative of the onset of spring—a time for fresh beginnings, fecundity, creativity, joy, and

81. West, trans., *Homeric Hymns*, 33–71.

play. It's a time when the earth awakens from its deep slumber, bursting with possibility and newness, opening itself up for renewal. Bursting with opportunity, the Maiden aspect is always protected, guided, and nurtured by the Mother and Crone. The maiden figure is also sometimes represented by Diana, Goddess of the Hunt and Lady of the Wild Things, a self-sufficient, wild, virgin goddess. The virginal aspects reflect unbridled potential, innocence, and oneness with the earth, and the Maiden figure helps us tap into our own limitless and boundless qualities.

Technique: Perform a Creativity Candle Ritual

All creation is an act of creativity, and all creativity is an act of creation. Creative acts are a kind of growing and gestation process, finally bursting into the world when they're ready. Is there a creative project that you've been waiting to begin for a long time but just haven't started? Get an orange or yellow candle and inscribe it with a five-pointed star or a triple moon symbol, as well as your initials. Set orange, white, or yellow flowers or petals around the candle and place the candle in a shallow bowl of sea salt. You can also rub the candle down with essential oils related to creativity and inspiration (see chapter 7). Begin by casting a circle of protection around you. Invoke the energy of the Maiden figure and ask her to help assist your creative process. As the candle burns, work on building plans or experimenting with the beginnings of your project. You can also work with the Star card of the tarot as representative of the Maiden figure, meditating on the image and incorporating elements of the card's symbolism into your candle design, or keeping the card out in front of you as you work on your creative project.

Technique: Tap into Your Sense of Play

Do one thing a day that appeases and brings out your inner child, welcoming a sense of delight and curiosity. It could be as simple as walking down the street with the eyes of a child for fifteen minutes, marveling at the streets, leaves, ants, people, and the simple shapes and colors in nature, as if you're seeing them for the first time. Invoke a sense of wonder at the most mundane things, marveling at the hidden beauty around you, whether it's in a blade of grass, the way a dog's ears flop as they run, or the small details of homes and buildings around you.

Technique: Perform a Self-Love Ritual Bath

We all look for validation from others at some point or in some way, especially from a lover or partner, colleagues, or family. But consider: Is your self-worth largely determined by others? If so, it's time to reclaim that power. Light a small pink candle (tea light, small pillar candle, or a taper candle) and write down a simple self-love mantra on a small piece of paper: "I embody love in all forms" or "I am a living embodiment of love; it dwells in me and through me in all ways" or "I am a child of the Divine Mother, loved and perfect just as I am." Take a sea salt bath and add rose petals, a few drops of rose oil, vanilla, ylang-ylang, or any scent or flower that you find most sensual (lily, violet, daffodil, and lavender are also great for this). While you're in the bath, imagine a pink light emanating from your heart, encircling your aura, and radiating outward to all things as the candle burns.

Technique: Seek Out New Knowledge and Skills

The Maiden is often associated with a kind of childlike innocence, and this symbolizes that we all have much to learn while we're on this earth. Remember, the Maiden figure is bold, unbridled, curious, unashamed. Perhaps there's something you've wanted to try for a while but didn't because you were too embarrassed or afraid of failure. Perhaps you've secretly always wanted to take up pottery, join a writer's workshop or a coven or a college course, learn about financial investments or philosophy, write or direct a short film, or learn to cook a complex dish—go after and follow whatever moves you, piques your interest, and awakens your curiosity. Approach everything you do with a sense of humility and innocence, knowing that despite all your knowledge, there's so much we don't know, and as long as we have breath, there's still more to learn, more to do.

Lessons of the Mother

The nurturing figure of the Mother is embodied in the summer season and onset of autumn, a time when the earth's fecundity is at its peak and overflowing in abundance. As the goddess of wheat and grain as seen in Demeter, Mother Earth brings life, sustaining us with her bounty, and because of this, it's a celebratory period. She provides for all, without question or judgment, without a scarcity mindset; hers is a giving, fruitful, rejuvenating energy, while also being protective of all living things. Demeter also taught mortals her rites and mysteries in the land of Eleusis, which are now known as the Eleusinian Mysteries. In this sense, Demeter, the Mother figure, is also a keeper of secrets and the greatest mystery rites of the gods.

Technique: Remember the Continuity and Unity Within All of Life

What are ways you can reenchant the world using your natural gifts? Everything on our planet has a purpose, from the microscopic bacteria to the tallest redwood tree, working together to form the earth's ecosystem. Everything is conscious. Consider how you are fulfilling your calling and purpose in the ecosystem of your life. How do your gifts, contributions, and spirit play a larger role in the spiritual and physical ecosystem of the planet and everything on it?

Technique: Use Your Creative Gifts

Make a list of your own potential "children" in the form of creative manifestations. What do you want to bring into this world? What have you already brought into this world? What would you like to give birth to? How can you use your abundance—your gifts, talents, voice, wisdom—to help yourself and others? In what ways can you embody the figure of the Mother, nurturing the world through your creations and creative activities? Your creations are your creative babies, so treat them as such—nurture, feed, and help them grow. Sometimes this may mean waking up in the middle of the night or early morning to tend to them; seeing your creations grow in the world takes work, often work that goes unnoticed, but they may one day grow into something beyond your wildest imagination and even better than you envisioned. You can also work with the Empress card in the tarot, as representative of the Mother figure, as you work on your creative project

Technique: Nurture Your Inner Goddess

Regardless of gender or sex, we all have an inner goddess within us; we all come from mothers, each and every one of us, and we contain their energy, too. We also all come from Mother Earth and contain her energy as well. How can you tap into that sacred energy to create space for more abundance in your life? Maybe that means communing with nature, taking that hiking trip, dancing under the moon. The Goddess is wild, howling, primal, and powerful—find time and activities to let your inner goddess roam free.

Technique: Heal Your Mother Wound

Sometimes the image of the Divine Goddess can be triggering for some, especially if they've had issues with their earthly mothers. Maybe you didn't have an ideal relationship with your own mother or have to relearn healthy maternal traits. Sometimes our earthly mothers aren't ideal (they're human, after all) and were only able to give what they could, flaws and all. Work on healing your earthly mother wounds, beginning with the understanding that you can't, couldn't, or perhaps shouldn't change them. What you can do, however, is empower and heal yourself and move beyond that cycle of hurt, shame, or abuse.

Lesson from the Crone

In contemporary witchcraft and Neopaganism, Hecate (pronounced *he-KAH-tay, HEK-ut, HEK-ah-tee,* or *he-KAH-tee*) is still honored as a wise Crone figure and the embodiment of the Triple Goddess. Unlike other goddesses or gods, Hecate also has a direct connection to the underworld. Many believe that it is Hecate herself who stands at the gateway between the underworld and Earth, and because of this, she has often been associated with ghosts, graveyards, sorcery, the moon, and crossroads. And because of her ever-present torches, she's associated with the element of fire, capable of purifying and lighting the way. Her spirit is often invoked when someone is going through a deep transformation, undergoing a long, precarious journey, or facing uncertainty. Here, she acts as a guide through the dark night and comes to the aid of those who find themselves at a crossroads in life.

As an archetype, Hecate shines a light on our shadow side and to what's no longer serving us, aiding in transformation—particularly when it comes to psychic or subconscious realms (or the emotional underworld). Bold, brave, and unrelenting, her spirit and archetype provide the necessary strength to venture into the unknown without fear, as her ignited torches and firm presence guide the way.

Technique: Make Time for Rest

The Crone represents the winter season, a time when the earth becomes still and quiet with cold, a time for contemplation, inner journeys, wisdom, and rest. Despite the illusion that everything is withered and gone, there's an incredible magic happening around the earth as it retires into its seasonal slumber. There are lessons in that profound stillness, inner power ripe for retrieval, and wisdom lies in her dormant seeds. There's also humor and candor found in the Crone figure, even a silliness at times, but above all, a gentle fierceness.

Technique: Practice Self-Acceptance

Wrinkles are just wisdom lines, time markers for your time on this planet. They are not mistakes or flaws. They are battle scars, symbols of strength, reminders of all the moments that led you to this one. Mass media, magazine campaigns, and the beauty industry have tried to train us to hide or change these so-called flaws, preying on the vulnerabilities and insecurities of others. Don't let anyone make you feel lesser than. As you embrace age, think of the Crone figure, her wisdom and freedom, her humor and confidence. She doesn't fret over lines or belly rolls or stray hairs—she's a powerful force ripe with knowledge and self-assurance. Her realm is both of the earth and beyond the earth, straddling the boundaries between life and death.

Technique: Accept the Impermanence of All Things

Everything changes, everything evolves, yet nothing, nothing is ever destroyed. Accepting the fact that time hurdles forward, with or without our consent, is a major lesson of the Crone. Change is inevitable and that's exactly as it should be. Work with the High Priestess card in the tarot as representative of the deep wisdom of the Crone, or try the Wheel of Fortune card, which represents the ever-changing ups and downs of life (nothing is inherently good or b d, but rather part of a unified whole, a circle, a cycle).

Technique: Honor the Dead

One thing the Crone figure teaches us is tha‘ death and loss are inevitable, natural aspects of life. Rather than turn away from death, we should honor those who've gone before us. Our loved ones never really leave us. Matter is neither created nor destroyed; it's simply *transformed*. Those who've passed before us are right there whenever you need them, like a spirit army surrounding you, guiding and protecting you. One way to honor them in the physical realm is to build an altar in your home, which can be set up every day or on special occasions like holidays, birthdays, reunions, and the like.

For instance, on Día de Muertos, the Day of the Dead, in Mexico, families set up *ofrendas* to honor their loved ones who've passed, which also coincides with All Saints' Day in the Catholic religion. Ofrendas include photos, candles, *cempasúchil* (marigold) flowers, and other mementos and tokens. Most funerals include an altar of some kind, displaying wreaths, flowers, photographs, and mementos. But the dead can be honored at any time throughout the year, right in your home, with sacred objects and symbols for those who've passed on.

PRACTICE:
A GODDESS RITUAL

This is a ritual to invoke the Great Mother Goddess and channel the energy of the Divine Feminine. Feel free to modify as you see fit, in whichever way works best in your individual practice.

Supplies

1-ounce amber-colored bottle with a glass dropper top

Essential oils of your choice, such as rose, cedarwood, bergamot,
    lily of the valley, sandalwood, vetiver, or myrrh

Dried herbs, such as red clover, motherwort, red raspberry leaf,
    mugwort, rose, or myrtle

Carrier oil like jojoba oil

Sea salt

Clean cloth to work on or an altar cloth

Incense of your choice (optional)

Dull carving knife or pencil

Small white or blue pillar, tapered, or pull-out candle
    (the latter burns for 7–10 days)

Rose quartz or clear quartz crystals

Bowl of spring water or filtered tap water

Preparation

Create your own custom Mother Goddess blend one drop at a time in the bottle. In a one-ounce bottle with a dropper, add approximately ten to twenty drops of your essential oil, depending on how strong you'd like the scent to be. You can also add a few dried herbs the bottle. Fill up the bottle halfway with your carrier oil, gently shake the bottle, and smell it again. Creating your own custom Goddess blend isn't an exact science; it's an art. Adjust with a few extra drops of various essential oils until you get your desired scent. Then fill the rest of the bottle with the carrier oil.

Step 1

First, use your light meditation to cleanse your aura and psychic energies (described on page 47). Focus on centering yourself. Next, cast a circle of protection around you by using your dominant hand to outline a circle of light around you and your working space. Then, sprinkle a bit of sea salt around your working area and the altar cloth and light your incense.

Step 2

Using your carving knife or a pencil, inscribe a triple moon symbol onto the center of the candle. You can also use any symbol that evokes the Divine Feminine for you, whether that's waves for water, a full moon, a five-pointed star, a specific flower, a tree, a crown, a circle, a vagina, a downward-pointing triangle, a spiral within a circle, and so on. You can also work with the symbols found in the Empress card in the tarot, as representative of the Mother figure.

Step 3

Anoint the candle with your sacred Goddess oil and either rub the herbs on the candle or sprinkle them around the candle. Next, place the crystals in a circle around the candle (or in the shape of a five- or six-pointed star, the latter representing the conjoining masculine and feminine energies). You can also draw a downward-facing triangle, symbolic of the Divine Feminine and mysteries of the womb, around the candle using either the crystals or sea salt.

Step 4

Add a bit of sea salt to the bowl of water and dip your hands in it, using the water to cleanse your hands and anointing your temples, forehead, and wrists. Now, place your feet firmly on the ground beneath you, connecting with the earth (even if you're indoors) through the soles of your feet. Feel the earth's cleansing and powerful energy rising up in your body.

Step 5

Light the candle and call upon the Great Mother Goddess: "Mother Earth, feed me your stories, your ancient truths. Build me back whole again. Whisper in the old tongue, remind me of your secrets, your wisdom. Deep in sleep, you come and to you I return. Nurture my body and spirit. I feel your presence in all things, your beauty and abundance, immense and limitless. I feel you in the rocks, the trees, the earth, and waters. I feel you in all living things, untameable and wild and pure. Great Goddess, Great Spirit of the Earth, be with me, protect me, guide me in the depths, between the spaces of light and dark."

Step 6

If you'd like to ask the Great Mother for assistance, you can invoke her in any way you'd like, but I recommend speaking your petition aloud and letting the vibrations of your voice carry out your call. As the candle burns, you can also ask for assistance and specific requests, including ways to acknowledge and honor yourself as a divine being and sacred vessel for creativity, or ways to give yourself and others more compassion. Ask for renewed qualities of grace, peace, and patience. Ask for prosperity and acceptance.

Step 7

When you're done with your ritual, say thank you three times and open back up your circle (the protective one you cast when you started) by drawing your circle in reverse using your dominant hand. Gather up your objects and dispose of any herbs or salt back into the earth, or burn them in a small cauldron when you're done, sending your petition to the Goddess. You can relight the candle if it's not burned out completely and come back to it whenever you'd like.

INTEGRATIONS

By turning back to the lessons of the Goddess, we reclaim a sense of personal power. And by doing so, we honor all of creation and the earth as holy, breathing, and conscious. Through this *consciousness of consciousness*, we shape a new cultural ethos and begin to see connections where first there were none. And by doing so, we're also actively revising existing power structures and preconceived dogma, beginning with inviting a sense of awe back into our lives.

By turning away from the Great Goddess figure, we have lost a sense of our connection to the Divine, as well as our sacred connection with the earth. But our connection to the Goddess, however she has been pushed down in history, can never be lost—she is always with us and within us. We only have to turn back to her, retrace her roots, and uncover her mysteries and sacred teachings. The attempted erasure of the Goddess has cost both us and the planet, but by actively assimilating her energies into our lives, through ritual, sharing ideas, and creating safe spaces for discovery and inquiry; retelling myths and bearing witness to each other; learning self-sufficiency; studying plant medicine; creating more green spaces; and valuing the creative arts and humanities (the acquisition of all new knowledge), we get closer to her and our own divine nature.

Like the Goddess, regardless of our gender, we each hold the power of creation and destruction within us. How we use this power within us is up to us to decide. For every action, whether individual or collective, consider: Is this adding value to my life or aiding its destruction? And if the latter, is this action perhaps contributing to the rebirth cycle? The Goddess upsets; she roars; she creates and destroys.

Just as volcanoes create new lands with flowing eruptions or the ocean takes over the domain of land, neither creation nor destruction is inherently bad—it's simply what we do with those forces that matters.

Another way we can invoke more divine Goddess energy in our lives is to support the women around us in all their successes and through their trials. Western society has pitted women against each other for far too long and kept everyone stuck in a scarcity mentality. Women are consciously and unconsciously pushed to compete with other women, especially if they're in our same circles or fields of work, but that isn't the way to go. The patriarchal world would prefer to keep women separated and skeptical of each other, rather than focus on the power of combining their talents and gifts to create something new. Don't let that be the case any longer.

There's space for everyone—and it's okay to take up room, be bold, shine your light, and also support others at the same time. Think of someone you may be jealous or envious of—whether it's their successes, beauty, family, living, or work situations—and tell them what you admire about them (I guarantee you they probably need to hear it more than you know). And remember that the successes of the women in our lives are successes for everyone. By building up and championing others, we're invoking the sacred Goddess energy that lives in all of us.

CHAPTER 7

THE HEALING POWER
OF ART AND COLOR

For the ancient Greeks, theater was a cathartic experience for the collective whole. By depicting tragedy on stage, with the viewer "safely" removed from the experience, the audience members in the ancient *theatron* could experience the entire spectrum of possible lived experiences—from death, love, chaos, and rivalry to fear, ethical dilemmas, and moral tests—all within the safe space of the theater. The theater, then, becomes a space for collective catharsis, a space where we set the ego aside, come together in a shared experience, and learn from the experiences of others.

This is true from a scientific perspective as well. According to Dr. Helen Riess, an associate clinical professor of psychiatry at Harvard Medical School and author of *The Empathy Effect*, the arts and empathy have a long-shared history.[82] "We often value art by how well it evokes emotions," she writes, adding later that "art may indeed be the greatest

---

82. Helen Riess and Liz Neporent, *The Empathy Effect: Seven Neuroscience-Based Keys for Transforming the Way We Live, Love, Work, and Connect across Differences* (Boulder, CO: Sounds True, 2018), 126.

connector for our divided world."[83] In fact, the part of the brain we use to understand narrative stories "overlaps with the part we use when exercising theory of mind, one of the foundations of cognitive empathy."[84] Theory of mind is generally defined as "the ability to appreciate on a basic level that another person has thoughts and feelings separate from your own."[85] Dr. Riess recalls a 2013 study where researchers at the New School found that "reading literary fiction led to higher scores on theory of mind testing than popular fiction," due to the richness and complexity of the characters.[86] She points out that it's not to say literary fiction is necessarily *better* than popular fiction, but literary fiction teaches us that not everyone thinks as we do.[87] Simply reading literary fiction—that is, engrossing ourselves in "made-up" worlds with nuanced characterization—helps us better understand and learn from one another.

Contrary to widespread thought, empathy is not simply "feeling bad" for others or taking on their emotional burden. Too often, we absorb the emotions and experiences of others as if they were our own, especially those who are highly sensitive. But this only leads to empathy fatigue and burnout—yet another reason why psychic self-defense and aura cleansings are so necessary for spiritual health. But practicing empathy doesn't mean feeling bad or claiming the pain of others, but rather holding space for others, actively listening to them, bearing witness to their stories, and accepting the inherent value of others *even when they're different from our own*. Empathy means responding with compassion and action, rather than simply reacting.

Instead, we should strive to cultivate *cognitive empathy*. Psychologists Daniel Goleman and Paul Ekman have identified three types of empathy:

83. Riess and Neporent, *The Empathy Effect*, 127, 130.
84. Riess and Neporent, *The Empathy Effect*, 134.
85. Riess and Neporent, *The Empathy Effect*, 22.
86. Riess and Neporent, *The Empathy Effect*, 133.
87. Riess and Neporent, *The Empathy Effect*, 133.

Cognitive Empathy: The ability to understand what a person is thinking or how they feel

Emotional Empathy: Reactionary, as discussed earlier, and sharing the pain of that person

Compassionate Empathy: Empathetic concern and when understanding leads to action[88]

When we couple cognitive empathy (logical, rational understanding) with compassionate empathy (rooted in concern and action), we're better serving our spiritual purpose.

Visual art, literature, storytelling, and theater are vital to fostering cognitive and compassionate empathy. In fact, art is incomplete without an active observer—it requires the "perceptual and emotional involvement of the viewer."[89] For instance, by engaging with and participating in the narrative arts—whether it's through reading fiction (with emotionally authentic characters), performing rituals, reenacting myths and stories in safe spaces, or experiencing visual artworks together, we form shared mental and emotional bonds.[90]

In this sense, art is a tool for collective healing. It becomes a tool not only for understanding others and ourselves but also for helping us strip away concepts of the individual self (or the ego). It also helps us consider our experience within the complexity of the cosmos, occasionally offering a transcendent or spiritual experience. In both its creation and reception, art unlocks wonder and curiosity, moving beyond the liminal and taking us into other realms of consciousness. Art's potential for transcendence, for deeper connection, is perhaps why, historically, those in power wish to contain or limit it, along with human potential.

---

88. Daniel Goleman, *Emotional Intelligence: Why It Can Matter More Than IQ* (New York: Bantam Books, 2020); Harvard Business Review, *Empathy: HBR Emotional Intelligence Series* (Boston, MA: Harvard Business Review Press, 2017).

89. Riess and Neporent, *The Empathy Effect*, 128.

90. Riess and Neporent, *The Empathy Effect*, 125–40.

Consider how many books have been banned in the US alone, a country with freedom of speech and the press built into its very constitution. Think of the censorship of art, film, and music throughout the centuries: it's because art is a powerful conduit. It can channel that which is hard or even impossible to express through language alone. Art is also a vehicle for the Divine and higher expression; it challenges the idea that things *are as they appear to be* on the surface. In other words, art takes us to other worlds, transports us, inducing self-reflection and curiosity, bristling up against the status quo of the accepted norm. For this reason, too, art can be a product of and vehicle for our higher callings.

When we seek out art, become curious and present with it, looking beyond apparent form, we become empathetic participants in the work, alongside its creator. In this sense, we're not merely passive observers; we're also building our intuition, expanding our vulnerability and emotional intelligence, and connecting to a small part of a much larger story. And by doing so, art becomes an active exchange, an exercise in empathy, a vehicle for spiritual awakening and healing.

STORY: A VEHICLE FOR AWAKENING

Mexico City and New York, 2018

In 2018, I attended an exhibition at Frida Kahlo's former home, La Casa Azul, which is now the Frida Kahlo Museum, in Coyoacán, Mexico City. The museum showcased her personal artifacts and clothing, and there was something deeply personal about moving through her blue house, seeing her personal things, her vivid artwork on the walls, her bed where she spent many years recovering from illness. After that initial visit, I began poring through her personal letters, finding any research material I could. Her work opened up something inside me, something powerful, but my brain wanted *words* and logic to understand this connection I had with her work. Perhaps I thought that if I could understand her better, it would illuminate something deeper not only about my inner psyche but also about the human condition at large. Then, only a few months later,

right in my neighborhood, the Brooklyn Museum put on a show entitled "Frida Kahlo: Appearances Can Be Deceiving." It would be the
largest US exhibition on her work in a decade.

Wandering through the rooms at the Brooklyn Museum, I became
visibly emotionally affected, overwhelmed by her works all over again.
After a series of accidents early on in life left her in chronic pain, she
transmuted and transformed this trauma and misfortune through art,
crafting and recrafting her sense of identity through self-portraiture. I
thought of her personal letters, the ones I had read over and over: the
fiercely strong woman depicted in the self-portraits was also undeniably fragile and vulnerable. Perhaps this is where her strength, and
subsequent beauty, came from. This ability to expose the rawness of
despair, to use it as a channel; to convey, through color and symbolism, the depths of personal suffering. I nearly stumbled out of the
museum in tears. I sat on a bench outside the museum, looking up at
its neoclassical columns and carvings, sobbing in awe, whispering to
the air, to Kahlo's spirit, "Thank you. Thank you. Thank you."

I wondered if, when she was creating, she knew just how impactful her work would become, how her work would transcend the personal and situational, and touch upon the universal. I wondered if
she knew how her art would become a vehicle, a connector, a channel between worlds. I wondered if she had been sitting on that bench
with me, would she say the pain of her life, the physical agony of it all,
was worth it to create such magic and movement in the world? All I
knew for certain, at that moment, was that through her artwork, I had
walked away changed, the colors of her work trailing behind me.

As a design editor and journalist, I've fortunately had the opportunity to utilize my sensitivities to design, color, and spatial layout in
intuitive ways, whether it's working on a print magazine layout, select-
ing editorial photos, or writing about the ways color, space, and organic
design in architecture and interiors have a profound impact on our
psychology, mood, and psychic states. Surprisingly, my sensitivities and

intuition have served me more in these arenas than traditional training or even schooling.

It's also come in handy while teaching art and culture: many of my college students had never visited an art gallery or critically analyzed a work of art before our class. Especially for first-generation college students (I'm one of them!), visiting museums felt a bit intimidating because they felt they didn't have the so-called proper artistic vocabulary to discuss the works. But I also knew that at one time or another in their lives, they had used the power of their intuition.

I'd ask students to analyze the hues, tones, and shading within artwork based first on how it made them *feel*. And more times than not, by focusing on their emotional and intuitive response, they were better able to understand the historical and cultural contexts in which the works were created. I'd start with simple questions: "What does this shade of blue mean to *you*? How does it make you feel? Is it a melancholic blue, or does it spark happiness and wonder? Why do you think the artist decided to use pops of bright pink within this triptych? What do you think of these particular shades of red?" and so on. Through seemingly roundabout ways, the students learned to rely on their intuition (sometimes called instincts, but I prefer to use the term *intuition*) to better understand an artwork, as well as explore their own personal connection to color. And through this, their ability to contextualize the painting's mood, style, and message also emerged.

Many of us don't realize just how much art is built into the everyday fabric of our lives. We communicate with each other through the conscious (and even unconscious) use of design and color all the time. For instance, design impacts the way we feel in spaces and places, influencing our psychology and emotional states, whether it's our workspaces or within our own homes. These nonverbal messages are just as much a part of our lives as our written, bodily, and verbal cues. So why aren't we thinking more deeply about them?

DEEP DIVE: THE MAGICAL, HEALING POWER OF COLOR

The greatest architects and designers in the world are masters at creating spaces that conjure specific feelings, sensations, and states of mind. Everything is intentional, well-thought-out, and precise—yet they just don't call what they do magic. They have to think of the multitude of ways space, color, and design influence our physical, emotional, and even psychic states. And if they don't consider the latter, well, in my opinion, it's just bad design.

Objects and experiences may not have inherent meaning without first passing through our perception—that is, our consciousness. We give meaning to things—to moments in time, to spaces, to objects. What moves us, what strikes passion and awe, what strikes a chord in our soul is subjective, but beauty can be found all around us. And if we open our eyes to looking at the physical world in a different light, even everyday objects can take on new meaning, allowing new depths of perception to emerge.

Some of the most inspiring principles of art, design, and color are found right in nature. When I visited Frank Lloyd Wright's desert laboratory in Arizona, Taliesin West, I was struck by how harmonious, how integrated, the architecture was with the surrounding landscape. It was there that I ran across a quote by this midcentury architect: "Nature is my manifestation of God. I go to nature every day for inspiration in the day's work. I follow in building the principles which nature has used in its domain." Nature, like artwork, reflects back to us something of ourselves, acting as a mirror.

In other ways, art acts as a catalyst for empathy and deeper spiritual connectivity, striking chords in us that require deeper exploration. If art is an active experience—requiring the viewer to actively and emotionally participate in and engage with the work—is it possible to use color itself as a vehicle not only for empathy but also for healing and deeper spiritual knowledge?

Color affects us on a deep, subconscious level, and we can consciously use it to tap into the greater frequencies both around and within us. Every color, hue, and shade contains its own unique vibration, which we can tune in to in order to gain deeper spiritual wisdom and insight. Consider all the colors present around you in this very moment, from the clothes and accessories you're wearing, to the color of the walls and décor, to the natural colors of the environment. Not only do these colors have a correlation with different emotions, but they also have magical uses, associations with chakra points, deities, planets, and psychic states of being. Think, for instance, about the color red: How does it *make you feel*? What's the first image that comes to mind? Is it fear, blood, anger, or chaos? Or is it invigoration, motivation, or passion? Where do you *feel* the color in your body? Depending on the distinct hue in your mind, the color red can evoke different emotions and images, as well as psychic states.

Color magic, which is rooted in intentionality, is about tuning in to the spiritual vibrations of color and using it to manifest your intention. There's a whole spectrum of colors that exist around us, including ones we can't even see, and these myriad hues influence our spiritual well-being, too. By consciously using color in ritual, including light visualizations, candle magic, and meditation work, we can realign with our higher intentions, goals, and spiritual callings. Color magic can also help align the chakras, unblock energetic centers within the psychic body, and positively influence our everyday consciousness and emotional states.

Whether it's painting an accent wall in your home, choosing a central hue for your living room, deciding on your clothes or jewelry for the day, or utilizing light visualization and meditation techniques, everything can be a magical act if done with intention. Color defies and transcends physical boundaries; color defies form and the limits of the mind, going beyond the intellectual planes.

But first, let's talk about how color is connected to energetic centers within the body, also known as chakras. First mentioned in the ancient Sanskrit texts known as the Vedas and later in Buddhist texts, the chakra system consists of seven energetic centers arranged along the spine: the root, sacral, solar plexus, heart, throat, third eye, and crown chakra. These energetic centers are circular (the word *chakra* translates to "wheel" or "circle") and are always in spinning motion, similar to a spiral. Interestingly enough, the spiral is a fundamental form of the universe: not only does the spiral show up constantly in nature all around us, within shells, pinecones, and even our DNA, but it's present throughout the universe at large, including the shape of galaxies like our own Milky Way, bristling and pulsating with energy. Our inner world mirrors our outer world, and vice versa.

In geometry, the spiral can be understood mathematically as the Fibonacci sequence, the golden spiral, or golden ratio. The Fibonacci sequence is a formula for the growth patterns of life, found all around us in nature and often used in art since it's so aesthetically pleasing, appealing to our sensibilities of form and symmetry.[91] Within the infinite pattern of this sacred form, if any part within the spiral became blocked or stagnant, it would affect the entirety of the spiral, affecting its growth and outward trajectory, inhibiting or limiting both flow and form.

The chakra system is similar: if one energetic center gets out of balance or stuck, it can affect the flow of all your energy. For instance, if your root chakra is blocked or out of balance, it can affect your crown chakra. Just as the blood carrying nutrients and oxygen moves through the body's limbs, our spiritual energy also must flow without impediment.

WORKING WITH COLOR MAGIC AND THE CHAKRAS

The chakra system dates back to the Vedic texts written over 3,000 years ago, and in recent years, it's become integrated into modern magical and witchcraft traditions as well. In contemporary times, the concept and energy work of chakras has continued to evolve to embrace color associations and symbology, especially in candle magic and rituals. The best

---

91. Elizabeth Hand, "Patterns in Nature: Where to Spot Spirals," Science World, April 25, 2019, https://www.scienceworld.ca/stories/patterns-nature-where-spot-spirals/.

thing is you have the power within you to help heal these energetic centers. Magic comes from within. As with all things, balance is key.

Here are some general techniques and ways to think about color as it pertains to your psychic, emotional, and spiritual well-being, as well as specific color rituals and meditations.

Technique: Working with Gold and Silver

Gold and silver are the colors of royalty, dripping sensuality, decadence, and celebration. But more than earthly desires and riches, they represent holy realms and energies of the sun and moon. Ever notice when you look at Renaissance art, you see a golden halo over the heads of saints and holy figures? This simple symbol, the golden halo, represents divine connection and enlightenment. It signifies a state of holiness and walking in truth.

For Illumination and Prosperity

Use the color gold to invoke the energy of the sun and prosperity and to illuminate higher truth. You can wear the color, use gold accents in your meditation space or study, or simply visualize the color around you. There's a reason why holiness is depicted with a golden halo in Western art. Gold was also spiritually significant for the ancient Egyptians, as it was considered to be the color of the gods' and goddesses' skin.[92] It's also the color used in illuminated manuscripts and holy texts from both Islamic and European traditions to represent the words of God.[93]

For Psychic Insight

Silver is connected to lunar energies, the subconscious, water, psychic knowledge, intuition, and emotions. Think of a dark, midnight sky on a full moon night. The shadowy earth has a silvery hue when it's bathed in

---

92. Jon Mann, "A Brief History of Gold in Art, from Ancient Egyptian Burial Masks to Jeff Koons," Artsy, October 19, 2017, https://www.artsy.net/article/artsy-editorial -history-gold-art-ancient-egyptian-burial-masks-jeff-koons.

93. Mann, "A Brief History of Gold in Art."

the light of the moon, revealing a softer, more elusive quality of reality. If the sun is sometimes regarded as masculine, the moon embodies the feminine. Use silver when you'd like to tap into your psychic powers or get clarity on your emotions.

Technique: Working with Deep Red, Reddish Browns, and Earth Tones

When you need to regain a sense of groundedness, safety, or calm (especially if you find yourself overanalyzing, overintellectualizing, or overthinking), meditating on and using deep reds, rich browns, and earth tones can help balance your root chakra. Alternatively, visualizing and meditating on a bright red can have a different effect altogether: either it's stimulating, invigorating, and passionate, or it can conjure up feelings of anger. There's a reason why people "see red" when they're extremely angry, and this is not the energy we want to harness and develop. Get specific about the shade of color you're working with to channel specific vibrations and emotions and to enhance particular psychic states.

Deep reds and browns are connected to the root chakra, *muladhara*, which is the first chakra, located at the base of the spine and pelvic floor, and is associated with the earth element. It's often symbolized by a lotus flower and helps with feelings of security and physical balance.

For Vitality and Passion

In Western color magic, a bright, bold shade of red is traditionally used in spells and energy work involving passion, sex, and control, as well as igniting old flames and sparking excitement. Of course, depending on your tradition, geography, and spiritual lineage, the associations with these colors may vary, not only from practice to practice but from person to person. Remember: *magic is individual.*

For Centering and Grounding

Meditating on a deep, rich hue of red or lush shade of reddish brown (not a murky, bland, or overly loud shade though) can help us feel more centered and secure in our bodies, helping us feel closer to our connection with the earth—especially for those working in the psychic and spiritual arts.

For Balancing and Centering Your Root Chakra

Begin by taking a ritual bath with sea salt, herbs, and essential oils of your choice. Either while in the bath or afterward, settle into the mind and visualize a deep, rich red color in your lower spine area and pelvic floor. Imagine that healing light releasing tension and opening that chakra point. If candle magic is in your practice, use a red candle and carve a downward-facing triangle and then draw a square around that. Next, draw a perfect circle around the square and add four petals, spaced evenly around the circle, on the outside. Add your name and astrological sign to personalize it. When you're ready to light the candle, continue the light visualization while the candle is burning. Add chants, mantras, or affirmations ("I am safe, grounded, rooted in my power. I am protected, loved, provided for. I have everything I need within me and around me. The earth anchors me."). Journaling for fifteen to twenty minutes can also help illuminate parts of yourself that feel "stuck" or out of sorts and point to the sources of these issues by bringing them out from the unconscious mind onto the page.

Technique: Working with Orange

Orange is associated with the sacral chakra, which is located in regions of the lower abdomen, and it's associated with sexuality, sensuality, emotions, and the element of water. Orange is the color of creativity, it *spurs something in the mind*, opening new pathways to reveal new dimensions, possibilities, and ways of seeing.

Interestingly enough, orange can sometimes have an irritating effect on some. Consider the nineteenth-century book by Joris-Karl Huysmans entitled *Against the Grain*: the reclusive, eccentric protagonist, Jean des Esseintes, declares that orange has "almost mathematical correctness— the theory that a harmony exists between the sensual nature of a truly artistic individual and the color which most vividly impresses him."[94] For Esseintes, orange was an artistic color, one that pulsated with vibrant, creative potentiality; it embodied that peculiarity necessary for artistic creation. However, he noted a peculiar drawback to the color: when "the eyes of enfeebled and nervous persons whose sensual appetites crave highly seasoned foods, the eyes of hectic and over-excited creatures have a predilection toward that irritating and morbid color with its fictitious splendors, its acid fevers—orange."[95]

Since orange is connected to our sacral chakra, when it's out of balance, consciously working with the color orange may reveal that this chakra point needs healing.

For Creativity

Surround yourself with a bright yet grounded shade of orange (like terracotta) when you're starting a new creative project. If a current project is lacking a little "oomph" or you're feeling uninspired, take a break and experiment with painting something using only various shades of orange. Start with a single shade of orange paint and mix in white and black paint to create five or six new values to work with.

For Thinking Outside the Box

If you're feeling stuck at work, change up the color palette on slideshow presentations to orange (even on a corporate deck). Try wearing the color or adding pops of orange in your home décor where you produce creative projects.

For Balancing Your Sacral Chakra

In Eastern traditions, orange is related to the second chakra, the sacral chakra (*svadhisthana*), and is connected to the kidneys, digestion, bladder, and sexual organs, as well as sensuality, sexuality, creativity, and

---

94. J. K. Huysmans, *Against the Grain*, trans. John Howard (New York: Albert & Charles Boni, 1922), 35.

95. Huysmans, *Against the Grain*, 36.

emotions. When these areas are overstimulated or in need of balance, visualize a healing orb of orange light cleansing and purifying these physical spaces. If it becomes too overstimulating, focus on a blue for balance (which the Impressionists often did to denote shadow in their paintings). You can also eat more orange-colored foods, such as yams, carrots, and turmeric, to help balance and heal this chakra point.

Technique: Working with Yellow

The color yellow is associated with our solar plexus (*manipura* in Sanskrit), the third chakra, and is connected to our emotions, power, will, self-esteem, assertiveness, identity, ego, courage, and confidence. Associated with the element of fire, it's found in the naval region, primarily the gut and upper belly regions within the body. Our solar plexus is the center of our personal power; it's connected to our personality, ego, and identity.

When our solar plexus is out of balance, we may feel a sense of powerlessness or insecurity. Some may have an "overstimulated" solar plexus, resulting in ego-driven behavior or an overinflated sense of self. When we feel emotionally out of control, anxious, or depressed, our solar plexus may be in need of healing. When our self-esteem is suffering, when we feel stagnation, when we're simply not motivated, or even when we experience digestive issues and anxiety, there's probably solar plexus work to do. Alternatively, if we find ourselves needing or wanting to control others or engage in manipulative behaviors, it can also signify this area is blocked or needs healing work. Like all chakra work, tuning in to this energetic center and healing any blocks can be emotionally transformative. Candle magic, breathing exercises, and meditative rituals, accompanied by other wellness practices, like yoga (especially twist positions) and a whole food diet, are all great ways to help rebalance, retune, cleanse, and strengthen this sacred center.

For Awakening Your Solar Plexus

Carve a downward-pointed triangle surrounded by a circle with ten pet-als on a yellow candle (evenly spaced) and burn it with the intention of awakening, opening up, and healing your solar plexus. You can also carve the sun symbol, stars, and other sigils involving growth, expansion, happiness, and empowerment. While the candle burns, meditate on the Sun and Empress cards in the tarot, noticing the artist's interpretation of the cards, staying open to the symbols, colors, and emotions it evokes within you.

For Stimulating Vitality

Since our solar plexus is located in our physical center, movement and exercise help this energetic center, especially when focused on the core, as well as deep breathing exercises and light walking in the sun. Consciously cook and consume yellow with intention, such as squash, sunflower seeds, bananas, cinnamon, and oats. As you ingest the food, concentrate on open-ing and cleansing your solar plexus. It helps to visualize the life cycle of the plant or vegetables: how each one starts out as a tiny seed and is nurtured by the earth and elements, relying on the sun for energy, which will now be transferred to you.

For Confidence, Peace, and Joy

Seek out yellow in the natural world, such as yellow flowers and plants found in nature, and become allies. You can also make solar plexus teas using ingestible yellow flowers, such as calendula, or those with yellow centers, like chamomile. Alternatively, you can choose a stone, crystal, gem, or resin associated with the solar plexus, such as amber, citrine, tiger's eye, and pyrite.

Pair this work with words of affirmation, either chanted or written out in a journal: "I am centered. I am whole. I am confident. I am radiant. I am enough. I am powerful. I use my power to help myself and others. I embody light and courage. The sun lives within my bones, in my belly, in my chest."

For Healing

Visualize a small, bright yellow ball of light in your belly area. As you breathe into that center, imagine that golden, radiant light expanding outward, flowing through all your limbs, and eventually extending beyond your body and settling around your auric field.

Alternatively, you can pick a natural yellow object to meditate on, such as a sunflower, daffodil, or marigold. Imagine the flower starting out as a seed at your center, growing and blooming inside you, and filling your body with a luminous yellow hue and light. Sit with this visualization for five to ten minutes per day while working on your solar plexus.

Technique: Working with Green

Green is associated with Gaia (or the Earth Goddess), Venus/Aphrodite, Fortuna (a.k.a. Lady Luck), Green Tara Goddess in Tibetan Buddhism, and the heart chakra. Green represents money, fertility, fecundity, financial success and wealth, luck, love, peace, and the elements of earth and air. In Eastern traditions, the heart chakra, known as *anahata* in Sanskrit, is symbolized by a six-pointed star with twelve lotus petals and governs our sense of love, compassion, and understanding. Meditating on a calming shade of green helps open and heal the heart center and also aids in grief, loss, and matters of love.

Since green is related to the heart chakra and associated with the various goddesses and archetypes, it's a good color to invoke the Goddess, Goddess energies, compassion, healing, and emotional well-being. The tone of the specific green you use is important here: it shouldn't be one that has a dreary or drab quality but a rich, deep or light shade that inspires a sense of joy and awe.

For Improved Finances

Green is best used for money spells, especially when coupled with sigils such as money pyramids and financial sigils (even something as simple as a dollar sign carved into a candle). Whether you're trying to welcome in more abundance, invite financial stability, or clear away debt, the color green can be used to psychically draw this energy toward you.

For Healing

Green is a powerfully healing color since it's most readily found in the natural world. Although finding it in abundance within urban centers can be quite the challenge with a limitation in green public spaces, forest bathing, or the art of mindful walks in the forest, can be especially healing for the mind, heart, and spirit. Studies have shown there are numerous physical benefits to forest bathing, as well, including lowering cortisol, stress hormones, and blood pleasure; alleviating stress and anxiety; and aiding in sleep, focus, creativity, and mood.[96]

Working with Pink

Like green, pink is also associated with the heart chakra and the goddess Venus (among other deities and archetypes in various magical traditions). It's often used for spells involving self-love, confidence, bringing along new love, healing matters of the heart, self-esteem, joy, empowerment, aiding in forgiveness, and working with the Divine Goddess.

While pink has a feminine energy, that doesn't mean it's meant for women or any specific gender—it's used to invoke, manifest, and align the feminine energies *present in all of us* or as a manifestation of love. All of us contain a spectrum of energies, and anyone, anywhere, can use the color pink to enhance their spiritual lives. The color pink (coupled with Spirit) is stronger and more luminous than you can imagine, replacing resentment with feelings of tranquility, acceptance, and unconditional

96. "Immerse Yourself in a Forest for Better Health," New York Department of Environmental Conservation, accessed June 4, 2024, https://dec.ny.gov/nature/forests-trees /immerse-yourself-for-better-health.

love. Pink is the color of forgiveness, which is the essence of love. We can send these healing energies as vibrational waves of color to others who may need it. Since color defies form, we can use it more easily for transcendental and healing purposes—plus it's much easier than sending something through the post office, that's for sure.

For the Home

Create a sacred space in your home for meditation. It can be situated near your sacred altar or just in a light-filled section of your living room or bedroom. Add items that spark joy and love and inspire reverence to a higher power, be it with Venus statues, singing bowls, bowls of water or crystals, incense, or photos.

For Opening the Heart Chakra

If you can, pull up a singing bowl playlist for the heart chakra on Spotify (but set your phone to "do not disturb"). Singing bowls tuned to F or F# notes are great for opening and healing the heart chakra. As you focus on the music, visualize the color pink: first radiating above you as a bright ball of light, then down on your body, and finally all around you. Next, imagine this light as a spiral coming directly from your heart center. Let the swirls of pink move throughout your chest, filling up your body, and eventually radiating outside of you. Let that color permeate the room, the street, the town you're in, eventually encompassing the entire globe.

For Cultivating Self-Love and Forgiveness

Focus on the bright, full, vibrant color of pink like an amorphous cloud filled with love and forgiveness. Move that sense of love anywhere you may need it to go: inward for healing or outward to those who may have hurt you, caused pain, misunderstood you, or angered you. I also find this color meditation very effective in "connecting" with others on a spiritual level—especially those with whom you've lost a connection or if things aren't going right on the physical plane between the two of you—as well as releasing anger. We're able to better communicate from a soul level when we embody this presence of love and compassion. Let the color radiate and extend that feeling outward; share it with others, sapped in a fullness that belongs to others just as much as it belongs to you.

Staying in this meditation for at least fifteen minutes, you will literally feel your heart center opening and feelings of anger and resentment melting away. Soon, the murky grays lurking within your heart space— wispy, unruly, heavy—will begin transforming into lush, soft pinks. If you get emotional during this time, it's okay. Cry, stretch, let it out. You're releasing a nest of emotions that are no longer serving your higher purpose, and it's okay to let it go. You can also chant aloud if that helps you in your practice: "I release all anger. I let that which is no longer serving me go. I give it back to the earth. I embody love in all ways. I am made of love and come from love. I forgive those who've caused me pain, and I ask for forgiveness in turn. I send this sacred message to the universe and to those who need it most."

Technique: Working with Blue

Associated with the throat chakra (*vishuddha* in Sanskrit, the fifth chakra), blue is connected to opening channels of communication, tranquility, and speaking your mind and truth. It's also associated with the god Hermes/Mercury, the Great Ocean Goddess, the orisha and queen of the sea Yemayá, the Divine Mother, Mother Mary, and the Roman goddess of peace Pax, as well as fecundity, protection, and unity. In Eastern traditions, the throat chakra is symbolically represented by a downward-pointing triangle and sixteen lotus petals.

For me, blue is the color that represents the first, the last, the always. It's the color of the ocean and sky. Blue is the color of peace, of protection; it's the color of healing, both emotional and physical. It's the color of our incredibly miraculous blue planet—a pale blue dot on the horizon of space, a tiny, fragile, lonely speck situated within a grand spectrum of light and darkness. The color blue represents *our first home*. And it's a reminder of the sacred things we must protect.

When ruminating on our solitary home planet from space, Carl Sagan wrote, "Look again at that dot. That's here. That's home. That's us. On it everyone you love, everyone you know, everyone you ever heard of, every human being who ever was, lived out their lives. The aggregate of our joy and suffering, thousands of confident religions, ideologies, and economic doctrines, every hunter and forager, every hero and coward, every creator and destroyer of civilization... every mother and father, hopeful child, inventor and explorer, every teacher of morals... every saint and sinner in the history of our species lived there—on a mote of dust suspended in a sunbeam."[97]

It's important to note there are so many variations, hues, and tones possible within a particular spectrum of color. Stay open to your own unique associations with blue and let that guide you. For instance, if I ask you to think of blue, what hue pops into your mind? Is it one similar to a warm summer sky or a deep ocean blue? A sea-green tropical blue? A turquoise stone from the desert? The muted pale blue of a French chateau? A deep navy color? Does it produce taste, a sound, a song?

For Strength

Wear the color blue for important business or social meetings where you need to convey and articulate something of importance. You can also wear blue stones on your person, especially necklaces with blue stones (like lapis lazuli, amazonite, larimar, blue topaz, or sodalite) that directly touch your throat chakra.

For Tranquility at Home

Paint an accent wall or entire room (ideally the bedroom or bathroom) to conjure a sense of peace. Make sure it's not a "loud" blue but has a soothing hue.

---

97. Carl Sagan, *Pale Blue Dot: A Vision of the Human Future in Space* (New York: Ballantine Books, 1994), 6.

For Balance and Healing

Create an altar for the Great Ocean Mother and petition her for healing, emotional balance, or issues with fertility by using a bowl of sea salt, seashells, blue and white stones, and any imagery of the sea.

For Peace

Carve a circle with a downward-pointing triangle in the center of a blue candle. Then carve sixteen lotus petals around the circle, as well as your initials and astrological sign.

Working with Indigo

The sixth chakra point, located on the forehead (in the brow area in between the eyes), is known as the third eye chakra or *ajna* in Sanskrit. It's associated with indigo or deep blue-purple and involves our awareness, psychic power, clarity, telepathy, clairvoyant knowledge, inspiration, the conscious and unconscious mind, intuition, imagination, intellectual work, and prophecy. As the "all-seeing eye," this energetic center allows us to communicate with the other side, spirits, and the Source.

Sometimes the brow chakra can feel warm to the touch and glow when you're working in the spiritual arts or engaging in psychic work, or even during heavy intellectual or artistic work. Purple or indigo is the color of wisdom, and so it can help us access communication with the divine energies present and beyond these physical forms. It's also a color of the Muses. In Eastern traditions, it's symbolized by a downward-pointing triangle surrounded by a circle with two lotus petals on the horizontal edges. The third eye is where wisdom comes flooding in, but it's also important to keep that center balanced, too.

For Communicating with Spirit

Mugwort, often associated with the goddess Artemis or Diana, can help open up channels to the spirit world and is often used for Delphic dreaming. Create a tincture with the freshly harvested herb: fill a mason jar with mugwort, cover it with 80- to 120-proof vodka or brandy, let sit in a cool, dark place for two to four weeks, and strain into a two- to four-ounce amber-colored tincture bottle. Alternatively, you can steep mugwort in hot water for a nighttime tea. Do not ingest mugwort if you are pregnant or want to become pregnant in the near future, as it can induce blood flow and menstruation.

For Improving Psychic Awareness

Take a small purple pillar or seven-day candle and carve a downward-pointing triangle surrounded by a circle with two lotus petals on the horizontal edges using a dull knife. Rub the candle with clary sage and lavender oils, as well as herbs of your choice (crackled bay leaf, rosemary, mugwort) or metal-based silver, lilac, or gold glitter.

For Your Third Eye

Charge an amethyst, a clear quartz, or a moonstone with the specific intention of strengthening your third eye. First, smoke cleanse the stone with palo santo, sage, copal, frankincense, rosemary, or any herb or resin of your choice, or you can leave the stone on your windowsill under the full moon or submerge it in a bowl of sea salt for two to three days. Carry the stone with you throughout the day or use it during meditation or spellwork.

Working with Violet or White Light

The color violet or pure bright light is connected to the seventh chakra or the crown chakra (*sahasrara* in Sanskrit). In Eastern traditions and magical practices, the crown chakra is the place where we connect to the Divine; it's located in the space *just beyond* our physical form, hovering above at the top of our crown (head). It's also connected to wisdom, transcendence, and divinity.

Have you ever noticed how newborn babies have a "soft spot" on the top of their heads, the sensitive space where the skull is not yet fully formed? As we've evolved as a species and our brains got bigger than our ancestors', this anatomical feature made childbirth easier as the mother pushes the baby from the birth canal; soft spots also help with the development of the skull and brain, since babies experience rapid brain growth during their first year of life.[98] And so, even after the soft spot on an infant's head begins to close up and become a fully formed skull, that space (and the space upward, just beyond it) remains significant all our lives. For me and many others, it's still the source of our divine connection.

The spiritual significance for this underdevelopment of a newborn feels especially unique. Babies are the closest to the Divine, for their souls just underwent a long journey from "the other side" into new earthly bodies. I like to think of it as the spot where our souls first entered our bodies, and the connection to higher realms is still directly present in that space; newborn children are the closest to the First Creator, the Source. When babies smile in their sleep, for instance, I think they're still communicating with the other side in those moments, smiling at the spectacle of wonder, protected by their spirit guides.

In general, the color violet, as well as the sacred crown chakra, can be viewed as a pathway toward enlightenment. It's the space where we access communication with our higher self, our spirit guides, our angels, and messages from beyond the veil. If we tune in to this energetic center while remaining grounded, we can experience transcendence, ecstasy, and enlightenment. It's from this space that we can channel divine messages, invoke wisdom from other realms, and keep in touch with who we are.

For Improving Meditation and Spellwork

Wearing violet, using it in your home décor (especially in wellness-centered spaces), and doing color visualizations can help promote and foster access to divine focus and wisdom. If we turn our gaze to this chakra point, focusing on what our spirit wants to tell us, we will see changes in our consciousness and access a higher vibratory state.

98. Erin Wayman, "Why Do Babies Have Soft Spots?" *Smithsonian Magazine*, May 7, 2012. https://www.smithsonianmag.com/science-nature/why-do-babies-have-soft -spots-82746501/.

PRACTICE:
A COLOR MAGIC RITUAL

Dr. John Miller, my friend and philosophy professor, was trained as a transcendental meditator, teaching classes on various techniques for many years, and emphasized working upward through the various spiritual realms or planes, moving through the lower physical vibrations toward the intellectual, and finally to the spiritual, by focusing on the chakra points and using the vibration of our voice to tune in to higher energy.

Before accessing and tapping into the transcendental state of the crown chakra (which is a state of pure joy, ecstasy, and peace), we should first move through the lower energetic centers of the body, followed by the other chakras, opening them one by one through visualizations, color meditations, and sound. Think of it like scuba diving or apnea (free diving): when you're descending or ascending in the water, you must equalize as you go through the various depths, adjusting the body and acclimating along the way.

Supplies
Meditation cushion or pillow
Blanket
Quiet room or a place in nature

Step 1
Sit in a comfortable position with your legs crossed, using a pillow or blanket, if desired. Start at the root chakra, visualizing a deep, enriching red hue or earth tones emanating from the base of your spine and bottom, anchoring and grounding you. Let that nurturing, warm color radiate around you, covering the floor, extending deep within the earth.

Step 2
When you're ready, move upward to your sacral chakra, visualizing a beautiful orange color moving through your hips, sexual organs, and kid-

neys, cleansing, purifying, and empowering those areas. Let this orange hue fill your belly. You can also imagine the color as a spiral, swirling through this region in your body.

Step 3

When you're ready, let the orange light move upward to the solar plexus, changing its color ever so slightly to a bright, healing, vibrant yellow. Raise your eyes under your closed eyelids a bit more. Let the yellow light turn into a bright sun, a cleansing force centered at the bottom of your rib cage, filling your belly with light and traveling upward and downward throughout your limbs. Let any emotions that may be coming up get "filtered" through this bright yellow light. Breathe deeply from your abdomen, and with each breath, imagine pure, energetic sunlight moving through you as a spiral or a wash of color.

Step 4

When you're ready, let the yellow light move slightly upward to your chest and heart area, transforming into a beautiful shade of green. Think of the rich hues of a forest, damp and fecund, letting the deep greens expand your chest and spread throughout your body. With each breath, draw in more of this pure green color. You can use mental images to assist: an expansive meadow on a warm day or a tiny fern that grows slowly into lush vegetation. If you notice emotions coming up, let them be "filtered" by this light, allowing them to move through you. Release your chest muscles, letting your heart expand open, perhaps even pointing it slightly toward the ceiling or sky as you breathe in.

Step 5

Let the green light travel toward your throat chakra, transforming into blue. Relax your throat, jaw, and chest muscles even further. Imagine a spiral of blue, like an ocean wave, move through your throat, releasing any blockages or tension. Stay here for a while, if you need to.

Step 6

Move upward toward your third eye, the space between your eyebrows, and focus on opening that space. Let the color blue slowly transform into a vibrant shade of purple, allowing new energy flow in this area. When you're ready, move even higher to your crown chakra, just above your head, imagining the purple hue transforming into pure white light or a bold indigo color. Let this color encase and envelop your body, connecting you to the spirit realm and also the earth. Stay open and curious to what comes to you in these moments. Accessing the crown chakra can sometimes feel disorienting, because you're breaking through barriers and illusions and entering a higher realm. Sit in this space for as long as you'd like.

Step 7

Just as you came up through each chakra point, use the spectrum of colors to work your way back into the body again, one by one, finishing with a deep, enriching red hue or earth tones to assist with the grounding process. Neglecting this step, just like coming up too quickly from a deep water dive, can produce strange effects, similar to oxygen deprivation and the buildup of nitrogen. As you go through each chakra point in reverse, with each breath, anchor yourself deeper in the earth. Before opening your eyes, wiggle your fingers and toes, stretch your neck, and place your palms firmly on the ground to reconnect with the earth.

INTEGRATIONS

When viewed holistically, color, art, and design can greatly impact our daily lives, whether it's actively seeking art at a museum or in the natural world, noticing our internal responses to color, or intentionally designing our spaces to manifest certain psychic states. If we remain present and open to its cues and clues, the visual and visible world has much more to offer than what's on the surface.

CHAPTER 8
CREATIVITY AND THE MUSE

To be human is to be creative; existence itself is a creative act. You could even say creativity is at the heart of nearly everything we do as a species. You don't have to be an artist to invoke more creativity in your life. As children of the earth, we have an infinite capacity for creativity, and each time we use it, we give birth to something new. Creativity can open doors in the mind, revealing new realms. It's the key to moving beyond the fixed, boring, colorless door of dogma and entering a kaleidoscopic world filled with untapped magical potential and possibilities.

As with empathy, I've been fascinated with the concept of creativity for many years: Is it a learned skill or innate? Is it something that resides deep within us, or does it come from outside of us? Are some people more creative (Does it run in the family? Is it personality type?), or can we conjure and cultivate it through exercises and practice? I think it's a mix of all these things, but regardless, the main question everyone wants the answer to is "How can we lead more creative lives?"

Minds far greater than mine have tackled these questions in interesting, nuanced ways, approaching the subject from angles ranging from the philosophical to the neuroscientific and even the magical. But in my own search for answers, I've found that one exercise—one simple practice—may be one key to unlocking the magic of creativity.

STORY: KEEPING A NOTEBOOK

New York, 2021

I stood at the head of the room, staring back at their faces, half covered with masks. "'Tell me about a complicated man. Muse, tell me how he wandered and was lost. ... Now goddess, child of Zeus, tell the old story for our modern times. Find the beginning,'" I read aloud to the class.[99] A siren blared from outside the window, a reminder of our place and time, a sound we'd all become strangely accustomed to. "You see, the ancient Greeks began their epic poems and stories with an invocation of the Muse, a goddess, or possibly sister goddesses, of poetry, dance, and art. They believed it's *through* the blessing of the gods that an artist can tap into creative insight, and that creativity comes from a higher realm. It was a gift that had to be given."

No response. Their eyes registered a blank. After months of sitting behind screens, finishing their senior year of high school learning from home, being in a college classroom was already strange, let alone hearing a teacher ask them to think about a passage from a book written some 2,700 years ago.

"But creativity doesn't always have to come from somewhere else, out there, in the ether, bestowed by the gods. While it's still a gift, it also comes from within. In fact, you already have it," I said into the silent room.

"So are we gonna write poetry?" a student asked.

"No. But you can if you want to. It's up to you. I asked you all to bring a notebook today because this is how we're going to begin each class. Sitting together, for five minutes, filling up blank pages."

"But writing what? What if we don't have anything to say?"

At this I smiled under my face mask. "You will. You'll see."

---

99. Homer, *The Odyssey*, trans. Emily Wilson (New York: W. W. Norton & Company, 2018), 105.

"What do you *mean* you want us to…just write whatever we want? For five minutes? That's it?"

"Exactly that. For five minutes. Even if you write the same word over and over, even if you have nothing to say. Just keep your hand moving on the page."

I explained that during these first five minutes, we were going to suspend time together, to think of ourselves as creators, to open ourselves up to whatever comes spilling out onto the page. "Don't censor yourself. Don't worry about grammar. This is for you. No one will read it but you, unless of course you want to share it," I'd said. No tablets, no phones, no computers. At first, the exercise seemed pointless, confusing, ridiculous even. When the gong of the five-minute timer sounded, they'd look up and eagerly wait for a response, a new directive, expecting to turn something in. Instead, I'd put away my own notebook and shift gears into the week's lesson.

Over the next couple weeks, like clockwork, their suspicion and doubt turned into something akin to magic. After coming in from the chaotic streets of Midtown Manhattan, setting down their bags, and hearing that five-minute timer, they'd dive into their notebooks with hands moving furiously across the page. They seemed surprised at just how much they had to say, at just how much they had to put down and release onto the page. They seemed surprised at how easy and natural it became, even after only two classes, and how much they actually enjoyed this tiny moment in time.

Soon, it all began to all make sense. They were finding words for things they didn't know were inside them: hidden emotions, rants, dreams, poems, epiphanies, self-reflections. Some wrote so-called practical things like to-do lists, which were just as important. Others sketched the outlines for a short story or rap song or possible screenplay. What I found in teaching this was that something else always emerged from these five minutes: they'd inevitably cross the debilitating threshold of writer's block and find themselves in a "flow state." How it happens, I don't know, but when the time was up, the majority of the class would still be writing. I'd then have to calmly bring them back to the moment.

I began this simple exercise for a variety of reasons, some of which were outlined in Julia Cameron's *The Artist's Way* (specifically the section on "Morning Pages"), Joan Didion's essay "On Keeping a Notebook," and the innumerable lessons taught by Dr. Miller. The notebook is a means to channel something higher, something hidden, something embedded within us. It's a blank slate, a tabula rasa, upon which to imprint parts of our essence, uncover the occluded or less obvious elements of the self. "Why did I write it down?" Joan Didion once penned in her famous essay on the subject. "In order to remember, of course, but exactly what was it I wanted to remember? How much of it actually happened? Did any of it? Why do I keep a notebook at all?" she wrote.[100] Her essay is riddled with questions, contradictions, and curiosities, but she eventually lands on the point of it all: it's about *keeping a record of one's life*, as well as keeping in touch with ourselves and feelings over time. And there's a sense of urgency in this: "I think we are well advised to keep on nodding terms with the people we used to be whether we find them attractive company or not."[101]

Even though I told my students the notebook was for them and only them—which I meant—there was also something else to be done with the notebooks. After a few free-writes, I started taking another five or ten minutes of class time for a new activity: "Would anyone like to share? No pressure." And as predicted, many of them would, despite not being required to do so. Soon, my students began opening up about their lives, their day, their fears, their dreams. This simple exercise provided a safe space not only for interior reflection but also for sharing the contradictory and complex experience of what it means to be human.

---

100. Didion, "On Keeping a Notebook," 192–93.
101. Didion, "On Keeping a Notebook," 203.

Each moment that followed became an opportunity for new lessons and ideas; it became a shared, collective, creative experience. Not just in active listening (a precursor for empathy), but also for helping them become more in tune with their inner thoughts. On a practical level, in an education setting, it also set the stage for us to then dive into close readings of essays, analyzing the nuance of the authors' words, following their trains of thought to a logical end, and exercising our critical thinking skills. We weren't there to standardize our thought; we were there to expand it.

DEEP DIVE: INVOKING THE MUSE

The topic of creativity—what it is and how it can be accessed—has been a topic of fascination for thousands of years. The word *inspiration* comes from the Latin word *inspirare*, which means "to breathe or blow into." Similarly, the Greek word *theopneustos* means "God-breathed."[102] To become inspired meant that the breath of God was blown *into* you, and so inspiration literally means to be "filled with the breath of God." In this sense, the creator of any artistic work is accessing a kind of divine wind, becoming a vessel for the gods. In another sense, these creative acts are like children being born into the world, immaculate conceptions born of a mingling between realms.

In our reliance on digital technology, so much of our modern lives is played out on or through screens. While these digital tools have been enormously helpful in streamlining daily life and productivity, there's much to be said of their drawbacks. Technology as a tool certainly has a big place in creativity, but an old-fashioned notebook helps us get in touch with our deeper selves, remaining present in the moment, in very different ways.

I first discovered the concept of channeling the Muse during one of Dr. Miller's lectures. He was the first one to posit to me the ancient idea that the Muse could be called upon for divine inspiration. Creativity, according

102. Maurice Gerald Bowler, *Claude Montefiore and Christianity* (Atlanta, GA: Scholars Press, 1988), 60.

to much of Greek thought, wasn't something that could be conjured within but was invoked, channeled, and bestowed upon you from the gods. Ideas, too, were gifts from the Muses, coming into the body from higher realms, into the top of the head, down the arm, and onto the page. Creativity, in this sense, becomes a rapturous, ecstatic act. The hand acts as an extension of the mind and spirit and, therefore, also becomes the hand of God or the Divine Muse. And while the process of creativity doesn't have to function in that way at all—it can be entirely secular—there's some truth to this: creativity is a manifestation of Spirit and a directed flow of concentrated, magical energy.

The Greek word *meraki,* Dr. Miller taught, means to do something with soul, creativity, passion, or love, to put the essence of ourselves into our work. Creativity is magic, but it's also discipline, focus, and seeing things through. When we're young, we have endless potential and imagination and creativity, but as we grow older, it somehow, for some reason, becomes harder. That's why it deserves conscious space in our lives—we must seek it out and cultivate it in our everyday lives, even in little ways. Sometimes getting in touch with the Muse simply means tapping into our playful side and seeing where it takes us.

Most of the time we're told that art or creativity is limited to the role of artists, but we all have the capacity for creativity. It's our nature to be creative. We come up with creative solutions every day without even realizing it. The way we balance our finances to stretch that extra dime at the end of month, the way we fix things around the house, the way we resolve interpersonal problems with tact, or the way we present ourselves to the world. Nearly everything we do first began as a form of creative exploration.

Accessing a flow state—where we effectively tune out the noise around us and tap into a nearly meditative state—essentially lies in our ability to open ourselves up and become vulnerable, whether it's to new ideas or to what's already brewing within us. But here's the thing: preparation is also key. Just like a baby can't be expected to write a sonnet without first learning and understanding language, or a woodworker can't build a table without learning how to use a chisel and hammer, we also have to learn new things in order to harness and make use of our innate talents. "A piano composition cannot 'come through' unless one has learned to play the piano; an inspiration for drawing or painting cannot manifest without the person first preparing herself as an artist. And so on," Dr. Miller once wrote in a letter. "So preparation is a necessary, but not a sufficient condition for creativity."[103]

When it comes to the Muse, we don't have to insist—or even worse, demand—that our pleas for inspiration must be heard, answered, and delivered. We are inherently creative beings already! Plus, no one has time to wait around all day for the Muse to show up at the mind's door and work its magic. In my experience, the Muse likes to work with a willing participant, with a creator who's prepped and ready to put in the work. Because while it starts with play, seeing it come to fruition— become manifested—takes work. And when it comes to both magic and creativity, that's what most people don't talk enough about. There's a well of creativity inside you and all around you, but sometimes you have to build the bucket, dip it into those waters, and pull that bucket up with effort and focus in order to access it.

Plus, if we just passively waited around for the Muse, practically nothing would get done. I can't tell my landlord, "Sorry, I don't have the rent because the Muse bailed on me this month. I'll try again in a couple of months." It's just not how the world works. As magical and ecstatic and transcendent as the Muse can be—as creativity can be—we can't always live in that state. It comes and goes; it moves like a spirit. But here's the thing: when it does come, we must grab on to it, flow with it, and hold on to it until it leaves. When it comes knocking, you better grab your bucket and drink up.

In her book *Big Magic*, author Elizabeth Gilbert proposes another notion on the subject: "I believe that our planet is inhabited not only by

103. John Miller III, correspondence with Amber C. Snider, September 1, 2020.

animals and plants and bacteria and viruses, but also by *ideas*."[104] For her, ideas are life forms with their own energy, will, and consciousness, swirling around us everywhere. Not only can they interact with us, but they also want to actively collaborate with us. Their one impulse, she writes, is to "be made manifest."[105] But it's only through our physical effort that these ideas, these life-forms, can be ushered out of the ether and into the "realm of the actual."[106] They're looking for someone to bring them to life. Creativity, she notes in a line that echoes the ancient Greek notion of the Muse, is "a force of enchantment—not entirely human in its origins."[107]

For Gilbert, the disembodied forms of ideas are always trying to find a home and trying to get people's attention. If they're ignored, well, then they'll just move right along to a more willing participant and open collaborator; to someone else who wants to earnestly work with them. Sometimes the ideas show up as fleeting, flickering thoughts, and sometimes they'll hang around for a while nagging at the corners of our sleeves throughout the day. Maybe they'll drop in very briefly just before dozing off to sleep or while we're in the shower rushing to get ready for work. And this isn't just limited to creative ideas, they can be any idea: mathematical, scientific, religious, technological, and so on.

In *Big Magic*, Gilbert recounts an idea for a novel she once had and how she chiseled away at the story for a while, developing the characters, setting, and plot, before ultimately shelving it, albeit temporarily. Eventually, she forgot about it after a while, and the book never came to fruition. But a few years later, with the beginnings of the manuscript collecting dust, she ran into another well-known writer, and as they caught up over coffee, she told Gilbert about the new book she was finishing up. She remarked how the story seemed to flow out of her during the writing process, and now it was nearly ready to go to print. To Gilbert's surprise

104. Elizabeth Gilbert, *Big Magic: Creative Living beyond Fear* (London: Bloomsbury Publishing, 2015), 34–35.

105. Gilbert, *Big Magic*, 35.

106. Gilbert, *Big Magic*, 35.

107. Gilbert, *Big Magic*, 34.

CREATIVITY AND THE MUSE 173

and near shock, it was almost the exact same plot, setting, and subject matter as Gilbert's idea, yet her author friend had no way of knowing this. She certainly didn't steal her idea, so how could this be possible? Gilbert realized it was because she *let the idea go*. She didn't treat it well and work to bring it to life, and so it jumped up and went on to the next available creator.[108]

Ideas, like creativity itself, have their own purpose, and they won't sit around waiting for us to get our act together. So when the Muse comes, grab a bucket, friends, and keep pulling up the water from that magical well until your arms get sore.

UNLOCKING CREATIVITY WITH SOUND

Sound has a unique way of transporting us into other states of consciousness. It can be used as a tool to tap into new creative insights, transcend space and time, and move deeper into the divine symphony all around us. Sound, even in space, is all around: the planets give out vibratory emissions that can also be translated into music (Jupiter sounds like a Gregorian chant, the rings of Saturn seem to sing, and even black holes produce an eerie, haunting echo from the abyss).

Pythagoras was thought to have said, "There is geometry in the humming of the strings, there is music in the spacing of the spheres."[109] Since everything in the universe has its own vibratory energy, we can use the power of sound to raise our own vibrations, access rapturous states of consciousness, and even heal. One way to experience the healing and therapeutic properties of sound is to partake in a sound bath with crystal singing bowls, a practice that has been around for thousands of years. Each bowl is tuned to a specific note and vibration, and when played together with intention, they produce a relaxing and calming effect in the body and occasionally a transcendent effect in the mind. Although the

---

108. Gilbert, *Big Magic*, 42–54.
109. Michelle Franklin, "Rhythm and Proofs: Finding Music in the Math," School of Physical Sciences, UC San Diego, May 19, 2023, https://physicalsciences.ucsd.edu/media -events/articles/2023/math-music.html.

exact origins of singing bowls are unknown (some say the practice began in Mesopotamia and then spread east to Tibet, India, and Nepal), the mystical experience of singing bowls seems to suspend time and space, allowing for a deep, meditative experience that helps unlock creativity.

If you can't attend a live sound bath session, try pulling up a chakra healing playlist on your music app (or meditation app). Using headphones does not have the same effect as sitting in a live session, especially as a collective experience, but technology can work to our advantage when needed. Sound can be broken down into units of frequency known as hertz.[110] I recommend starting with the root chakra, for a sense of grounding, by playing music at a frequency of 396 hertz (Hz) or the C note for singing bowls. For heart healing, try 639 Hz or the F note. You can also, of course, invest in a couple of singing bowls and play them at home. When I feel off balance, I spend twenty to thirty minutes listening to a playlist or frequency to help balance and fortify certain chakra points, and I feel an immediate difference in my mind and body afterward. For enhanced creativity, try listening to music that's at 288 Hz or the D note.

Music has the power to alter our state of consciousness—it can turn a dull afternoon or boring dinner into a romantic escape, promote an artistic flow, allow for people to feel more at ease with each other, bring people together in shared memories, and evoke camaraderie. The truth is, we do not live in a silent world, yet we can consciously curate the sounds around us to elevate our consciousness and spirit.

When we harness the power of sound for specific intentions, it becomes a magical act. Sound, combined with good design, also has the power to unlock a higher human potential and perhaps assist with communication beyond the veil or between worlds.

Consider this rather strange, albeit fascinating, fusion of magic, art, and science: in 1954, a man named George Van Tassel began constructing a giant wooden dome known as the Integratron in the Mojave Desert.

---

110. "Understanding Sound," National Park Service, July 3, 2018, https://www.nps.gov /subjects/sound/understandingsound.htm.

It was intended to be a place for healing, gravity suspension, and time travel. The design, he claimed, came from his telepathic communication with extraterrestrials and the writings of Nikolai Tesla. But the location was also significant: it was built on the "intersection of powerful geomagnetic forces that, when focused by the unique geometry of the building, concentrate and amplify the earth's magnetic field."[111] In fact, the location was intentional: magnetometers reportedly "read a significant spike in the earth's magnetic field in the center of the Integratron."

The dome's design was meant to include an installation of "64 aluminum dirods, or extended beams, intended to spin and generate electrostatic energy," which could apparently help recharge human cell structures and prolong life.[112] But it never came to fruition. Van Tassel, a former aeronautical engineer (who worked for Lockheed) and test pilot for Howard Hughes, died before the building was fully realized. Today, the Integratron is on the National Register of Historic Places by the National Park Service and owned by three sisters who facilitate sound baths in the structure.

The site is regarded as a near-perfect acoustic space. According to the *New York Times*, "its curvilinear dome and reverberating wood...act as natural amplifiers, a surround-sound stereo system in the shape of a building," allowing for sonic healing.[113] Reporter Jody Rosen described it as follows: "You may not subscribe to Van Tassel's belief...that the Integratron is capable of rejuvenating your cells and reversing the aging process. But an Integratron sound bath will startle your ears, and, perhaps, awaken your imagination. The crystal singing bowls have a ventriloquial effect: Their tones seem not to emanate from the instruments themselves, but to hover and dart in midair, an effect that is enhanced by the Integratron's awesome

111. "About: The History of the Integratron," Integratron, accessed November 5, 2022, https://www.integratron.com/history-about/.

112. Chris Nichols, "The Stranger-Than-Fiction History of the Integratron," *Los Angeles Magazine*, November 5, 2019, https://lamag.com/lahistory/integratron-desert-dome.

113. Jody Rosen, "Welcome to the Integratron," *New York Times*, August 20, 2014, https://www.nytimes.com/interactive/2014/08/20/style/tmagazine/welcome-to-the-integratron.html.

acoustics.... It is, aesthetically speaking, extraterrestrial: a transportative encounter with music, an experience of pure sound not quite of this earth."[114]

Sound also has benefits for patients dealing with dementia and Alzheimer's disease. Numerous studies throughout the years have shown that music can help boost brain activity, help with the recall of memory and emotions, and improve behavioral issues within these patients. As with sound baths, live music is more effective than recorded music, and even short-term music therapy has been found to help alleviate symptoms of depression and anxiety and improve mood and cognition.[115]

WORKING TOWARD A MORE CREATIVE LIFE

Whether through writing, painting, color, or song, there are millions of opportunities to invite creativity into your life. Try out as many as you can to find the one that connects with you.

Technique: Quiet Your Mind, Open Your Vibrations

While there's no true substitute for experiencing the healing vibrations of music in person, consider how you can use sound to assist in your creativity, paying close attention to the frequency you choose. In our digital world, we can easily access volumes upon volumes of sound—a few taps on your phone and you can be transported to a stormy night, a waterfall, a bird-filled forest. There are plenty of apps online, many of them free and accessible, that include sound baths by amazing artists with playlists consisting of healing tones, some of which can truly enhance your creative life.

114. Rosen, "Welcome to the Integratron."

115. Balakrishnan R. Nair, William Browne, John Marley, and Christian Heim, "Music and Dementia," *Degenerative Neurological and Neuromuscular Disease* 3 (September 1, 2013): 47, doi:10.2147/dnnd.s35762; Ronald Devere, "Music and Dementia: An Overview," Practical Neurology, June 2017, https://practicalneurology.com/articles/2017-june/music-and-dementia-an-overview.

Technique: Listening with Intention

Using sound with intention can help open parts of the brain associated with creativity, relaxation, and altered states of consciousness. As you listen, see where you feel the music in your body: Is it in your hips? Your heart? Limbs? Forehead? Imagine the energy of the music working to open up your third eye chakra, located directly on the forehead in between the eyes, and moving upward through the crown chakra. Set the intention to unlock a deeper creative flow in your everyday life.

When people say "go with the flow," we tend to think of a moving stream, a body of water, but I also imagine this to be similar to flowing with the notes on a sheet of music. Acknowledge the pauses and moments between sounds.

Technique: Try Morning Pages

One of the best exercises in Cameron's book *The Artist's Way* is to write three pages a day every morning.[116] Not only is it a great way to channel unexpected creativity, but it can be used to tap into your higher self as well. Before looking at your phone, checking emails, or scrolling through social media, spend the first twenty minutes of your morning writing down whatever comes to you. You may start out with nothing to write. So what! Write down the same word over and over. Eventually, something magical happens, especially midway through page one or about five minutes into the exercise. Reread your morning pages after seven days to reflect on what is there.

Technique: Seek Out Art

When you go to an art gallery, look for reflections of yourself or even *the absence* of yourself in the artworks. Consider the hand or mind behind the work—the creator, story, and history behind the piece. If you find an artwork that resonates with you, or if it brings up any strong feeling, sit with it for a while, letting the image, idea, or visual experience settle into

116. Julia Cameron, *The Artist's Way: A Spiritual Path to Higher Creativity* (New York: TarcherPerigee, 2002).

your bones. While looking at the smooth curvature of a marble sculpture or admiring the strange blue color palette of an oil painting, take note of your feelings and sensations that emerge in the moment. Perhaps it's a slow, vibrating crescendo bubbling up, an epiphany, a feeling of ecstasy, a dull numbness, or even a sense of apathy. Reflect on why and how the artwork produces this sensation in you. If you feel nothing at all or the absence of feeling, consider that, too. Stay open, but most of all, stay curious.

The work of artists like Hilma af Klint, Remedios Varo, Salvador Dalí, Frida Kahlo, William Blake, Leonora Carrington, and countless others is steeped in spirituality, symbolism, and mysticism. Take a day trip to a museum and see their works in person. Purchase one of their art books and meditate on one of their images each day for a month, or if you're strapped for time and cash, search for their work online and explore their paintings that way.

Technique: Imitation Painting

Pick a painting or artwork by one of the artists listed above. What story do you think it's trying to tell? Do any aspects of the painting bring up certain memories? Sensations? Scents? Notice the brushwork, line work, and any symbolism you may find. Now, take one element from the painting—the line work, color palette, subject matter, composition, title—and create your own artwork inspired by that singular element.

Technique: "Invoke the Muse" Painting

Play is at the heart of creativity. I believe that a sense of play, coupled with practice, focus, and dedication, is what makes one an artist. But even if you're not an artist, it's good to try new things as an adult, and you may even surprise yourself along the way. First, set an intention for the painting: It could be as simple as "I want to see my inner child," "I want to explore the origins of the universe," "I want to channel Mother Earth," "I want to see the moment of conception," or "I want to understand the essence of the color orange." This exercise is bound to produce something beautiful, comical, or surprising. Don't overthink it and just let your hand guide you as you explore color, shape, texture on the paper or canvas.

PRACTICE:
EXPERIMENTING WITH AUTOMATIC WRITING

Automatic writing involves tapping into the subconscious and accessing "stream of thought," but perhaps just as compelling, it was regarded as a tool to channel messages and ideas from the spirit realm. The work of nineteenth-century psychologist and philosopher William James had a deep and lasting impact on the concept of automatic writing.[117] One of James's most dedicated students, the modernist poet and writer Gertrude Stein, took his ideas and used them to create one of her most revered literary works, *Tender Buttons*, cementing her place as one of America's greatest avant-garde artists. Automatic writing also has therapeutic benefits, as it's still used today as a way to channel thoughts and feelings that are otherwise hard to access.

Years ago, while doing automatic writing, I ended up using some parts of it as the basis for a short story—so you never know what may come of it down the line. Here's how to try it.

Supplies
Pen and paper
Quiet room
Chair or desk

Step 1
Go to a quiet room and get settled in a comfortable, seated position with your pen and paper. You can sit at a desk or anywhere you're most comfortable writing. Clear your mind and take slow, deep breaths, in and out. If a stray thought comes into your mind, acknowledge it, and then

---

117. "William James," Department of Psychology, Harvard University, accessed June 4, 2024, https://psychology.fas.harvard.edu/people/william-james.

let it go. I recommend speaking your intentions aloud at this point and casting a protective white light around yourself (see the light meditation on page 47). Ask your spirit guides, angels, ancestors, the Goddess/God, Divine Light, or the universe to assist you and help reveal what you need to know in that moment for your ultimate highest good.

Step 2

Pick up the pen and concentrate on the page. Try not to let your rational mind take over—forget about logic, spelling, or censoring yourself. It's very similar to the free write, but this time, you're giving your hand over to the higher realm and being led by Spirit. Let your hand move freely across the page. Close your eyes if that feels more comfortable, especially if it helps you concentrate on *not* concentrating.

Step 3

If you start writing gibberish, that's okay. If your words aren't making sense, that's okay! Symbols or numbers or even other languages may come to you. Just let it flow and whatever comes, comes. Eventually, you'll notice that words may start to form. You may find yourself hearing an inner voice—it's okay to ask questions and let those answers reveal themselves on the page.

Step 4

This practice works to unveil parts of our unconscious as well, so there may be some things that come through that aren't, well, so pleasant. If something makes you feel uncomfortable, stop the automatic writing session and do a light meditation, say a prayer, or do a cleansing ritual. Recenter yourself and focus on the highest good. Take and use only what works for you—discard the rest. If something doesn't feel right, don't push. Just try again another time and keep the power of the light around you. Remember that you are a divine child of the universe.

INTEGRATIONS

Creativity is an essential part of our essence, and we can exercise this innate talent every day in novel ways, whether it's in the conscious selection of our clothes, coming up with unusual conclusions to processes at work, or invoking a sense of spontaneity in our routines.

We are inherently creative by nature, and although there are no prescriptive, set-in-stone ways to conjure creativity from within, a few things can help: staying open to your sensitivities to visual cues (or cultivating an openness toward it), carrying a notebook with you or jotting down notes in your phone every day, and paying attention to your inner child, who yearns for spontaneity, room for play, and creative attention.

The Muse—how it functions and what it exactly is—may always remain a mystery. Perhaps it comes from a certain region in the brain, or a cross-firing of neurons through different regions, or our spirit or higher self, or maybe it's a state of mental and emotional being. Or maybe, like Gilbert says, creative ideas are actual living, breathing entities looking for a way to manifest in the world. Or maybe the Muse consists of ancient spirits from other realms, companions to us human beings, endowing us with their presence and inspiration, or divine breath. Whichever the answer, our survival has long been attached to our ability for creativity— whether it's adaptation or problem-solving, as well as our capacity to create beauty and pleasure in the world. So remember: stay curious and stay creative, and never let the monotone of the world drum it out of you.

CHAPTER 9
FINDING YOUR SOUL IN DARKNESS

Caves have an ancient association with the search for enlightenment. To enter a cave often involves embarking on a perilous journey through strange, uncharted, often eerie or even terrifying territories. In one sense, the cave acts as a metaphor for birth and the mysteries of the womb, a place with hidden secrets of Mother Earth. In another, it's a raw place to discover yourself, to turn inward, to grow. Caves can be places from which to find the soul and heal emotional wounds, a symbolic journey of returning back to the womb to find healing. Knowledge, it is said by the Asaro tribe of Papua New Guinea, is just a rumor until it lives in the body.[118] Sometimes we can glean soul insights through physical rituals involving this symbolic journey of returning back to and reemerging from the earth.

Sometimes, counterintuitively, caves can provide their own kind of clarity: you must confront the shadows in order to find the light. While mysterious and often uncomfortable, darkness holds its own unique

118. Valentina Stoycheva, "Hack Your Unconscious: Why Negative Feelings Linger," *Psychology Today,* November 13, 2019, https://www.psychologytoday.com/us/blog/the-everyday-unconscious/201911/hack-your-unconscious-why-negative-feelings-linger-0.

wisdom, and that's where the healing power of the *temazcal* comes in. A temazcal is a dome-shaped structure made of stone and mud (sometimes volcanic rock) and has been used as a sweat lodge and an Indigenous ritual site for countless years. It's a space for both physical and spiritual healing, for reflection and reconnection.

Like a cave, the temazcal is symbolic of not only the womb from which we once emerged but also Mother Earth. It's representative of the Great Mother Goddess, whose arms are always open to us. The ancient, Indigenous ritual involves burning medicinal herbs on fiery volcanic rocks at the center of the closed dome, sending prayers to spirit guides and the elements, chanting, singing, and offering thanks to the Grandfather Fire burning outside the temazcal entrance.

In the temazcal, you must become like a child—humbling and readying yourself to open, release, and receive. By returning to the belly of the earth, you're entering into the unknown territory of the soul, a place to retrieve and reclaim what is hidden, to uncover that which feels lost. You're reentering the original womb, a symbolic journey of the life cycle. It's here, in this place of fire, air, earth, and water, that you can shed the illusions that you think define you—old wounds, shame, guilt, heartache—and reawaken to your calling.

STORY: RETURNING TO THE WOMB

Yucatán Peninsula, 2019

Each time I visited the Yucatán Peninsula, something in me reawakened, as if I was called repeatedly to this land by an unseen source. This time, I was there as a travel writer, to document and share what I experienced with readers, but I wasn't expecting to walk away changed yet again. *Tread lightly*, I told myself, *but dive deep.*

While there, I met with two women healers who led a temazcal ceremony, an ancient, healing earth ritual in Latin America that is still practiced today. Sharing any story of this kind requires a kind of vulnerability, reflection, and ultimately surrendering. Every place, every culture, has its own spirits, its own traditions, and I knew to be mindful of those energies and practices as I moved through the world. My own spiritual practices involve reconnecting with the Great Goddess, Mother Earth, the Divine Feminine, which in turn has helped me reclaim a part of my own wild nature and divine power. Although the specific ritual of the temazcal was not my own, it felt like a further unfolding of this reconnection and re-membering.

Our ritual was led by a Mexican healer named Cristina, who began her awakening in Michoacán, a state with eight *pueblos mágicos* (magical villages). There, with a tribe of the Red Road in the mountains, she practiced her sacred art and medicine work. Now, standing at the entrance of a freshwater cenote, she raised her hands for a blessing, asking the guardians of the land to assist our journey. Smoke from copal, a sweet resin used throughout the region, and sacred herbs poured from a chalice as we walked the gravel path to the cave-like dome up ahead. A fire raged just outside the entrance, despite the sweltering jungle heat, surrounded by palm leaves, medicinal herbs, and flowers.

"Temazcal is a ritual that moves energy, which is why we begin by recognizing and asking permission from guardians and protectors of each cardinal direction, while saluting and humbly paying tribute to each energy, each element: earth, water, fire, and air," Cristina said. "We raise our faces and hearts to heaven, to Mother Earth, and to the very heart of existence. This is how we also recognize each other and those elements inside ourselves." She explained how the word *temazcal* comes from the word *temazcalli* of Nahuatl origin, which means "steamhouse." "Within the *temazcal*, the council of village elders made decisions about the future of their tribes; midwives came to accompany women to give birth to their babies." Healers also use these rituals for women's postpartum recovery sessions, in order to close hips and restore balance in the body.

Volcanic rock was hauled in with an iron pitchfork, sparking and glowing a faint orange hue, as Cristina placed it in the center of the dome, shifting it into place with small antler horns. Medicinal herbs, woods, and resins were added—lemongrass, rosemary, palo santo, jasmine, sage, and copal—a dazzling array of sparks reminiscent of stars in the dark. "We enter the temazcal as little seeds to finish gestating as the beings we want to become: free, conscious, healthy, and at peace," she said. "It's an opportunity to give birth to ourselves. The fire enters through the grandmother stones to bring us their message of healing to the physical body and the heart. The entire ritual is a re-creation of how we were once in the womb of our biological mother, giving us an opportunity to release memories or blockages that we have implanted during gestation or the environment in which we were born into," said Cristina.

As the heat intensified, she sprayed herbal-infused cenote water onto the volcanic rock with a thick palm branch. "Now we will close the first door," she said. The round skylight in the dome above us was then closed, sealing in the steam and heat, and wrapping us in darkness. *Breathe, breathe,* I told myself, my heart like a drum inside my chest. I had to find a way to calm myself in the heat. A cacophony of sizzling water, drums, and songs filled the space, with even more darkness with the roof door now closed. A breeze would feel like the greatest luxury in that moment, even a wisp of air, a cool breath. The heat seemed to never end. The answer was simple: surrender.

"I want each of you to say your name, the names of your parents, and what you'd like to heal," Cristina said. The perfumed mineral water steamed on the rocks, rising, raging, dancing, mixing with our sweat, our words. I named my mother, my father, but my thoughts soon turned to the myriad women in my life, the ones who'd made unimaginable sacrifices to pave the way for my existence. The long lines of women, my grandmothers, their mothers, and their mothers, stretching back generations across time.

I thought of my aunts, my own flesh, inseparable from them, the sound of my mother's heels clicking on the linoleum floor at five every morning, quietly pulling me out of bed in the cold to take me to the sitter's house, coming home exhausted and weary from work, yet somehow managing to put together dinner while I tugged at her skirt below. I heard the sound of my aunts' laughter in the evenings, beautiful and strong, sitting around the living room drinking coffee, twirling strands of hair, legs tucked under them. I saw the hands of my grandmother, her skin papery thin with age, slicing up cantaloupe and patting my back, offering a comfort I still ache for today. The scent of her clothes musky and rose, my godmother bouncing her crossed leg in the chair as she rocked me back and forth, singing *rocky, rocky, rocky* when I needed comfort. I thought of the bonds of female friendship, how this same woman was there for my mother throughout her pregnancy, just two wide-eyed girls who met at work many years before, and stood by her through countless moves and lonely nights. I thought about how it takes a village, literally, to raise a child, and how lucky I was to be a part of that village of women, how all the best parts of me come from them. I thought of how they taught me to be strong, tough, resilient, and loving. How the sacrifices of birth, not just the hero's journey of defying death, are perhaps the most sacred of all. I felt their legacies, silences, joys, simple pleasures, traumas, and courage pumping through my veins. *I am them, they are me.*

Within those moments of the deep, earth-black darkness, I wanted to go back and hug the child my mother once was—to tell her that she was impossibly loved right from the beginning. How she'd fall in love and make children from that love, and that it would be hard, but she'd overcome every hardship. I felt a surge of gratitude for everything she did to make life beautiful, commuting long hours, raising two children largely on her own, never sheltering me from the harshness of the world, knowing I'd be stronger for it. I thought of her most sacred teachings: not to worry, despite my seriousness, to learn to laugh at life's trials, and to let things go. But most importantly, she taught me how to forgive, or try to forgive, even if the person didn't deserve it, even if they hurt you beyond measure. I wanted to tell my mother's inner child that one day, her daughter would think she was the most beautiful person on the planet.

Cristina said that to relive the moment of the maternal womb allows us to "observe, liberate, and heal diverse self-limiting programs or beliefs," and this resonated. Yet I still yearned to reach across time, or through time, to heal all the generations before me. More rocks entered from the door, heavy and steaming, the sound of drums and singing. "Now we will close the second door."

The cave becomes symbolic of the underworld of ourselves. "The temazcal allows us an environment of deep introspection and personal reflection. It allows us to see ourselves in all our nuances, recognize our own shadow, put ourselves to the limit of our known abilities before entering, and teach us that we can always discover something new about ourselves—that is, taking a step beyond what we thought possible," Cristina said. And sometimes that means going deep into the inner reaches of our psyche and soul to heal what the "outside" world has tried to imprint there.

In the belly of the earth, I realized that I had been putting up a hardened exterior for the world when all I really wanted was to be soft. To be a woman in this chaotic world means guarding yourself at all times, yet I wanted to eliminate fear and anger, to throw it all into the fire. My whole life I had been trying to find a sense of safety. I had been angry at what the patriarchal system had done to women, for the worldwide systemic abuse against us, the injustices and attempts to strip us of our power, the rampant inequity. There was so much justified anger in the world, and rightfully so, but I knew this was not the answer. Nature, Mother Earth herself, was also a victim of such force and greed; she, too, ached with this pain and suffering.

Anger is a gift, a survival tactic, a necessary part of evolution, but it can also be a poison. And healing is not a destination; it's a continuous practice—a relearning and unlearning. It's something elusive that you have to seek over and over again, digging deep and chiseling away at the layers.

Ritual healing is also a kind of postcolonial unlearning. A country like Mexico knows the effects of colonialism only too well. Yet Mexico is not a *product* of colonialism; it is a *survivor* of it. These ancient Indigenous rituals of the Americas, including some of the sites and temples in which they were originally performed, have managed to survive hundreds of years after Hernán Cortés landed his ship. They are very much still alive.

"Life on the planet and in the Milky Way will continue; the wheel of life will continue to rotate, with or without us. Anchoring and recognizing children of mud, of corn, remembering humility when we see our feet and feel that our hands have been given to serve others, we will reconnect again to existence itself," Cristina said. As above, so below, I thought. We are a reflection of that which we surround ourselves with; the state of the world is also a reflection of us. This is perhaps what the mystics mean when they speak of oneness, of wholeness: we are not separate from nature—we are nature. And when we take from it, we are taking from ourselves.

"We need to anchor ourselves to Earth and recognize that we are a part of Her. We are not separate from Her and, of course, we're not superior. Yet the human species is devastating [our planet] and taking from [it], and we are causing an imbalance. It's imperative and urgent to remember that we have come here to be happy and live in the totality of that which we are a part of," Cristina said. Eventually, the temazcal doors opened. "It's time," Cristina said, "to unite in a single heartbeat."

Releasing fear and letting go. In the end, sometimes, that's about all we can do anyway. The temazcal is an extension of Mother Earth, a womb in which to become reborn, a place to begin anew. It was a place to *re-member* the awe-inspiring, to discover the secrets of the soul, and realize that while we're here on this earth we have so, so much more to do.

DEEP DIVE: PLATO'S ALLEGORY OF THE CAVE

The Allegory of the Cave is one of the most widely read allegories in Western philosophy. It was written by one of the greatest minds in ancient Greece, both a student of Socrates and a teacher to Aristotle: the fifth-century BCE philosopher Plato. The allegory begins with a group of people living in a cave. They are prisoners, with their necks chained in place, unable to move or turn around to see what lies beyond the cave. They're only able to gaze ahead at the dancing interplay of shadows that appear fleetingly upon the walls. They have spent their entire lives in this place and do not know of anything else. They believe the shadows to be the only reality—or the real, true world.

But behind them, a great fire roars. And beyond that, there's a passage, a tunnel, out of the cave. "Between the fire and the prisoners is a road above their level, and along with it imagine a low wall has been built, as puppet showmen have screens in front of their people over which they work their puppets."[119] These images are cast upon the wall, and the prisoners consider themselves wise, being able to recognize the shapes by names, priding themselves on knowing how reality actually works. Their entire experience is limited to those flitting, flickering forms—they don't realize these images are mere *representations* of reality.

But then one day, a single man breaks free from the chains that bind him to the wall. He turns around and sees a great blazing fire behind him, the sight of which is excruciatingly painful, since he has never seen such brilliant light before. Up until this point, he had only known the shadows. Imagine, then, that someone drags him up and out of the shadowy cavern. In this brilliant light of day, of reality, it takes a long while for his eyes to adjust to the sight of it. He must see things as reflections in water first, but after some time, he's able to first make out faint outlines,

---

119. Plato, *The Great Dialogues of Plato: Book VII*, trans. W. H. D. Rouse (repr., New York: Signet Classics, 2015), 365.

then objects themselves. He's able to survey the night sky and moon, the seasons, but still cannot look upon the bright sun of day just yet.[120]

Then, finally, he can make out the sun for the first time, not as a shadow or reflection, but as a source of all things—the "cause of all things they saw" in the cave.[121] The source of all reason and beauty, goodness and enlightenment. Excited at this discovery, this entirely new reality that lies just beyond the cave, the man naturally wants to go back and tell the others. He pities them in their state. But the prisoners are still trapped in a world of superficiality and arrogance, congratulating each other on being the best at recognizing shadows and remembering their shapes, deciphering their patterns and order.[122]

Imagine, then, how the enlightened man will be received by his peers once he tells them of the wonders just outside the cave. As his eyes again struggle to readjust to the darkness of their domain, he seems like a raving lunatic, and they make a laughingstock out of him.[123] A fool who went on a solo journey, who ruined his sight, and now speaks of impossibilities beyond the cave! The prisoners, in their ignorance and bewilderment at the man's words, instead try to kill the man who tries to relieve them of their place in the cave and get them out. Although he tries to liberate them from their chains, relieving them of the constant darkness and shadows, sharing the knowledge of the real and good, or *reality as it is*, he is condemned for it.

Socrates—the primary speaker within Plato's works, as well as his real-life teacher—was also condemned to death for his philosophical teachings by the government of Athens. This happened nearly four hundred years before the birth of Christ, yet we see this trope of the "wise

120. Plato, *The Great Dialogues*, 366–67.

121. Plato, *The Great Dialogues*, 369.

122. Shawn Eyer, trans., "Translation from Plato's Republic 514b–518d ('Allegory of the Cave')," *Ahiman: A Review of Masonic Culture and Tradition* 1 (2009): 73–78, https://scholar.harvard.edu/files/seyer/files/plato_republic_514b-518d_allegory-of-the-cave.pdf.

123. Eyer, trans., "Translation from Plato's Republic," 73–78.

one as martyr" all throughout human history. Socrates's teachings and philosophies were regarded as impious, as corruptive forces. He was officially charged on these accounts, found guilty, and subsequently executed in the year 399 BCE. Socrates's disciples offered him a way out of death by means of escaping prison, and yet he chose to die for his beliefs and submit to punishment.

We've seen this trope over and over, not only in literature but also through other historical and religious figures: martyrs throughout history who've sacrificed their lives for truth or whose lives have been taken; leaders like Martin Luther King Jr. who tried to save others from disillusionment, who've sought to change the existing status quo. Today, like Martin Luther King Jr.'s dream, Socrates's teachings are foundational cornerstones of Western thought.

Now we don't have to be martyrs, nor should we all hope to become them. But the point is it's never easy to leave the metaphorical cave. It's not easy to leave the comfort of ignorance, to go against the grain, or go out seeking the truth of who you are. It's also not easy to simply be okay with not knowing—and admitting that. How many people find themselves deeply uncomfortable when confronted with a question to which they have no answer?

Unlocking your divine potential, awakening to your soul calling, like the journey out of the cave, can be uncomfortable, arduous, complex, and riddled with doubt. It's easier to stay cozy in our patterns, engrained religious dogmas, and belief systems, to go along with the masses, stay quiet, and not stir up trouble. But no great tale, nor life story, begins or ends with the advice of "Do what everyone else does."

Seeking knowledge is, in itself, a radical act. To *know thyself* involves a radical journey, and it takes courage. If, according to Plato, we're restricted to our senses and perceptions, catching only fleeting glimpses of the higher, spiritual reality around and within us, sometimes we must go inward—deep within caverns—in order to unlock the soul's mysteries.

The Soul's Immortality

In one of his best-known dialogues, *Phaedo*, Plato retells the lessons of his teacher Socrates, as he speaks of the soul's immortality and its temporal confinement in the body. He believed that our bodies are vessels for the soul, and that reality, as we know it, is misinterpreted through the faulty, clumsy lens of the body. Our corporeal form restricts and limits us to our senses, which in turn deceive us and veil our true nature.[124] Philosophy, according to Socrates, can help set the soul free.

Plato believed that the soul, or our higher self, dwells in an eternal realm of absolutes, a realm whose reigning essence is absolute love, beauty, goodness, and truth. However, in this earthly plane, we experience the shadowy fragments of these absolutes, yet we believe them to be our true reality.

In his *Allegory of the Cave*, Plato showed that those shadows are mere illusions. And while we can't truly know the nature of ultimate reality in this life while limited to our senses, we can get hints of it in other ways. We can sometimes see through and beyond the veil and feel, with some semblance of certainty, absolute truths of the universe. We can sense the perfection of nature, the harmony of the universe amid the chaos, the complete unity of all things—even if we've never, not even once in our waking world, experienced such a thing.

Some things go beyond and transcend the rational mind. There's no language or rationale for it, yet we still *know* certain things—we perceive them in other ways. Call it intuition, ESP, or gut feelings, but I also call it a "soul knowing." When we look through the lens of the soul, we begin to view the world with a sense of divine wonder and get beyond the limitations of the corporeal mind. In the words of Socrates, "the soul itself sees that which is invisible and apprehended by the mind."[125] And by seeing things through the eyes of the soul, we get closer to reality *as it is*—not as it appears to be. Socrates's genius also stems from his understanding that,

---

124. Plato, *Phaedo*, in *Euthyphro, Apology, Crito, Phaedo*, trans. Harold North Fowler (Cambridge, MA: Harvard University Press, 2005), 287–88.

125. Plato, *Phaedo*, 289.

despite all his knowledge, he knows nothing at all. Even with an entire lifetime dedicated to learning and questioning the world, the questions always far outweigh the answers.

In Plato's *Apology*, Socrates remarked that no evil can come to a good person, whether living or dead, since the only real, lasting damage we can do is to the soul.[126] The physical world will fade, and we will be reborn again; however, our soul is what we are, our true self and eternal essence.

Our purpose here is to continuously learn, evolve, and achieve what the Buddha referred to as enlightenment. Our purpose is to learn kindness and love, to endure and overcome suffering, to help those in need, to learn and grow, to develop higher states of consciousness, to know the Divine, and to expand our soul. Knowledge is an active force; it's always reaching for something more, beyond itself. Yet the temple of wisdom is not a destination; it's a process of constant discovery, an endless path. And sometimes when you come to the center of knowledge ("aha, there it is"), it manages to slip away again, opening up yet another series of pathways and possibilities.

Just as we once thought, not so long ago, that the smallest particle in the universe was the atom, consisting of electrons, neutrons, and protons, we now know there's an ever more mysterious, smaller reality beyond that, made up of neutrinos and quarks, and possibly even a *smaller* reality beyond that. The more we learn about our reality, the more questions arise. Questioning is at the heart of mystical wisdom, and it's the driving force behind our spiritual evolution.

Our time here on Earth is an endless unraveling of experience, a constant search for meaning. At the heart of it all, much of that is really an effort to understand our soul purpose. When we strip away the illusions of reality, we come across another land, another place entirely, one full of magic and possibility. Stumbling in the dark, we come across the glimmers of the Divine within us. *As within, so without. As above, so below.*

---

126. Plato, *Apology*, in *Euthyphro, Apology, Crito, Phaedo*, trans. Harold North Fowler (Cambridge, MA: Harvard University Press, 2005), 145.

We each contain a map with answers of the universe. It's embedded within us, in our DNA, in our mind, in the inner workings of our soul. The answers are *within*. Knowledge is not only found out there in the cosmos but also deep within the self. Yet we must all find the Divine on our own—in our own way—even if that means walking through darkness to find it, even if that means beginning with denial and doubt. Our purpose is to fully participate in this earthly experience, to seek the truth for ourselves, and stay open to the lessons of the earth.

WORKING WITH WAYS TO RESTORE THE BODY–MIND–SOUL CONNECTION

In life, we all go through valleys: sometimes long, arduous periods of confusion, sometimes grief and indifference, or sometimes just apathy. Although we may not see it at the moment, these periods are also sacred times, but the trick is to not stay in those valleys forever. Just as the natural world is cyclical, constantly moving, retreating back into itself, hibernating, and becoming still, we, too, need those periods for our own growth.

Technique: Embrace Solitude

As much as we need community, we also need solitude. The world is full of distractions and diversions, but spending time with yourself and really getting comfortable in that space is so important for spiritual growth. Alternatively, spending too much time alone isn't ideal either, but striking a balance is key. We need time to ourselves to process our thoughts, to hear the pulse of life within us, to go inward and reflect.

Technique: Talk to Your Higher Self

If you could interview your higher self, what would it say back to you? What advice does it have? What would it want you to know? What does it need at this moment or in the near future? If you could interview your soul, what would it say back to you? What would activate soul bliss for you? Write out a list of questions for your higher self and then play the role of a journalist for an hour or so, asking each question aloud to yourself. Wait with a pen in hand to hear the responses come through and jot them down. You may be surprised by what you find.

Technique: Honor the Natural Rhythms of Your Body in Times of Change

Just as the man in Plato's allegory of the cave had to readjust his vision to both the light and darkness, we also need to allow our bodies to readjust to extreme change, especially in times of grief or hardship. We are not meant to be on 24/7. It's a lie we've been told, to constantly produce and be productive, to always be seen and see others. Give yourself permission to retreat inward, to rest, to enter into the proverbial cave of yourself to find equilibrium again and restore your strength.

Technique: Reconnect with Nature

Tapping into the energies of the earth under our feet is one of the most effective ways to heal and reconnect with our soul. Many of us, especially city dwellers, are cooped up in small spaces with limited access to the lush, green world out there. It's not always easy for urbanites to get out into the wild, but we can use what we have around us: parks, green spaces, wooden areas for walks, promenades near the water, and the like to reconnect, reground, recenter. Living magically doesn't always equate to complicated spells or long rituals, but rather it can be simple mindfulness—noticing the beauty in the everyday and staying present to it all.

Think of your feet as superhighways to receive and transport energy through the body, as well as dispel it. Plant your feet firmly on the ground, in the soil, on the sand, on a bed of leaves, and release any negative or pent-up energy. The thing is, Mother Earth is so abundant and accepting that She can take it all in—and still give back so much strength. Even a languid, meditative walk in the park or woods can reset us and reconnect us with our soul calling. As you walk, notice the trees, the wind, the grass under your feet, the movement or stillness around you. Listen to what the earth and elements are telling you in these moments.

Just as lightning seeks and strikes the ground to release the chaotic energy of the skies into the earth, we too can channel the energy in our bodies that's no longer serving us and release it into the ground. We regain our power and strength by taking in the gifts of the earth from our feet, channeling the wisdom and strength there, and releasing what no longer serves us. By reconnecting with the earth, we reclaim our inner magic, restore our inner sight, and realign with our higher calling.

Technique: Record Your Dreams

The mind only processes a fraction of its sensory experiences throughout the day, and sometimes recording our dreams (literally, writing them down) can help us process our inner reflections, fears, and anxieties. Each week, look back at your entries and notice any recurring symbols or patterns. By bringing these unconscious messages to the forefront of our minds, we're better able to process and integrate them.

Technique: Soul Art

When it comes to the somewhat chaotic tasks of adulting, too often we forget the magic of play—not to mention, the spirit world is more humorous than we may think. If the nature of the soul is joy and peace, try to unlock that with silly, playful exercises. Break out your watercolors, Play-Doh, air clay, fingerpaints, acrylic paints, or just a regular no. 2 pencil and start an artwork based on one of these prompts:

- What does your soul look like? If it had an outfit, what would it wear? What color is it? What's its shape or essence?
- What place is your soul drawn to? Is it a landscape, another dimension, a country, a particular home?
- Paint or draw a vision from one of your recent dreams. Keeping a simple dream journal helps with this.
- Think of a favorite person in your life: a family member, a lover, a partner, a teacher. Now draw or paint a picture of their spiritual form, without paying regard to their physical form. Think

of their essence, their favorite things and objects, their tone and voice, their mannerisms, the energy that radiates from their eyes. Try to tap into who they are underneath the veil of physical illusions.

• Construct a visual representation of a sacred soul sanctuary for yourself. If you were going to design a room for the unique purpose of soul expansion, rest, inner reflection, or to receive divine wisdom, what would it look like? After you've constructed this space on the page, you can mentally go there whenever you'd like to reconnect with your higher self and guides.

PRACTICE:
CONDUCT A PERSONAL RELEASE CEREMONY

Candle magic can help us release what is no longer serving our higher purpose and channel energy with specific intention. Since many of us don't have the luxury of creating a giant bonfire in a field and conducting a fire release ceremony, there are simple, safe rituals we can do in the comfort of our own home.

Supplies

Paper

Pen

Firesafe dish (a small cast-iron cauldron works well)

Small votive or small pillar candle (a 2" × 3" or 2" × 6" candle works well), in a color aligned with your specific intention; see step 2

Essential oils of your choice (frankincense, tulsi or holy basil, cedar, lavender, copal, sandalwood, vetiver, and myrrh all work well for this) mixed with a carrier oil like jojoba (see step 3)

Incense of your choice

Dried herbs or flowers (see step 4)

Step 1

Write down all your fears, traumas, or heartaches on a sheet of paper and then scan the page to find similarities between them. Narrow and condense the list down to one definitive sentence, but rephrase it as a positive intention that represents everything you'd like to let go of and write it down on a tiny slip of paper.

Step 2

Get a firesafe dish (a small cast-iron cauldron or a cast-iron pan that's reserved for magical purposes only) and a white candle (or you can use any color that represents your intention). Blue has a calming, protective, peaceful effect; yellow or orange can be used for emotional work or to ignite change; black for banishing; purple to channel higher wisdom; and so on.

Step 3

Rub the candle down with essential oil, ideally blended with a plant-based carrier oil that you've already made. If the essential oil is already blended with a carrier oil, you should need only about a quarter-size amount to rub on the candle. If it's straight essential oil, a few drops will do.

Step 4

Next, light some incense of your choice and rub the outside of your candle with crushed herbs: hawthorn leaves or rose for emotional issues and matters of the heart, cinnamon for banishing, calendula or bay leaves for prosperity and insight, lavender for peace and calm, rue or rosemary for cleansing and clearing, mugwort or motherwort for women's health, and so on. Alternatively, you can also add herbs around the candle.

Step 5

Do a short meditation (an abbreviated version of the one described in chapter 1) to center yourself and focus on what you'd like to release. Burn the paper, and as you do, focus on the dissipation of this fear, moving away from you, into the air and out of your mind-body-spirit.

Step 6

Give thanks when you're finished and let the candle continue to burn until it goes out on its own. If you have to put it out, don't blow it but snuff it out to seal in your intention. Light it again when you're ready and let it burn until the candle is fully burned out.

INTEGRATIONS

The temazcal, for me, was about releasing fear. It was about honoring the uncomfortable parts of myself and making peace with them. It was a ceremony of release, while also honoring the generations of women who've walked before me. But I knew one ritual wouldn't cure me of fear, nor would fear cease to visit again—it was something I'd have to work on again and again, perhaps until my breath finally gave out. But I knew that to release fear—even if in the abstract or as a first step—required me to be entirely present. To remain present in the moment and push through the uncomfortable, whether it was the heat, or the visions, or the tension that lived in my body, or the imposter syndromes, or judgment of others, or the hustle to survive. I had to be present in fear, to sit with it and offer it room, to let it make its case and then politely tell it, "Sorry, but you gotta go." There was no room for fear, however much it insisted on creating its own apartment in my mind and body. After all, it wasn't paying rent and the lease was up.

We all need safe spaces for release and healing, whether it's through ritual baths, getting wild in nature, or a candle ritual. Remember that in tough times, the only constant in the universe is change, and you can use those valleys to come out on the other side with new insight and greater depth. The journey may be uncomfortable, just like in Plato's cave, but you will eventually find the passageway out. And you just may find wonder on the other side.

CHAPTER 10
REINCARNATION AND SOUL CONNECTIONS

Over the course of my early academic years, one subject radically changed my worldview: the possibility of reincarnation. Hints of reincarnation are all around us. There is a continuous cycle in nature, in day and night, in the seasons, in the evolution and dissolution of galaxies—energy is neither created nor destroyed. In the fall, leaves fade and wither away, becoming bare and seemingly lifeless by winter, but once again, in spring, they are reborn, giving birth to new life. After death, there *must be more life.*

The possibility of reincarnation allowed for numerous chances, alternatives, lessons to learn over and over until we somehow get it right. Reincarnation didn't justify suffering in the world, nor the problem of evil, but it provided a framework for a world view that felt more real and true than any other. It allowed for a sense of balance, mathematical precision; a cosmic equation, working out over space and time; a language working in the backdrop of the universe.

Plato believed that we chose every aspect of our lives before coming to this earth: every moment, every step, every forking path of our journey is part of a larger purpose. We've lived innumerable times, over and over. While at some point in that cycle we may eventually evolve beyond these earthly existences, the soul itself is immortal. And perhaps life is just working through every possibility, until we learn the lessons we're meant to.

Plato argued that we must have known perfection in another existence or realm, since absolutes of this kind don't exist anywhere in the world. The mere fact that we have a concept of perfection at all—that is, absolute goodness, absolute truth, absolute love, absolute justice, and absolute beauty, despite the fact that we've never experienced perfection here on Earth—is reason enough to consider reincarnation. For him, it's one basis for proof of the soul's immortality. As taught through his teacher Socrates, Plato believed we must have learned these concepts of perfection somewhere else.

If life is temporary and cyclical, with death eventually coming for everything and everyone, where, then, do we get the idea of perfection if we've never seen or experienced it? My first philosophy professor and dear friend Dr. Miller once wrote, in a philosophy handout on Plato's *Phaedo*: "If we do in fact have knowledge of absolutes, that knowledge must have come from another existence, an existence where the soul was not incarnated in the present or another similar physical body. But do we have knowledge of absolutes? Yes, Plato would argue, because we judge that what we experience in this realm is not perfect. To know what is not perfect, we would need to know what was perfect."

In Plato's *Meno*, Socrates questions a servant (most likely an enslaved boy) on mathematical principles, although the boy had no previous schooling on mathematics or geometry. Through a series of questions, Socrates was able to pull out the correct answer from the boy. This led Socrates to conclude the boy's knowledge of geometry had to have been remembered.[127] As the ancients say, *ex nihilo nihil fit* ("out of nothing, nothing comes"). The answers must have been present within him all along, somewhere deep within his soul, and rather than having to be

127. Plato, "Meno," in *The Philosopher's Handbook: Essential Readings from Plato to Kant*, ed. Stanley Rosen (New York: Random House Reference, 2009), 415–23.

learned, they merely had to be remembered. Perhaps, even, from a past existence.

Most people have, at least once in their life, experienced an intense connection with a stranger and even an immediate feeling that they've always known that person before. These experiences seem to testify to a larger fate and destiny, as well as preexistence of the soul, that possibly, in another life, in another realm, we wanted to meet these people again, and that our separation becomes all the more joyous for finally reuniting once again. Memories of these former lifetimes lie deep within us and can be triggered by people, places, or conversations. Sometimes they're too strong to brush off as mere coincidence.

Consider, too, child prodigies, those with uncanny musical ability, artistic talent, or mathematical genius. Consider Mozart, who began to write musical compositions at age six and composed his first symphony by the exceptionally early age of eight. Preexistence of the soul, where extraordinary talents were perfected and mastered across lifetimes, could be an explanation.

If the soul is eternal, it must have existed before this lifetime, whether on this earth (as reincarnation suggests), in another realm, or as a part of the Divine Source from which it came. Maybe even a combination of all three. If this may seem strange at first, consider the common experience of déjà vu or love at first sight: something inside *tells us* we've either been here before or known that person before, somewhere and somehow. Sometimes, these soul connections can also be uncovered through regressive hypnosis, meditation, or ecstatic experiences. Or sometimes, this knowledge comes swooping in like a gust of wind, a sudden burst of knowing.

For instance, have you ever walked up to someone on the street, had a chance encounter at a café or bar, or spied someone from across a crowded room and felt that you had met them before? The uncanny feeling of déjà vu creeps up and you find yourself wondering, How do I know them? Where do I know them from? There's also an intense urge to be near them, to get close, to catch up even, despite you never actually having met before. Maybe there's something familiar about their gaze, their stance, the way they move their hands when they speak, the flick of hair over their eyes. Perhaps there's a spark between the two of you, an ease, a quiet understanding that drifts back and forth like a river, an easy flow of words, an exchange of *knowing*. Something about them pulls you, draws you in, and makes you feel like you've returned home. Maybe it's because the soul remembers.

I believe that long ago, before we each came into these bodies, we once knew every person in our life today. We chose to see them again, making pacts with each other to reunite. Despite earthly life being only a second in the scheme of eternity, a quick flash, some souls we can't bear to be separated from; others we're drawn to because we have karmic ties, unfulfilled promises, and lessons to learn again and again. Every person serves a purpose and we, in turn, serve a purpose for them. We're here to teach, guide, challenge, love, and learn from each other.

The thing is, we can have profound soul connections with someone, but that doesn't mean they're meant to be our forever person. These deep soul ties, perhaps from another life, may mean that there are still lessons to be learned in this incarnation. But sometimes it's not meant to be a prolonged physical connection. I've learned, for instance, that there are some soulmates whose purpose might be to show us what we *don't* want in a partner, or that when the learning is over, the relationship is, too. We may have been born to be together again, but to our temporary dismay (and I promise you it's temporary), that may mean only for a brief moment in time. Endings are lessons, too.

We tend to think of life in terms of all or nothing, at least when it comes to romantic relationships. But sometimes the most powerful, impactful, and life-changing relationships are also transitory, ephemeral, and temporary. This, I believe, is because the universe always has something bigger and better in store. The universe has higher plans. When the learning is done, so goes the connection, but the soul connection can never truly be severed. Our ties are not bound to time; they're not subject to conditionals.

Love transcends time and space; it can open doors and worlds. I knew there were lessons to be had and made, however short lived, and to go along with whatever fate wanted to show me. Maybe the lesson would be quick or maybe last a lifetime; maybe a soul mate person is someone who breezes through your life only to awaken your senses and remind you of your purpose.

We'll meet many soul mates in our life, and some of them may not stay around very long. That's because soul mates are other forms of soul lessons. They're here to teach us something about ourselves. Or maybe they'll come to simply teach you one of the hardest lessons of all: letting go.

STORY: THE SOUL REMEMBERS

Brooklyn, 2017

One chilly November evening in Brooklyn, while I stood underneath a tree outside a speakeasy jazz bar, a young man approached me and asked if the music was any good. The moment our eyes met, something in me shifted: a sudden soul recognition, like two primordial rocks colliding among the stars, destined to crack each other open and create new worlds. Love's initial, lingering impact, a swirling flurry, a stop in time.

From that moment there was a deep-seated feeling of knowing and remembrance from very long ago, and the more time we spent together, the more it seemed as if we were just beginning to awaken. Soon, we began a relationship, but what seemed like memories from previous lives would come in flashes, in lovemaking, in dreams, in plain daylight. Some were memories that I didn't have, memories that didn't even *belong* to me. One night, while I sat reading Van Gogh's letters, I looked up at his face and saw a myriad of people flash before me: I saw him as an old man, a different man, a young man, another ethnicity, from a different time period, countless people in his face, his eyes. They were all different, and yet still him. I wondered if these were all the people I had once known him as before, different variations stretched across time and space. It startled me—a dizzy feeling washed over me as I looked into a million faces he embodied. Time seemed to stand still.

Our love played out like a strange symphony over the years and led me to places and encounters I never would've imagined. One morning, only a few months after our initial meeting, I found myself sitting in the garden of a house in Mérida and wrote in a notebook: *I have the urge to text my best friend and tell her the following: I know what happiness is. I finally know a sense of place. How can I hold on to this teaching? Why does it feel like I've been here before?* I had never been to the house before and yet the place—the trees, sounds, walkways—reminded me of home. It was like being wrapped in a dream, moving through the scenes of life as if I was acting out a play that had already been written.

Three years later, I returned to the stucco garden house in Mérida. But this time, I went to gaze upon the face of the man I once loved and say goodbye for good. I had gone there to grieve, to pick up the fragile, ravaged pieces of myself, and string them back together in the best way I knew how. I went there to heal the parts of myself that were unraveling, lost, hidden. I knew I had to revisit the past in order to start again. But I didn't know I'd also be saying goodbye to a very different kind of soul mate.

The house was a dream with cool polished concrete floors inlaid with mosaic tiles, a clean white bed, and a hidden garden enclosed in a high stone wall. The bedroom doors opened to the garden, a star apple tree whispering in the night. During the day, the white-yellow blossoms of the plumeria tree, grown sparse in winter, still flickered like stars inside their thick green leaves. Purple plants crowded the garden bed along the walkway—determined and confident, swelling under the January sun. I paced the walkway each day, barefoot and wild, dreaming of fictional worlds, trying to piece together a novel and the reason for love's inevitable end.

In the span of three years, the house seemed changed. But perhaps it wasn't the house at all, just the people inside it. My ex-lover and

I hadn't seen each other in nearly a year, a year that the pandemic took away. But so much had happened that we knew we couldn't get it back. We wanted to rekindle something lost, to see the beautiful parts of ourselves reflected in the other, mirror images, but we knew nothing would be the same. Too much had happened, too much change for us to hold.

Then, suddenly one day in the Mérida garden, I received a text message from my neighbor back in New York saying that a letter had been pushed under my door. Each year, without fail, I received a birthday and Christmas card from Dr. Miller, as well as multi-page typed letters. In between holidays, I'd rejoice at finding one of his lengthy letters in the mail or in my email inbox, complete with philosophical ruminations, details of his lunches with friends, the retelling of discussions held over wine, insight into numerological readings. Somehow, despite the stretch of time and miles, he always knew exactly what I needed to hear, read, and learn at that moment. It was as if there was a cord between the two of us, with a small bell attached on the end, and he could hear its ringing—always right when I needed it.

I turned back to my computer screen, now dark and dimmed under the noon sun, revealing the dust and oil streaks on its surface. My own face reflected back in the black mirror: at once young and old, anxious and at ease, filled and hungry. The afternoon heat kept rising in the thick underbrush of the trees. I watched a few birds chase each other through the plumeria branches. A giant iguana peeked his head from a hole in the stone wall. The sky was a perfect clear blue overhead, mirrored in the cool, shiny face of the pool at my feet.

Ding. A photo of the envelope from my neighbor came back: a single rectangular card stamped "Return to Sender" in bold letters. It wasn't a letter from Dr. Miller at all. It was the Christmas card I had sent him a few weeks back. It was then that I knew: I had been sent to Mérida, seemingly on a whim, to write and grieve something else entirely: another loss, the death of a soul mate.

A few days later, after unanswered calls and receiving only "Voice-mail full," my heart sank. I then scoured the internet and found his obituary online. He passed away on January 1 at the age of 83.

Every so often, if you're really lucky, someone comes into your life and rattles the very foundations of your being. From the moment you meet, you're forever transformed. Their teachings lay a pathway for who you'll become, who you'll strive to become. Perhaps they'll also give you clues to who you've always been. Dr. Miller taught me soul lessons I am still uncovering to this day.

As a guide, a teacher, a light in the shallow murkiness of the world, he showed me that the nature of the soul is eternal and that everyone we meet serves a purpose. His teachings were streetlamps, markers of time. He lit something within me—a seed of knowledge, which I will never stop pursuing as long as I have breath. He saw deep in the depths of life, the marrow of reality, pulled out pearls, and gave them freely to the masses. Jesus once said, "Do not cast your pearls before swine."[128] And yet, Dr. Miller's love of teaching, his love of love, his love for fellow man, meant he *must* do so. It was a moral and ethical imperative to use one's gifts—and his was the art of teaching—to help others. He freely cast precious gems, truths, gifts to the world without expecting anything in return. A modern-day Socrates.

Death is never final. This I knew all too well, long before I began this journey. A few weeks after Dr. Miller's passing, I gathered up his letters and papers back at my Brooklyn apartment during a winter storm. I heard his voice: "You are love. I am love. We come from love." And I knew that one day I'd see him again.

DEEP DIVE: THE MYTH OF ER

In Plato's *Republic*, book 10, a solider named Er dies and goes onto the afterlife. In a beautiful meadow, souls are reunited with each other and joyously regale or lament the stories of their previous life on earth. There

128. Matthew 7:6.

are two openings in the sky and two in the ground, from which souls came and went. Some souls are pure and clean; others are travel-worn, dusty, and tired; some cry out over the conditions of their previous lives, while others recount the beauties and wonders of the heavens.

They spend several days in the meadow before journeying on to meet the Fates. The souls are instructed by Lachesis, the daughter of Necessity, that they will soon begin a new round of earthly life; however, they are to choose the next life themselves. No one in heaven, no divinity, no one else would choose their life for them—the choice was all their own. They were masters of their own lives. Heaven, in this sense, is blameless.

Er is instructed to not choose a lot for himself, as his task is to bring back to earth all that he has witnessed there. He watches the souls select their next incarnation, with every variety of life lots to choose from: lives filled with power and prestige, beauty and riches; lives of obscurity, with some ending short or midway; lives of virtue; lives of tyranny. Each life is combined with other inevitable qualities, like health or sickness, happiness or grief. Some souls choose to become animals or wild creatures that mirror their inner nature. The souls' fortunes are at stake in this moment of choice, yet each soul does not know which will be a good or easy life, nor which one will produce more spiritual fruits. Er is moved to pity, laughter, and astonishment at the sight of each soul choosing their next life according to the habits of their former lives.

The souls also choose their guardian *genius*, a kind of spirit guide who escorts them through life and helps them fulfill their chosen path. Then, they drink from the waters of Lethe, the River of Forgetfulness, before returning back to Earth. The souls go back like shooting stars to their next life, forgetting everything they have seen and heard there, but Er was told not to drink. He soon found himself awake again at his own funeral and told the tale of what he had seen.[129]

129. Plato, *The Great Dialogues*, 491–501.

DÉJÀ VU AND SYNCHRONICITY

Déjà vu is a funny thing, especially when it happens upon meeting a stranger. I've always thought that déjà vu means that you are exactly in the right place at the right time and that you're fulfilling your soul path, which you decided long ago. If our soul, our higher self, already knows exactly what will happen—if we choose every moment, every person, each step along the way—then these experiences are a kind of remembrance. We're remembering something we promised ourselves a long time ago.

Perhaps we also wait for certain souls in order to cross back over from the other side, choosing to learn new soul lessons together in our next incarnation. Perhaps we decide our next lives alongside certain individuals or groups of people, choosing to know them again, to reconnect. Others we may have deep spiritual ties with, stretched out over a series of lifetimes, and some we may owe karmic debts to, and they to us. Everyone has a role to play, however small or large in our life. In this sense, we also choose our soul mates and they choose us, for many, many different reasons. Whether that person stays in your life for an extended period or just a brief visit isn't the point—you were meant to reunite in this life.

All around us are signs that point the way. When déjà vu occurs, or a knowing encounter with another, it's a sign, a guidepost, that we're on the right path. Which brings us, naturally, to the question of soul mates. Perhaps what we call soul mates are those whom we've known from a previous existence. Perhaps in another life, they were your mother, brother, lover, teacher, partner, or best friend.

The idea of a soul mate doesn't always have to be romantic, but sometimes we feel these kinds of connections stronger than others because there's a visceral, powerful exchange of energy and remembrance. Even the possibility that we once knew a love in another life, another time, bound by some mysterious soul tie, has captivated us as a species, a concept that's played out throughout literature, film, and art. Even the biggest cynic, at one point or another, has asked themselves upon meeting a love interest, "Are they the one? Could they be my soul mate?"

"If we listen, the universe (God, the Mother, the Masters, whoever) will 'speak' to us," Dr. Miller once wrote in a letter.[130] "Maybe it's an inadvertent remark by a friend or even a stranger, maybe a song on the radio, maybe a rainbow or butterfly; but we 'know' that it's not accidental or coincidence, but rather a sign. 'All things work for good for those who love God,' St. Paul wrote, echoing Plato's idea that whatever happens or exists, happens and exists for a purpose, goal, reason, or some 'good.'[131] That's what we must be aware of if we are to comprehend our world properly. The Good, or the Idea or Form of the Good is, for Plato, the 'highest Reality.'[132] Let those with eyes perceive! Those who are not so inclined may see but not understand."[133]

When we open our eyes and see all the evidence the universe is giving us for our own preexistence and divine nature, that everything works toward a higher purpose, we will ultimately live our lives differently, spend our time more wisely, and develop better habits, values, and morals. We will hold sacred our inclinations toward people and places, knowing that they are of another time and are dear to our very soul. We will admire the irony in all things and no longer brush things off as mere coincidence. With preexistence and reincarnation, there is no room for self-pity, judgment, or fear of an eternal damnation.

We are all part of a continuous journey toward enlightenment, self-realization, and spiritual evolution. Earth is a school, providing innumerable opportunities for lessons in the guise of setbacks, tests, and trials, which we may have to repeat over and over. Perhaps it's so we can try out every possibility, every choice, in a vast multiverse, or perhaps it's so we can learn soul lessons to raise our consciousness while on this planet.

130. John Miller III, correspondence with Amber C. Snider, August 8, 2016.

131. Romans 8:28 (New International Version).

132. Eyer, trans., "Translation from Plato's Republic," 73–78.

133. John Miller III, correspondence with Amber C. Snider, August 8, 2016.

If, according to Plato, we choose our own lots, our fate, what we do with this life is our own. Our actions in this life will dictate the future, perhaps not only in this life, but beyond. We may have karmic debts, left over from previous lives or this one, and our experiences serve to balance the whole, just like an algebraic equation. The character you're developing now and choices you make influence who you'll eventually become.

The word *personality* comes from the Latin word *persōna*, meaning "mask." It's the face we present to the world, the persona we display, a costume for who we really are. Social media propagates a celebration of the ego or persona—it's merely a performance of our various masks. We wear our happiness, health, beauty, and occasionally our grief on the stage of social platforms, but rarely do we get to glimpse each other as we truly are. But what is the true self beyond this mask? What lies behind or beyond it? Consider the meadow in the Myth of Er: in that field, after this life, there are no masks. It's your spirit that others will recognize. How are you cultivating a life now, in this incarnation, where others will recognize you later on?

The prospect of laying aside that mask is terrifying, since it can shatter self-perception and that of others. But fear is like a fortress and becomes a barrier to self-actualization. We're living in a technological world that prides itself on so-called authenticity, but it's rarely the truth. The Sufi author Kabir Edmund Helminski once wrote, "The personality can be either a means of binding us together in solidarity with other human beings or a means of separating us from others through its habits of rudeness, exclusivity, superficiality, comparison, and judgment. We can be the kind of people who harmonize with others and bring them into productive relationships, or we can be divisive, exclusive, envious, competitive, and suspicious, labeling people as 'other,' seeing them as objects."[134] When we get caught up in outward perceptions or how we're received, it takes away from the real soul work and moves away from the idea that you are already exactly as you should be.

134. Kabir Edmund Helminski, *Living Presence (Revised): The Sufi Path to Mindfulness and the Essential Self* (New York: TarcherPerigee, 2017), 116.

WORKING WITH THE LESSONS OF ER

If we've chosen our lives before, then everything in our life—our hardships and setbacks, our joys and loves—is part of a larger plan. If we've chosen our path before in other existences, nothing is inherently unfair or wrong—it's simply a learning opportunity for the soul. We're here for growth, to expand and utilize our creative potential, to build our talents and use them to better the world. If reincarnation is true, there is no room for self-pity, only compassion; there is no room for blaming others for our hardships or misfortunes, but we can use them as catalysts for change and soul growth.

Life presents a seemingly never-ending series of challenges, and each time it does, we're given the opportunity to level up. Hardship is a universal struggle—it's inevitable, but it's what we do with the struggle that matters. When things don't go our way exactly, when the world doesn't conform to how we wish it to be, these expectations are a major source of disappointment and unhappiness. The Buddhists teach that attachments are the source of disappointment. While this is true, how can we reframe our reactions and experiences of hardship so we can better handle them in our daily lives, while also paying attention to our possible evolution of spirit?

When faced with the injustice or pain of the world, Dr. Miller taught me to not ask, "Why is this happening to me?" but instead ask, "What is this teaching me right now? What is the lesson I am to learn here? Why is this happening *for* me?"[135] If we're here to learn and experience the fullness of the world, in all of its contradictory, harsh dichotomies, we should look at each experience as a lesson to level up our consciousness. This, he taught, is also the key to happiness.

In an attempt to live our own truth, it's also simply not rational or reasonable for us to expect others to share our viewpoints. In fact, it's egocentric to think that others should share our beliefs, and we can't (and shouldn't) force others to change their views and accept ours. "Acceptance:

---

135. John Miller III, correspondence with Amber C. Snider, October 21, 2019.

that's a key. Others are who they are, and we can't make others or the world fit our desires," Dr. Miller once wrote.[136] This is also true when we consider the plot of our own lives—acceptance is key, and not insisting the world fit our expectations of how we want it to look or be. I've found that magic works in a similar way: When you send your intention out there in the world, either through spellwork, prayer, or spirit petitions, don't get fixated on a particular outcome. The universe may have something much better, greater, in store for you. Trust that the universe has your back.

When faced with the impossible difficulties of the world—in those moments of questioning, "Why this is happening to me?"—here are some techniques to use them as opportunities for soul growth.

Technique: Acceptance, Not Passivity

"We are responsible for our own consciousness," Dr. Miller wrote. "No one can inflict an insult on us unless we accept it. *Detachment*: that's the key."[137] But if expectations and attachment are the roots of suffering, which we also learn most readily from the Buddhist tradition, that doesn't mean we should passively accept whatever the world throws at us. Consider the words of Black American writer James Baldwin, who wrote of the problems of systemic racism and the internalized grief, anger, and bitterness it caused him, in his prolific 1955 essay "Notes of a Native Son." His conclusion, at first glance, may seem contradictory, but it is riddled with a powerful truth: "It began to seem that one would have to hold in the mind forever two ideas which seemed to be in opposition. The first idea was acceptance, the acceptance, totally without rancor, of life as it is, and men as they are: in the light of this idea, it goes without saying that injustice is a commonplace. But this did not mean that one could be complacent, for the second idea was of equal power: that one must never, in one's own life, accept these injustices as commonplace but must fight them with all one's strength. This fight begins, however, in the

---

136. John Miller III, correspondence with Amber C. Snider, October 21, 2019.
137. John Miller III, correspondence with Amber C. Snider, October 21, 2019.

heart and it now had been laid to my charge to keep my own heart free of hatred and despair."[138]

Baldwin knew that we cannot change others. Injustice is a rampant, unavoidable part of life. But *that doesn't mean* we should be complacent or passive when faced with its evil. We must use all our gifts—our minds, spirits, and bodies—and the collective power of the community, to reel against it with action. We're called to confront hate without harboring it within our hearts, without allowing it residence in our spirits. Consider how you can use your spiritual gifts to invoke change through positive action, which also paves the way for soul evolution in the next life. What are the causes you feel most passionately about? Is there an organization you can volunteer for or a cause you can rally behind or teach others about? How do you effectively teach those around you (friends and family) a higher, more progressive perspective? Sometimes this may mean changing your approach and tone. Getting creative with it. But don't just post about it on social media; do something action-oriented that is aligned with invoking and inspiring positive change.

Technique: Respond, Rather Than React

Our character is largely determined by how we respond to hardship, whether it's a sharp word from a stranger or a life-altering decision. Everyone is reacting or responding to their own internal monologue and record of experience. And most of the time, it's not personal. Dr. Miller taught that instead of reacting to unsavory situations, we should respond to them, since it implies a conscious decision, rather than rash reaction. It's not an easy thing to do, to consciously respond to life's incessant arrows, but we're faced with opportunities to practice this wisdom every day. It's about living proactively, rather than passively, and empowering ourselves rather than playing into a series of reactions.

"Let us follow the wisdom of the wise and commit ourselves to learning to live proactively. We may be sure that each day, maybe a hundred

---

138. James Baldwin, *James Baldwin: Collected Essays* (New York: Library of America, 1998), 84.

times, we shall all have the opportunity to learn that lesson again and again," Dr. Miller wrote.[139] If someone hurts, upsets, or triggers you or does something to throw you off your center, do not react to their bitterness, but try to cultivate compassion and understanding for them (remember: most everyone is just reacting according to their experience). Imagine them as a small child, innocent and stubborn, and still learning. Then respond accordingly. When you walk away, do your light meditation to cleanse your energy. For bigger decisions, take time to consider them from a higher perspective before taking any leaps: take a sea salt bath, light a white candle, and recalibrate alone in nature. If you need a little extra motivation or courage, try adding cinnamon to your daily tea or light a red or orange candle for a few days, with the intention of providing clarity on next steps and a positive action plan.

Technique: Go Beyond the Mask

We don't need to perform for or convince others of anything. Real connection begins, with ourselves and others, when we break through beyond the masks and illusions of the world. We all want to be understood—it's a universal trait—but rather than focusing on outer receptions (which we can't control), focus on aligning your inner self so that it becomes manifest in your outward persona.

While the masks we wear are necessary for survival, set aside time to go inward and examine who you truly are, when no one is watching. Take time off social media, stop comparing your *mask* with others. Take time to ponder your own nature, as a microcosm of the macrocosm, and your unique place in this world. Remember the words written at the Temple of Apollo at Delphi: "Know thyself." Consider: What am I here to do? How am I to use my gifts, talents, and energy for a higher purpose? How does my persona, or mask, help fulfill this calling? Is it being used to serve me or contradict me?

---

139. John Miller III, correspondence with Amber C. Snider, October 13, 2019.

Technique: Recenter, Regroup, Realign

Most of the time, it's our ego that reacts negatively to a situation, not our higher selves. It's not easy to *not* take things personally, when everything feels so deeply personal, especially for highly sensitive, intuitive folks. We can become overstimulated and feel into things more deeply, and so practicing conscious responding is a necessary companion to our innate gifts.

"The spiritual journey from beginning to end can be characterized as the overcoming of fear," wrote Helminski. "A whole philosophy and methodology could be developed around this fact. Fear shapes the false self and fuels its desires. Our preoccupation with fear is the greatest obstacle standing between us and the abundant life we might know."[140] Fear has an evolutionary purpose—it's undeniably integral to survival—but there comes a time when we must choose which state to reside in, which state of being to give power to. A state of fear or love? They're both difficult in their own ways, but one is infinitely more rewarding and akin to our nature than the other. Consider how each experience in this bodily incarnation is part of a lesson of the karmic whole—each step like a level in a video game, moving toward higher consciousness.

Allow yourself time and space, even just a few moments, to pause and regain your power and wisdom and reconnect with yourself. Breathe in for three counts, hold for three counts, and exhale for three counts. As you do so, imagine a white light surrounding you, consisting of pure loving energy radiating from above, dispelling any and all fear, anything holding you back.

Technique: Learn from the Past

Our concept of time is limited to past, present, and future. The truth is, all three exist at once, but some of us get stuck or fixated on the past. So how do you let go of the hope that the past can be anything different from what it is? To paraphrase the German philosopher Hegel, the owl of Minerva spreads her wings and flies at dusk, meaning wisdom often

---

140. Helminski, *Living Presence*, 156.

comes after the fact.[141] Wisdom can carry us only after the experiences of the day have come to pass.

When we practice acceptance, detachment, and conscious response, we're better able to view the lens of the past with a sense of compassion and learn from it. "We don't always—or even often—know why what happens happens," Dr. Miller wrote in a letter. "Often, it is only in looking back over what has occurred that we gain an insight into why it was, ultimately, for our good, our learning and growth."[142] Similar to a gratitude journal, at the end of the day or week, start writing down what you've learned from various moments after some time has passed. You can focus on the individual day or week, or move further back in time to moments much deeper in your past (your childhood, teens, early twenties, major life transitions, memories of individual people, etc.). Think of each moment as a kind of awakening or uncovering, a lesson to grow from rather than hold on to. Acknowledge how it's shaped your identity, give it thanks, consider its potential higher purpose in your life, and then let it go.

Technique: Follow Your Own Unique Life Path

No two spiritual paths look alike, and some of us may begin our journey with doubt, which is actually a healthy alternative to blindly following any dogma. Whether or not we believe in a higher power, we all still want to understand the meaning of life and answer the biggest question of all: Why am I here? Denial and doubt, too, can be tremendous teachers on the journey to any discovery, whether it's scientific or spiritual.

Dr. Miller helped answer this question many years ago: "Each must find his or her answers from within. Of course, one can learn from others, but ultimately it will be what resonates with your deeper or higher consciousness that will provide the 'answers.' When you resonate with an answer, you know that it is the answer 'for you.' Those answers are within

141. Georg Wilhelm Fredrich Hegel, *Hegel: Elements of the Philosophy of Right*, ed. Allen W. Wood, trans. H. B. Nisbet (Cambridge: Cambridge University Press, 1991), 23.

142. John Miller III, correspondence with Amber C. Snider, July 18, 2019.

you, at the deepest or highest and most sacred level."[143] We interpret our experiences according to our worldviews, belief systems, and unique interior lens. "In this sense, what we believe is *our own truth*, not 'The Truth' but 'our truth.' It is not that there is no Truth, but how we come to it or apprehend it is always in our *own way*. So it is absolutely *unreasonable* to expect others to share—maybe even to respect—'our truth,'" he wrote.[144] And our experiences may reveal, over time, the keys to unlocking the answers to life's most interesting questions. In the words of Socrates, "the unexamined life is not worth living."[145]

We are free to choose our path ourselves—and that is a gift. Everyone is a participant in the great play of life, and we're part of that whole. Shakespeare once wrote that "all the world's a stage," so whether you wrote the script of your life or not, take ownership of your journey and revel in the mysterious connections that bind people together, that unravel, that make our story unique. Claim your life as your own—find boldness in it, cultivating the belief that you are exactly where you should be in your journey (never early or late). Do not waste time comparing yourself to others or trying to be like anyone else; work on empowering your uniqueness and celebrate those differences instead.

Technique: Transmuting Obstacles into Lessons

If it's true that we've all lived many times before and we shall do so again, think of the various obstacles or trials you've faced so far in your life. Could or *should* any of them be learning opportunities? Write down three major obstacles you've faced in your journey and then write down three obstacles you're currently facing. Are there any similarities between them? Any patterns?

Next, write down three potential lessons you can gain from both past obstacles and current ones—try to be positive about it, but don't force it.

143. John Miller III, correspondence with Amber C. Snider, April 5, 2018.

144. John Miller III, correspondence with Amber C. Snider, July 19, 2019.

145. Plato, *Apology*, in *Euthyphro, Apology, Crito, Phaedo*, trans. Harold North Fowler (Cambridge, MA: Harvard University Press, 2005), 133.

For instance, maybe one obstacle is that you have a difficult time with your family or one family member. Regardless of blame, these obstacles also come with new lessons for soul growth *for you*. Maybe the potential lesson here is learning to practice and maintain healthy boundaries with your loved ones, or learning to respond, rather than react. Or maybe someone's feelings may be more hurt than they're letting on, or they simply don't have the tools for healthy communication. Write down the possible lesson(s) to be gleaned from this obstacle—try to think and feel through your higher consciousness for the answer.

Technique: Create Affirmations

Create affirmations around the prior lesson so that the lessons remain at the forefront of your consciousness until they become second nature: something like "I am practicing and maintaining new, healthy boundaries with my loved ones. I choose to respond to issues rather than react to them. I acknowledge the feelings of others and my own. I am aware that not everyone is equipped with the same tools and accept that not everyone communicates the way I do."

Remember that knowledge is just a rumor until it lives in the body. Let this new awareness become alive in your body until it's fully known and in alignment with your actions. In this way, we can better glimpse what we're here to learn, conquer, and grow from and become more in tune with our higher purpose.

PRACTICE:
HEALING AND SEVERING KARMIC BONDS

Even though, at the highest level, we are all connected in some way—like the stars within the Milky Way connected against the vast tapestry of the black sky, forming patterns and influencing planetary movement—sometimes we need to disconnect ourselves from certain people. Maybe it's because the learning is over between you or nothing can be repaired, or all they cause you is pain. If that's the case, it may be time to cut the psychic cord between you and this person.

Sometimes the bond we have with someone is so strong that it creates a psychic cord that attaches itself to our auras. And sometimes, if the connection is very strong, one or both people can feel the pain of the other, as well as their energetic pull and influence. When you know it's in your best soul interest to let someone go entirely, when it's a necessary part of your spiritual journey, you can cut psychic ties with them using this technique so they're no longer connected to you physically or emotionally. Don't, however, sever the heart or soul cords between you and another person, as you might not want to sever those connections indefinitely.

Supplies
Sea salt
White or blue candle

Step 1
Take a sea salt bath to cleanse your physical body and aura. Afterward, when you emerge from the bath, light a white or blue candle.

Step 2
Next, start with a light meditation (see page 47) and visualize a purifying, protective, cleansing light around you. Then, when you're ready, visualize your various connections with that person. Start with your physical body: Can you "see" any cords coming from your body, connecting you to that person? They may have a silvery look to them or a darker shade. If it was a sexual relationship, you may notice these cords coming from your genital region or womb. Now, mentally visualize a pair of scissors and cut those cords that connect you to the person. There may be several, and here, you can use the light of the candle, moving it around in different places, to help burn away those cords. Visualize each cord falling away and being absorbed into the white light, moving away from you in love and peace, not anger.

Step 3

I do not recommend severing the heart or soul connections between others, as noted, since we may have karmic or soul bonds with others that serve a higher purpose. The point here is to heal emotionally and psychically, separating your mental and emotional planes from that person. If you notice any cords coming from the very top of your head or heart area (heart chakra), use the power and energy of the light meditation (and your will and focus) to purify those cords, raise their vibrations, and send out only peaceful, radiant love in those areas, rather than "cut" them. In this way, you change the vibrational patterns between you and that person, rather than severing any soul connections.

Step 4

You may have to do this practice several times in order to feel disconnected from that person. Each time, you may feel lighter and more at peace, as each cord falls away. I find this technique especially useful when focused in the sacral or solar plexus areas, where emotional cords tend to congregate. Soon, you'll feel yourself less connected to and bothered by that person, whether you were tied together by heartbreak and emotional wounds from a romantic love or by toxic energy from a person in your past whom you were very close with.

INTEGRATIONS

Let's do a philosophical thought experiment from the nineteenth century. Imagine, if you would, that you're sleeping soundly in bed one lonesome night and suddenly a spirit appears to you at the foot of your bed: it has a message, a revelation, a secret from beyond. The spirit speaks and tells you that you are destined to live your exact life, down to the simplest, minute details, over and over again for the rest of eternity.

Every moment you've ever lived, every hardship you've overcome, every person you've met, every laugh, tear, and moment—every single thing that has made up your entire life—will happen again, over and over for all time. Now, would you spring up from your bed and bow to the spirit, proclaiming, "You are an angel!"? Or would you scream in horror and curse the spirit, casting them away as a demon?

Nietzsche made this point in the nineteenth century, and despite being a devout atheist, his point seems, at least to me, profoundly spiritual.[146] Think about the revelation he posits—are you living a life that you'd want to repeat over and over? If not, you might want to do something about it while you can. Live a life worth living over and over, so that despite the difficulties, harsh edges, and painful dark nights, you would do anything to relive it again.

146. Friedrich Nietzsche, *The Gay Science: With a Prelude in Rhymes and an Appendix of Songs*, trans. Walter Kaufman (New York: Random House, 1974), 273–74.

CHAPTER 11
ON DEATH AND DYING

Death is the separation of the soul from the body. While I already discussed reincarnation and the state of rebirth in the previous chapter, what about death itself? The experience of dying and confronting that unknown? "To be generated into life is for the soul to once again be attached or conjoined with the body," Dr. Miller once wrote in a handout for class. If death is the soul's temporary separation from the body, what happens on the so-called other side? So far in our human timeline, the answer to this question has been left up to mystics, prophets, and philosophers, but over the last forty years, studies led by world-renowned researchers, neuroscientists, and medical doctors at major universities (such as Raymond Moody, Elisabeth Kübler-Ross, Ian Stevenson, Brian Weiss, Bruce Greyson, and countless others) have made strong cases that after death there is indeed more life.

Swiss-American psychiatrist Dr. Elisabeth Kübler-Ross garnered eighteen doctorates for her work on dying, death, and grief, ultimately becoming a trailblazer for near-death experience (NDE) research. She and her team studied twenty thousand cases of people from all over the world who had died and come back to life and found that there were several common denominators in all their experiences.[147] Using collected cases from a variety of religious and cultural backgrounds, including people from different countries and ages ranging from two to ninety-seven years old, there were striking similarities among those who've died and returned back to their bodies. This variety of data was to ensure that nothing could be construed as "religious" or any other social conditioning.[148]

Before 1968, death was typically understood as the absence of a heartbeat and breath, but "brain death" (when all brain activity ceases) has since been used as a definition in hospitals.[149] At the point when a patient was declared clinically dead, the majority of NDEers, as they're called, reported they felt their spirit or soul leave their body, but they still maintained consciousness with an acute sense of awareness—visual, auditory, and an ability to *move through* the physical constraints of the world.

In her collection of essays entitled *On Life after Death*, Kübler-Ross describes how innumerable patients who've had a near-death experience have been able to recall, with astonishing accuracy, the immediate details surrounding the events of their death. Upon returning back to the body, they can recall conversations heard in the room; the precise medical processes of the doctors; details of objects around them they wouldn't have been able to see, such as colors, clothes, patterns, and the jewelry of nurses, doctors, and onlookers; and minute details of the scene surrounding their death. Previously, these cases were readily dismissed as projections or wishful thinking.

Without serious study, this phenomenon could, of course, be attributed to many factors. Perhaps they had seen the nurse, doctor, or individual who tried to save them beforehand. Or had they picked up on physical details because part of their consciousness was still somehow present? Knowing this as a scientist, Kübler-Ross decided to also conduct studies

147. Elisabeth Kübler-Ross, *On Life after Death* (Berkeley, CA: Celestial Arts, 2008), 2.
148. Kübler-Ross, *On Life after Death,* 46.
149. Ryan Montoya, "What Is Death, Exactly?" *Scientific American*, October 18, 2019, https://blogs.scientificamerican.com/observations/what-is-death-exactly/.

involving those who were legally blind to further reduce claims for "wishful thinking" or projections. She found that even those without light perception before their NDE were able to recall specific visual experiences of what was happening around their body at the moment of death, including "the color of a sweater, the design of a tie … and designs of people's clothing."[150] Recalling these details upon coming back to life was something "a totally blind person would never be able to do" in their physical body.[151]

STORY: THE WHITE BRIDGE

On the Other Side, 1970s

I've never had an NDE, but my father has. After years of struggling to connect with him and understand his absences and never-ending riddles, I decided that it was in my best soul interest to forgive him. Three things I knew for certain: (1) If reincarnation was true, as I saw evidence for all around me, I was bound to meet him again in yet another life. (2) If I didn't learn the lessons of forgiveness and love now, I would have to repeat them over and over. (3) For some reason beyond my understanding now, I *chose* him to be my father. Perhaps my lesson was to learn how to love unconditionally.

I felt as though I'd be bound to him in each life, returning to learn the same thing or balance out whatever karmic debt we had between each other until I fully learned unconditional love. In the swells of my anger, disappointment, and sadness at all he had done and not done, I knew that I had to forgive him. I didn't want to repeat these lessons in the next life, and whatever karmic connection we had had to be healed. The path of acceptance and forgiveness, for me at least, will be a lifelong journey, but I also know that each person in our life serves a purpose, an opportunity for a soul lesson.

In one of my attempts to connect with him on the phone one evening, parsing through the family history and deciphering his riddles, he

---

150. Kübler-Ross, *On Life after Death*, 49.

151. Kübler-Ross, *On Life after Death*, 49.

said something very plainly, with striking coherence: "I died before. I guess it's what they call a near-death experience. I had one of those." He began to tell me the story of his NDE, and as he did, his voice became determined, straightforward, as if confessing something very important that he had long buried.

When he was nineteen years old, while swimming in Savage River in Maryland with a group of friends, his foot got caught in a rock. The strong pull of the rapids took him under, and he yelled out for help. His friends tried to unlatch his foot from the rock, but each time it wedged down even further into the crevice. After many attempts, his body finally went under, thrashing and pulsing in the water. So he gave up and let go.

He then described a serenity washing over him and said he felt at peace. He thought of his parents and his girlfriend at the time, before deciding in that instance that they'd all be okay with him gone. "My parents have five other kids. They'll be all right," he thought, and so he let the water consume him. He drowned.

"They say you see a tunnel with a light at the end of it. But that's not true at all. Or at least, that didn't happen to me," he said. Instead of a tunnel, a white bridge made of wooden planks appeared before him. Although it seemed like a regular bridge, something was strange about the handrail. It was *also* shaped like a bridge, with steps going upward along the handrail. The bridge was less than a city block ("maybe half a block"), and when he got about a fourth of the way across, he saw a figure standing at the end of it.

It was his grandmother.

She had died a few years back, and he immediately recognized her face and hair. It looked as though she was in a "cloud" or a mist (the same phenomenon as described by Dr. Raymond Moody), and she was wearing a white, grayish flowing dress that seemed to blend with the clouds behind her. Yet he recalled seeing the crisp outlines of her ironing, which set her body apart from the mist.

Before he could reach her across the bridge, she told him to stop. But this was not with vocal language: "I never saw her lips move, but it was her voice. Clear as day." Her face looked solemn, and she simply said, "It's not your time yet. You must turn back."

When he turned back, it was at that moment that he "woke up." His body was on the opposite bank of the river on the gravel, a trail of blood left on the rocks. When his body completely relaxed to death, his foot must've become unstuck from the rock, he reasoned, and washed ashore. By then, his friends had already called the ambulance, but when they got there, he refused to go with them. He knew he had seen part of the "other side" of death and returned. He would live.

My father, a blue-collar tradesman, never studied near-death experience, nor esoteric or Eastern philosophy. He also wasn't the type who just happened to keep up with the latest scientific research of NDEs. Yet his story bore striking similarities to everything I had studied about the phenomenon, with astonishing accuracy mirroring the common model of an NDE. He has since recalled this story several times to me without any variation.

What I find perhaps most fascinating is how his story never wavers each time I ask about it. His voice suddenly becomes clear: there are no riddles, no evasions. I asked him if he had ever told anyone else about the experience and he responded, "Only my friends who were there that day. But other than that, no, I never spoke of it. I didn't think people would understand what happened to me. I didn't want them to think I was crazy or weird." When I asked him what the experience taught him, he said, again very plainly, "It taught me not to be afraid of death."

DEEP DIVE: NEAR-DEATH EXPERIENCES

Dr. Kübler-Ross notes that an NDE typically involves the person hovering above themselves, witnessing the scene with absolutely no pain or fear, and sometimes even wanting to comfort those trying to rehabilitate them or grieving over them. Interestingly, some NDEers seemed to have an ironic sense of humor at the absurdity of the entire death situation in this out-of-body state.

Many NDEers describe encountering a loved one they had known in their life who had previously died or the appearance of a spiritual figure to help guide them. What's particularly fascinating here is at this stage, no one ever encountered someone who was still living. It's not as if their life partner or a still-living beloved parent figure suddenly appeared: it was always someone who had previously died. Even more, they never encountered a spiritual figure outside of their religion or spiritual practice. For instance, a Catholic may encounter Mary or Christ, but an atheist wouldn't. Regardless of their religious affiliation, they were never alone: they were "guided" by either a loved one or a spiritual being during this transition. The major takeaway from this is that each person had someone (or many figures) to guide them through the transition, awaiting them, in a manner proper to their comfort level. Whoever or whichever figure was regarded as the most loving and revered in their waking life "met" them during this transition from body to an ethereal form.

The next striking similarity between these cases was a transition involving a tunnel, river, bridge, or the like. Some even describe it as a black vacuum, fitting their bodies and sucking them into a kind of vortex, before then experiencing an all-encompassing bright light with incredible sensations of love and peace, and the complete erasure of pain, anxiety, or fear. "This all occurs at the time when we have no measurable signs of brain activity," Kübler-Ross writes.[152] At this point in the death transition, most everyone is met with a spirit guide, sometimes called a guardian angel, or again, someone whom the person has known before but has previously passed on.

Kübler-Ross describes the dying experience as "almost identical to the experience at birth," regardless of one's religious affiliation, upbringing,

---

152. Kübler-Ross, *On Life after Death*, 47.

or cultural background.[153] The human body is like a cocoon, and death is the release of the body from its encasement, just as a butterfly emerges into existence. It's "moving from one house into a more beautiful one." You will "release the butterfly, your soul to speak," and at this stage you're "supplied with psychic energy."[154]

During the NDE, the person will encounter a peaceful, loving light and rarely want to turn back: "In this light, you will experience for the first time what man could have been. Here there is understanding without judging, and here you will experience unconditional love. In this presence, which many people compare with Christ or God, with love or light, you will come to know all your life on earth was nothing but a school that you had to go through in order to pass certain tests and learn special lessons."[155]

Like Plato's Myth of Er, each person will face a judgment—but not one of condemnation or to provoke guilt or a primary segue to hell. It's described like a movie reel of one's experiences on Earth: every moment will be played before you, instantaneously, and you will bear witness to what you've done with your precious life. Every instance, every memory, every loved one, every beautiful or embarrassing or transcendent or mundane moment will be seen again.

Yet the interesting aspect is, especially in contrast to the Christian notion of judgment, that all of this is done sans judgment. "In this light, in the presence of God, Christ, or whatever you want to name it, you have to look back on your entire life from the first day until the last," Kübler-Ross writes.[156] "During this review of your earthly life you will not blame God for your fate, but you will know that you yourself were your own worst enemy since you are now accusing yourself of having neglected so many opportunities to grow."[157] It's very similar to a "television screen,"

---

153. Kübler-Ross, *On Life after Death*, 2–3.
154. Kübler-Ross, *On Life after Death*, 3–4.
155. Kübler-Ross, *On Life after Death*, 11.
156. Kübler-Ross, *On Life after Death*, 11.
157. Kübler-Ross, *On Life after Death*, 12.

and "you will be given an opportunity—not to be judged by a judgmental God—but to judge yourself, by having to review every single action, every word, and every thought of your life. You make your own hell or your own heaven by the way you have lived."[158]

Many NDEers are given a choice to come back—to fulfill a promise, fulfill a duty, continue a task, or to simply express their will to live in this incarnation again. This could be to continue education, raise children, help a family member or friend, or have a strong desire or will to continue on. Dr. Kübler-Ross summarized her decades-long research on death and near-death experiences in the following: "Most important of all, we must learn to love and be loved unconditionally."[159]

What Lies Beyond the Threshold

Dr. Raymond Moody, psychiatrist, author, and forefather of near-death research, published his findings in his seminal book *Life after Life* in 1975, which at the time rocked the world. Just like Kübler-Ross, he unexpectedly found a very similar chain of events that occurred when someone died and came back to life. Before rigorous scientific and medical studies were conducted on the subject, NDEs could be easily written off as wishful thinking or a hallucinatory reaction to oxygen deprivation, or, worse, patients could be labeled as "crazy."[160] In fact, this is still the case in many medical circles. Often NDEers were hesitant to speak of their experiences. Dr. Moody hesitantly posited that death is not an "annihilation of consciousness," but perhaps a progression into another higher realm. He continues, "Some say that death is annihilation of consciousness, others say with equal confidence that death is the passage of the soul or mind into another dimension of reality." He does not wish to "dis-

---

158. Kübler-Ross, *On Life after Death*, 35.

159. Kübler-Ross, *On Life after Death*, 65.

160. Raymond Moody, *Life after Life: The Bestselling Original Investigation That Revealed "Near-Death Experiences"* (New York: HarperCollins, 2015), 84.

miss either" but rather to elucidate the results of his medical and scientific research.[161]

Moody was skeptical of NDEs, but over the course of many years, after amassing many different cases of NDEs and independently interviewing each survivor about their out-of-body experiences, he discovered many shared similarities between them.[162] Interestingly enough, many people had never spoken of their experiences before or had only told very few people of the details of their brief life after death. As in the research of Kübler-Ross and the experience of my father, NDEers expressed a kind of shame involved in speaking of things that language itself could not encompass or express, fearing that they may be judged or dismissed by others. Despite this reticence, they all agreed that the singular experience had a profound impact on their life, "especially [their] views about death and its relationship to life."[163]

In his research, Dr. Moody noticed a series of similarities within each case, which he used to create a "model" or "composite" of NDEs.[164] Now, keep in mind this is years before most medical schools or reputable research universities took this phenomenon seriously. Around the same time, in 1967, the University of Virginia School of Medicine's Division of Perceptual Studies was formed, and they, too, have been researching "phenomena that challenge mainstream scientific paradigms regarding the nature of human consciousness," most notably near-death experiences, ever since.[165] Originally led by Dr. Ian Stevenson, and later carried on by Dr. Bruce Greyson, the crux of their work involves evaluating empirical evidence on whether consciousness survives death by analyzing data collected from those who've had "extraordinary human experiences."[166] Today,

161. Moody, *Life after Life*, 6.
162. Moody, *Life after Life*, 7.
163. Moody, *Life after Life*, 13.
164. Moody, *Life after Life*, 13.
165. "Division of Perceptual Studies," University of Virginia School of Medicine, accessed March 1, 2024, https://med.virginia.edu/perceptual-studies/.
166. "Division of Perceptual Studies."

NDEs, and the phenomena they produce, are so widely reported that other prestigious universities, scientists, and doctors have taken notice.

But consider how, in 1975, this was revolutionary in many ways. It also stands to note that in order to move forward and conquer new ground in any subject, research, or scientific or creative endeavor, we must acknowledge the innovators and thinkers who've walked before us and paved the way.

Moody emphasized that each case was unique, and no one experiences every single aspect of the "model" NDE.[167] One similarity between cases was that at the point of death, the person will hear a loud buzzing sound, hear a "loud ringing," or experience a "whirling state."[168] One woman described hearing music: "majestic, really beautiful sort of music."[169]

This last sentiment, in particular, made a lot of sense to me. Shortly after learning of the death of my teacher Dr. John Miller, I returned back to my apartment in New York, sat on my green velvet couch, and broke down in tears. Staring out the window, I asked him to give me a sign—something, anything, to let me know that he was okay. Moments later a voice came to me, like a whisper, but as clear as day: "The music, the music is so beautiful here!" Although it was a whisper, it seemed like a shout at the same time, an ecstatic version of his voice. After his voice dissipated and became a lone echo in the chambers of my mind, I knew he was okay. He, the man of opera, transcendent sound lover, lover of musical ecstasy and symphonic bliss, was in a place where the sounds were more magical than ever. Wherever *there* was, he wanted me to know that the sounds —"The sounds!" he shouted—were magical.

Similarly, this focus on majestic music was also described by Dr. Eben Alexander, a neurosurgeon who had a near-death experience and later wrote about it in his book *Proof of Heaven*: "Then I heard a new sound: a *living* sound, like the richest, most complex, most beautiful piece

167. Moody, *Life after Life*, 13–14.
168. Moody, *Life after Life*, 20–21.
169. Moody, *Life after Life*, 20–21.

of music you've ever heard. Growing in volume as a pure white light descended it obliterated the monotonous pounding that, seemingly for eons, had been my only company up until then."[170] He, too, was guided through a profound experience that changed the course of his life when he emerged from death. In his communications with loving spirits on the other side, including what he called "Om" or God, he was told that there is "not one universe but many—in fact, more than [he] could ever conceive—but that love lay at the center of them all."[171]

At the moment of death, Moody also found that NDEers find themselves outside their body, seeing it from afar as well as the "immediate physical environment," almost like a "spectator," and in some cases, they watch as others try to revive them.[172] Like Kübler-Ross found with thousands of cases, NDEers can *see* their bodies after death, noticing minute details and bearing witness to the scene of their deaths. They recall shouts, the backs of people's heads, different angles of the scene, their twisted body parts on the pavement after accidents.[173] Yet there isn't pain involved, but rather a sense of timelessness. Afterward, they find themselves "moving very rapidly through a long dark tunnel," an "utterly black, dark void," or a "dark valley."[174] Dr. Alexander described it was an "inky darkness that was also full to brimming with light."[175] Some even, like my father, describe it as a bridge. At some point at either the moment of death or after passing through this tunnel, another phenomenon occurs: relatives and loved ones who've already passed on appear before them.

---

170. Eben Alexander, *Proof of Heaven: A Neurosurgeon's Journey into the Afterlife* (New York: Simon and Schuster, 2012), 38.

171. Alexander, *Proof of Heaven*, 48.

172. Moody, *Life after Life*, 12.

173. Moody, *Life after Life*, 28–29.

174. Moody, *Life after Life*, 12, 23.

175. Alexander, *Proof of Heaven*, 48.

A Spirit Guide or Being of Light

Dr. Moody reported that most, if not all, patients returning from death claim a sensation of being drawn into an all-encompassing, compassionate, calming light.[176] They each describe this light as the most loving force they've ever encountered. Upon returning to their earthly bodies, after crossing over to the other side, nearly all NDE survivors report some kind of experience with this light.

In many cases of NDEs, both Dr. Moody and Dr. Kübler-Ross have described NDEers encountering a being of light on their journey: a "loving, warm spirit of a kind he has never encountered before—a being of light—appear before him."[177] The identity of the light being can vary from person to person, especially according to their religious backgrounds, just as Kübler-Ross later reports; some may say it's Christ or God, whereas others say it's a figure of pure love and light.[178]

This light being acts as a spirit guide and asks questions about what the NDEer has done with their life, if it was worth it, and if they're ready to die.[179] Again, this is done without judgment, without malice, and only with love. The line of questioning reminds me of Mary Oliver's famous poem "The Summer Day": "Tell me, what is it you plan to do with your one wild and precious life?"[180] Perhaps there are many prophets among us.

A panoramic, instantaneous playback of their life ensues, guided by this being of light, and they are confronted with their life on Earth: "This review can only be described in terms of memory, since that is the closest familiar phenomenon to it, but it has characteristics which set it apart from any normal type of remembering," writes Moody.[181] It's

176. Moody, *Life after Life*, 51.

177. Kübler-Ross, *On Life after Death*, 46, 60–61; Moody, *Life after Life*, 12.

178. Moody, *Life after Life*, 55–56; Kübler-Ross, *On Life after Death*, 61–62.

179. Moody, *Life after Life*, 56–61.

180. Mary Oliver, "Poem 133: The Summer Day," Library of Congress, accessed June 24, 2024, https://www.loc.gov/programs/poetry-and-literature/poet-laureate/poet-laureate-projects/poetry-180/all-poems/item/poetry-180-133/the-summer-day/.

181. Moody, *Life after Life*, 58.

"extremely rapid," and visual memories "follow one another swiftly," but some describe no chronological or temporal order at all. Rather, it is an immediate remembrance. Every image is "perceived and recognized," as well as the emotions associated with the memory.[182]

This life in review is without judgment or condemnation. "Through all of my research, however, I have not heard a single reference to a heaven or a hell anything like the customary picture to which we are exposed in this society," Moody writes.[183] The purpose of these flashbacks is to show meaning in each of the moments, the inherent lessons within each; to show when we were foolish, selfish, loved, helpful, loving, joyous, melancholic. It's taking stock of each individual moment that makes up the totality of our lives and always with the emphasis that the meaning of life is to *love one another unconditionally and help others.*

Interestingly, there's also an emphasis on the importance of knowledge and using this life to acquire as much knowledge as possible. There's a sense that this caveat also extends to other worlds: the meaning of life is to love and learn—and then *keep* loving and learning throughout all existence.

The After-Effects of NDEs

Does a person change after these encounters with death? Is there any difference in their new waking hours? After experiencing an NDE, is one's life imbued with a sense of mystery, renewed passions, goals? In a study published by the *Journal of Humanistic Psychology*, researchers found that those who had experienced an NDE became "more concerned with the welfare of others," as well as experienced a deeper appreciation for nature and an "increase in awareness of paranormal phenomenon."[184]

---

182. Moody, *Life after Life*, 58–61.

183. Moody, *Life after Life*, 133.

184. Gary Groth-Marnat and Roger Summers, "Altered Beliefs, Attitudes, and Behaviors Following Near-Death Experiences," *Journal of Humanistic Psychology* 38, no. 3 (Summer 1998): 110, 118.

Researchers "investigated the extent and types of altered beliefs, attitudes, and values of 53 subjects who reported having a near-death experience" and then compared them to a control group of 27 individuals who had experienced life-threatening incidents *without a near-death experience*.[185] They also involved their significant others in the study to corroborate and rate any noticeable changes in their partners, both before and after the NDEs or life-threatening incidents. While both groups had reported that they had undergone significant life changes after these events, the "magnitude of change was greater for the NDE group."[186]

No one should, of course, willingly seek out an NDE, just to experience a shift in perspective or glimpse into the afterlife. Many who come back from these experiences feel a kind of isolation among others who haven't shared the same experience and are hesitant to talk about it for fear that they'll be labeled crazy or deemed to have lost touch with reality.[187] But chances are, if you ask around, you, too, may encounter many, many people who've had an NDE.

To quote Dr. Alexander and the higher lessons he brought back with him, he learned that the "world of time and space in which we move in this terrestrial realm is tightly and intricately meshed with these higher worlds," consisting of other dimensions with beings of advanced intelligence.[188] These other worlds are not entirely separate from ours, as they are deeply intertwined with the same "overarching divine Reality." And the discovery of the knowledge he acquired in these other realms, their immediacy and profundity, was enough to give him "food for thought for ages to come."[189]

---

185. Groth-Marnat and Summers, "Altered Beliefs, Attitudes, and Behaviors Following Near-Death Experiences," 110.

186. Groth-Marnat and Summers, "Altered Beliefs, Attitudes, and Behaviors Following Near-Death Experiences," 116.

187. Groth-Marnat and Summers, "Altered Beliefs, Attitudes, and Behaviors Following Near-Death Experiences," 122.

188. Alexander, *Proof of Heaven*, 48–49.

189. Alexander, *Proof of Heaven*, 49.

WORKING WITH THE LESSONS OF LIFE AND DEATH

During his lectures, Dr. Miller would summarize the findings and conclusions of Kübler-Ross's NDE studies and the knowledge brought back from the thousands of people who've died, crossed over, and come back to life again. Years later, he wrote to me: "Each of us has our own particular 'path' to walk, our own experiences to have, etc. But there are general goals for us all, like developing the capacity to love, to forgive, to give, and to develop the 'virtues,' most of which are expressions, in one form or another, of love."

"Remember what the research of Elisabeth Kübler-Ross, MD, showed regarding the near-death experience? People who had NDEs generally agreed that there were only four activities that made life truly worth living," he continued.[190] And so here are the four most profound lessons of death I've learned and have carried with me for nearly twenty years. Whenever I'm confused on my journey or not sure of my next steps or my place in the world, I remember these four simple truths.

Technique: Develop Agape

First, we're here to love each other unconditionally and develop an *agape*, or godlike love for all. This is easier said than done, but simply remembering this in moments of despair or difficulty helps us see the bigger picture. It's not about seeking love out there or even searching for romantic love, but *embodying* love in all ways. No matter the ways we've been wronged or the hurts others may have caused, when we shift our perspective and gaze to this truth, practicing seeing others through an agape lens, something starts to shift.

Technique: Develop Our Talents

Second, we're here to develop and maximize our talents and abilities. Each of us is born with a set of talents and abilities, some of which I believe are innate, while others are learned. Either way, while we're here

190. John Miller III, correspondence with Amber C. Snider, July 30, 2013.

on Earth, it's our moral imperative to grow and use these talents. This also means embracing our individuality, our uniqueness, our quirks and even strangeness—and figuring out how we can use these gifts for a higher purpose. By truly embracing and acknowledging our full selves and even dormant talents, we better align ourselves with our soul purpose.

Technique: Be of Service

We're also here to find a way to be of service. Like embodying unconditional love, helping others on their journey is part of the essential reason why we're here. We've all needed help at some point in our lives, and innumerable people have shaped our life path along the way. Whether it's your first-grade teacher, a kind neighbor, a friend, a mentor, or a grandmother, so much of what we were able to accomplish is only possible through the kind assistance from someone else. Consider how you can pay it forward and give back in what I like to call "big, little, and small" ways. Never underestimate how words of advice or a kind act can profoundly impact someone else's life.

Technique: Help Others Develop Their Talents

And finally, with the other three truths in mind, we're also here to help others develop their talents. In a sense, this differs from being of service. Consider your career or a particular talent you may have: Would you have truly known you had a gift or knack for something without someone else recognizing it and acknowledging it—at some point—along the way? Sometimes we come to know ourselves and our abilities *through* others, and while we certainly don't need validation from the world, it's very rare that any human is an island unto themselves. Just as you've relied on others to grow and understand your own talents, consider how you can encourage others to discover their own hidden abilities and potential.

PRACTICE:
CONFRONTING DEATH, PRACTICALLY SPEAKING

Death is a subject that no one wants to really talk about. Whether or not one believes in an afterlife, the reality is death is inevitable. What truly happens beyond the threshold is unknown—it is unknowable—but there are practical steps we can take now in this life to prepare for our own death. Part of being of service to others means taking responsibility for our lives and making things easier on our loved ones after we're gone.

In my own experience dealing with the loss of a parent, my father, I was struck by just how much I didn't know when it came to the practical, bureaucratic, and legal aspects of death. I thought I understood grief but had absolutely no idea how difficult it would be to handle the actual death process. While the following could be the subject of an entire book, here are some basic tips for how you can prepare for your own death and help ease the burden on your loved ones.

Supplies
Computer and secure internet connection
Optional: Estate lawyer or estate planner
List of your personal affects, belongings, and accounts

Step 1
Create a living will. Even if you only have two dimes to rub together, as my grandmother would say, it doesn't matter. When you leave this Earth, you're going to leave behind bills, a home (either a mortgage or lease), clothing, artwork, bank accounts, an email account, a cell phone with a password, and debts or assets. Someone has to take care of it all, and if you don't have a will with a named executor or personal representative, it becomes part of the probate process known as intestacy. This is an enormously difficult process, both emotionally and legally, and no one should have to make difficult (big or small) decisions while in the midst of grief. So do your loved ones a favor and create a living will right

now—either write it on your own and get it notarized or do it through an estate lawyer.

Step 2

Have a health plan. Put your last wishes in writing, including your organ donation desires, a "do not resuscitate" plan if that's your desire, whether or not you want a spiritual or religious figure to offer a blessing, and so on. Each state has different requirements, so ideally all this should be in your living will and looked over by an attorney, but you can also simply look up your state's laws to find out if there are specific forms, notary requirements, and whether or not these forms have to be filed at your local Register of Wills.

Step 3

Name an executor, personal representative, and/or power of attorney in your will. If, for any reason, you're unable to make decisions for yourself while you're alive, they'll be able to speak on your behalf, and in the event of your death, they'll be able to efficiently handle the practical aspects of your passing. Also, give a copy of your living will to this person.

Step 4

Secure all your practical matters. Consider your closest loved ones coming into your house after you've passed and having to clean up everything you've left behind in a state of grief. One of the most loving things we can do for our friends and family while we're still here is making sure our "practical business" is handled beforehand. Set up a POD beneficiary (payable on death beneficiary) on your bank accounts. Create a secure list of your bank accounts, passwords (including your phone password and email), assets and debts, names of your mortgage company or landlord, utility and insurance accounts, and any details you'd like to share with your loved ones that can help ease the process for them. Keep it in a safe place and give a copy to your most trusted family member, friend, or power of attorney.

Include what you'd like done with your personal effects (all your stuff); any individuals, charities, or programs you'd like to give your money to (if there's extra leftover after the funerary services); where you want your books, manuscripts, and cherished items to go; and so on. You don't have to be on your death bed to handle this. It should be done as soon as possible, ideally while you're healthy and sound of mind.

Step 5

Create more detailed instructions for your last wishes, including your funerary services, any songs you want played, and any spiritual/religious/church affiliations. Would you like to be buried or cremated? Is there money put away for that and where? If you'd like to be buried, what would you like to wear? Do you want an open or closed casket? What would you like to include in your obituary? Possibly create your own or at least write down a list of life accomplishments that you'd like to see included in your obituary. These small yet big details add up, and if you've already outlined them in writing, it truly takes away the burden of decision-making for your loved ones in their time of grief.

INTEGRATIONS

None of us truly knows what's waiting on the other side. But rather than simply pondering the possibility of a heaven or dreaming about the afterlife, we'd all be a lot better off if we tried to create that reality while we're here right now. Some say that heaven is right here on Earth. While I believe the soul is eternal and that we'll move on to another state of being after this one, why not use our gifts, the tools of nature, the gifts of the earth, and our physical consciousness to evolve and grow while we still have time? If Earth is a giant school, we still have much to learn. There's important work to be done still, but I know one thing for certain: it starts and ends with love.

CONCLUSION
THE WREN

On New Years' Eve, while visiting family for the holidays, a wren perched himself on a wreath outside my mother's front door. We didn't notice him nestled there when we arrived home that evening, and when we opened the door, he came swooping inside. It seemed like he was waiting for us. His little wings fluttered up to the window enclave, carved high above the sitting room, and there he settled on a large plant. We tried everything to help him find his way back out, but he seemed determined to stay. We kept the front door open so he could feel the breeze, put a speaker playing bird sounds outside, and gently rustled objects in the room so he'd begin to fly again. But instead, he stayed, like a little prince in his tree, staring down on us.

We marveled at his plump body, at his wise and inquisitive face, and how of all nights, this one, at the beginning of the new year, he decided to join us.

All birds have spiritual significance, and when they become a guest in your home, they tend to portend *something*. "Maybe it's my brother coming to say hello," my mother said, thinking of her recently passed sibling. "Maybe it's Nanny," I said, thinking of my grandmother. We knew the wren's presence was significant, that it was a sign, but we didn't know exactly what. After many failed attempts to help him outdoors again, we finally told him goodnight and let him rest up on his perch.

The next morning, New Year's Day, the little wren was still there, and when we opened the front door again and continued on with our morning, he flew out without us knowing. He went as suddenly as he came. A few weeks later, when I learned of Dr. Miller's death, his date of passing struck me: it was January 1, 2021.

I didn't know it then, but the wren is a harbinger, a messenger of rebirth and spring, representing immortality and protection.[191] Interestingly enough, wrens are also associated with musicians, writers, and poets (a.k.a. the Muse). Small, energetic, and quick-thinking, they're known for their cleverness and ingenuity, as well as being social, loving, and happy birds who enjoy life.[192] The Celts, ancient peoples who were greatly in tune with the natural world, believed that when someone in their tribe died, they could transform into these animals upon their death. And in the Celtic zodiac, people born between June 10 and July 7 are represented by the wren, which Dr. Miller's birthday also would've fallen under.[193]

I was amazed at this and knew then that Dr. Miller would never truly leave me. His spirit would live on, and he would continue to be there, as my muse and mentor, my forever Socrates and friend. A few months before he left this earth for the next realm, he sent me a poem, and the last line read: "LOVE remains, though hidden deep from sight." In all my continued questions, in my search for divine truths, I knew one thing for certain: that at the beginning and end of all roads, love remains.

He gave me a gift, too many gifts to ever be contained in a single book, and I knew he would continue to show me the way, alongside many other

191. Katelyn Wilde, "Wren Symbolism and Meaning (Spirit, Totem and Omens)," *Sonoma Birding* (blog), accessed January 21, 2021, https://www.sonomabirding.com/wren-symbolism/.

192. Wilde, "Wren Symbolism and Meaning."

193. Avia, "Celtic Zodiac Sign Wren," Whats-Your-Sign.com, January 20, 2018, https://www.whats-your-sign.com/celtic-zodiac-sign-wren.html.

loved ones who've already left this world. He would guide me, just as the trees do, the wind, the sacred waters of the earth, on this journey toward knowing, toward becoming, toward love, toward my soul purpose.

The student-teacher relationship is sacred, and we'll each encounter many teachers on our individual journeys and someday, perhaps, become teachers in our own way, too. But my hope is that we all remain students of life, ever questioning and curious, for as long as we're here. My journey of awakening, of discovering my purpose through magic, curiosity, and creativity, has always been a process of becoming. It's led me down some strange, beautiful roads. What first began as questioning the dogma of organized religion has since brought me to a threshold, a doorway, where there are many, perhaps even infinite, paths to the Divine and sacred knowledge.

It's my hope that this book has helped you, even in the simplest of ways, expand your ideas of what's possible and encourage you to be bold in your search for truth and beauty. It's my hope that you will continue to tap into your innate magic, wisdom, and intuition and, above all, acknowledge the divine current and consciousness within all things. *Occult* simply means "that which is hidden," and it's my hope that you, too, uncover the infinite hidden mysteries within and beyond. Blessed be.

ACKNOWLEDGMENTS

This book is dedicated to Dr. John Miller, my Socrates, whose life teachings and spiritual lessons were the catalyst for and inspiration behind this book. And to my mother, my original priestess, best friend, and first love, I'm so happy we chose each other again in this life. I'd also like to thank the following people and organizations during the making of this book: To Stacy Rapp, the head witch of Enchantments, for all her support and guidance over the years, and all the witches I made magic with there over the years. To my acquisitions editor Heather Greene for championing my work and helping me craft this vision into reality, and to all the wonderful, talented minds at Llewellyn Publications. To Shannon McKuhen for the beautiful book cover, to my production editor Lauryn Heineman for her savvy edits, and my publicist Kat Neff. To Jessica Hundley for her thoughtful, beautifully moving foreword and for supporting this book. To the community of Prospect Heights in Brooklyn for always keeping it real and supporting me in this long writing process. To all my aunties, who have shaped me with their guidance and strength and stories. To Vicki, my second mother and rock, thank you, and to my auntie Tina for all her wisdom and love.

Thank you to Rachel, Esme, and Nikki for your inspiring friendship over the years. To Victor for capturing my visual essence and knowing just what magic I need. To my stepfather Ron for accepting and loving me as I am (even as a liberal, feminist witch) and for your unwavering support. To Jim and Denise for your support, love, and guidance (see you at the lake). To my Nanny for all your love and guidance from the other side. And to all my loved ones who've crossed over (I know you're all still around and looking out, thank you).

To Meredith for your friendship for all these years and for always keeping it real. To Dahlia for being the first one to say, "Write a book to Dr. Miller," which was perhaps the original catalyst for the book. To the tree outside my Brooklyn window for being my constant companion.

To Mercy University for two faculty development awards that helped with the research of this book and for facilitating one of my great loves, teaching. To City College of New York, specifically the English Department, for providing a world-class public education and for helping shape my own academic journey. To all the teachers I've ever had, for the selfless instruction you've given and believing in the power of education even when the system makes it difficult, I tip all the hats to you. I'd like to thank all the librarians at the Brooklyn Library for keeping all those books in stock, in storage, and available to the public. And to anyone who's ever donated to a library, you're all angels in my eyes.

To the Portland and Oregon Tourism Boards for sending me to your beautiful region and believing in my journalistic vision. To Phelim for providing a beautiful garden house in Mérida (at a discount) when I needed to write. To the Hawaiian Tourism Board for sharing your beautiful island and culture with me, and to Micah and all the aunties of Waimea for welcoming me with open arms. To Rocio for the trip to Cuba that changed my life.

To *Atmos* magazine for commissioning the story "Yemayá: Learning to Surrender" and continuously producing incredible nature-based stories and great journalism. Thank you to the editors at Fodor's Travel for commissioning "The Myths and Legends of Hawaii" and for all your support. And shout-out to every publication who has ever rejected a pitch, for you taught fortitude and resiliency and have empowered me to keep going.

To Richie, Phil, and Manish, for your laughter, pep talks, and love. To Ryan C. for your kindness and support of my work. To Pete and Michael from our old CT crew, thank you for all the advice and encouragement over the years. And finally, to my brother Tommy for roughing the storms with me and remaining the greatest gift of my life.

BIBLIOGRAPHY

"About: The History of the Integratron." Integratron. Accessed November 5, 2022. https://www.integratron.com/history-about/.

Alexander, Eben. *Proof of Heaven: A Neurosurgeon's Journey into the Afterlife*. New York: Simon and Schuster, 2012.

Almaguer, Itzel. "Yaxche: The Tree of Life." Historical Mexico. Sam Huston State University. Accessed June 4, 2024. https://historicalmx.org /items/show/141.

Avia. "Celtic Zodiac Sign Wren." Whats-Your-Sign.com. January 20, 2018. https://www.whats-your-sign.com/celtic-zodiac-sign-wren .html.

Baldwin, James. *James Baldwin: Collected Essays*. New York: Library of America, 1998.

Becerra, Daniel. "The Canonization of the New Testament." In *New Testament History, Culture, and Society: A Background to the Texts of the New Testament*, edited by Lincoln H. Blumell, 772–86. Salt Lake City: Deseret Book, 2019. https://rsc.byu.edu/new-testament-history -culture-society/canonization-new-testament.

Bonansea, Bernardine, and Godehard Bruentrup. "Panpsychism." *New Catholic Encyclopedia Supplement* (2012–13): 1–3. https://core.ac.uk /download/pdf/131204105.pdf.

Born, Max, ed. *The Born-Einstein Letters: The Correspondence between Albert Einstein and Max and Hedwig Born from 1916 to 1955*. Translated by Irene Born. New York: Macmillan, 1970.

Bowler, Maurice Gerald. *Claude Montefiore and Christianity*. Atlanta, GA: Scholars Press, 1988.

Brumfiel, Geoff. "Researchers Say Time Is an Illusion. So Why Are We All Obsessed with It?" NPR. December 16, 2022. https://www.npr.org/2022/12/16/1139780043/what-is-time-physics-atomic-clocks-society.

Cameron, Julia. *The Artist's Way: A Spiritual Path to Higher Creativity*. New York: TarcherPerigee, 2002.

Campbell, Joseph. *The Hero with a Thousand Faces*. Commemorative ed. Princeton: Princeton University Press, 2004.

Carroll, Ryder. *The Bullet Journal Method: Track Your Past, Order Your Present, Plan Your Future*. New York: Penguin, 2018.

Caruth, Cathy, ed. *Trauma: Explorations in Memory*. Baltimore, MA: Johns Hopkins University Press, 1995.

"Ceiba Tree: Sacred Tree of Life of Maya People and Universal Concept in Ancient Beliefs." AncientPages.com. April 14, 2021. https://www.ancientpages.com/2017/06/12/ceiba-tree-sacred-tree-of-life-of-maya-people-and-universal-concept-in-ancient-beliefs/.

Crookes, David. "Can Our Brains Help Prove the Universe Is Conscious?" Space.com. February 23, 2022. https://www.space.com/is-the-universe-conscious.

"Dark Matter." CERN. Accessed October 11, 2023. https://home.cern/science/physics/dark-matter.

Denning, Melita, and Osborne Phillips. *Practical Guide to Psychic Self-Defense: Strengthen Your Aura*. St. Paul, MN: Llewellyn Publications, 2002.

Devere, Ronald. "Music and Dementia: An Overview." Practical Neurology. June 2017. https://practicalneurology.com/articles/2017-june /music-and-dementia-an-overview.

Didion, Joan. *Slouching Towards Bethlehem.* New York: Farrar, Straus, and Giroux, 1968. Reprint, New York: Picador Modern Classics, 2017.

———. *The White Album.* New York: Farrar, Straus and Giroux, 1979.

"Division of Perceptual Studies." University of Virginia School of Medicine. Accessed March 1, 2024. https://med.virginia.edu/perceptual -studies/.

"DOE Explains … Dark Matter." Office of Science. US Department of Energy. Accessed July 23, 2024, https://www.energy.gov/science /doe-explainsdark-matter.

Donne, John. "No Man Is an Island." All Poetry. Accessed June 2, 2024. https://allpoetry.com/No-man-is-an-island.

"Dori Laub M.D." Trauma Research. Yale University. Accessed June 4, 2024. https://traumaresearch.yale.edu/dori-laub-md.

Einstein, Albert. *Living Philosophies.* New York: Simon and Schuster, 1931.

"Einstein's Quantum Riddle." NOVA. PBS. January 9, 2019. Video, 53:40. https://www.pbs.org/wgbh/nova/video/einsteins-quantum-riddle/.

Eyer, Shawn, trans. "Translation from Plato's Republic 514b–518d ('Allegory of the Cave')." *Ahiman: A Review of Masonic Culture and Tradition* 1 (2009): 73–78. https://scholar.harvard.edu/files/seyer/files /plato_republic_514b-518d_allegory-of-the-cave.pdf.

Fedrizzi, Alessandro, and Massimiliano Proietti. "Quantum Physics: Our Study Suggests Objective Reality Doesn't Exist." Phys.org. November 14, 2019. https://phys.org/news/2019-11-quantum-physics-reality -doesnt.html.

Franklin, Michelle. "Rhythm and Proofs: Finding Music in the Math." School of Physical Sciences. UC San Diego. May 19, 2023. https://

physicalsciences.ucsd.edu/media-events/articles/2023/math-music
.html.

Gilbert, Elizabeth. *Big Magic: Creative Living beyond Fear*. London: Bloomsbury, 2015.

Goleman, Daniel. *Emotional Intelligence: Why It Can Matter More Than IQ*. New York: Bantam Books, 2020.

Grant, Richard. "Do Trees Talk to Each Other?" *Smithsonian Magazine*, March 2018. https://www.smithsonianmag.com/science-nature /the-whispering-trees-180968084/.

"Gray Whale." Discovery of Sound in the Sea. University of Rhode Island. Accessed June 7, 2024. https://dosits.org/galleries/audio -gallery/marine-mammals/baleen-whales/gray-whale/.

"Gray Whale." NOAA Fisheries. Last modified April 13, 2023. https:// www.fisheries.noaa.gov/species/gray-whale.

Griffin, Wendy. "The Embodied Goddess: Feminist Witchcraft and Female Divinity." *Sociology of Religion* 56, no.1 (1995): 35–48. https:// doi.org/10.2307/3712037.

Groth-Marnat, Gary, and Roger Summers. "Altered Beliefs, Attitudes, and Behaviors Following Near-Death Experiences." *Journal of Humanistic Psychology* 38, no. 3 (Summer 1998): 110–25.

Hand, Elizabeth. "Patterns in Nature: Where to Spot Spirals." Science World. April 25, 2019. https://www.scienceworld.ca/stories/patterns -nature-where-spot-spirals/.

Harvard Business Review. *Empathy: HBR Emotional Intelligence Series*. Boston, MA: Harvard Business Review Press, 2017.

Hegel, Georg Wilhelm Friedrich. *Hegel: Elements of the Philosophy of Right*. Edited by Allen W. Wood. Translated by H. B. Nisbet. Cambridge: Cambridge University Press, 1991.

Helminski, Kabir Edmund. *Living Presence (Revised): The Sufi Path to Mindfulness and the Essential Self*. New York: TarcherPerigee, 2017.

Homer. *The Odyssey*. Translated by Emily Wilson. New York: W. W. Norton & Company, 2018.

"How Ancient Trinitarian Gods Influenced Adoption of the Trinity." United Church of God. July 22, 2011. https://www.ucg.org /bible-study-tools/booklets/is-god-a-trinity/how-ancient-trinitarian -gods-influenced-adoption-of-the-trinity.

"How Trees Secretly Talk to Each Other." BBC News. Video, 1:47. June 29, 2018. https://www.bbc.com/news/av/science-environment -44643177.

Huysmans, J. K. *Against the Grain*. Translated by John Howard. New York: Albert & Charles Boni, 1922.

"Immerse Yourself in a Forest for Better Health." New York Department of Environmental Conservation. Accessed June 4, 2024. https://dec.ny .gov/nature/forests-trees/immerse-yourself-for-better-health.

Isenberg, Wesley W., trans. "The Gospel of Philip." The Gnostic Society Library. Accessed June 4, 2024. http://gnosis.org/naghamm/gop.html.

Kaku, Michio. *Parallel Worlds: A Journey through Creation, Higher Dimensions, and the Future of the Cosmos*. New York: Vintage, 2006.

Krishnamurti, J. "Choiceless Awareness." Krishnamurti Foundation America. Video, 28:49. Accessed January 13, 2024, https://www.kfa .org/teaching/choiceless-awareness-2/.

Kübler-Ross, Elisabeth. *On Life after Death*. Berkeley, CA: Celestial Arts, 2008.

Lambdin, Thomas, trans. "Gospel of Thomas." *Marquette University*. Accessed October 30, 2023. https://www.marquette.edu/maqom /Gospel%20of%20Thomas%20Lambdin.pdf.

Llanes, Hector. "Are the Gnostic Gospels Reliable Sources?" Grand Canyon University. March 3, 2015. https://www.gcu.edu/blog /theology-ministry/are-gnostic-gospels-reliable-sources.

Mambrol, Nasrullah. "Lacan's Concept of Mirror Stage." *Literary Theory and Criticism* (blog), April 18, 2021. https://literariness.org/2016/04/22/lacans-concept-of-mirror-stage/.

Mann, Jon. "A Brief History of Gold in Art, from Ancient Egyptian Burial Masks to Jeff Koons." Artsy. October 19, 2017. https://www.artsy.net/article/artsy-editorial-history-gold-art-ancient-egyptian-burial-masks-jeff-koons.

Maybee, Julie E. "Hegel's Dialectics." Stanford Encyclopedia of Philosophy. Last modified October 2, 2020. https://plato.stanford.edu/entries/hegel-dialectics/.

Melina, Remy. "Gray Whales Adapted to Survive Past Climate Changes." Livescience.com. July 6, 2011. https://www.livescience.com/14931-gray-whales-adapt-habits-survive.html.

Mercier, Vivian. "Samuel Beckett and the Sheela-na-gig." *The Kenyon Review* 23, no. 2 (Spring 1961): 299–324. https://www.jstor.org/stable/4334122.

Monroy-Ríos, Emiliano. "Chicxulub Crater and Ring of Cenotes." Karst Geochemistry and Hydrogeology. February 7, 2023. https://sites.northwestern.edu/monroyrios/some-maps/chicxulub-and-ring-of-cenotes/.

Montoya, Ryan. "What Is Death, Exactly?" *Scientific American*, October 18, 2019. https://blogs.scientificamerican.com/observations/what-is-death-exactly/.

Moore, Glen, and Cassandra Atherton. "Eternal Forests: The Veneration of Old Trees in Japan." Arnold Arboretum. Harvard University. May 18, 2020. https://arboretum.harvard.edu/stories/eternal-forests-the-veneration-of-old-trees-in-japan/.

Moody, Raymond. *Life after Life: The Bestselling Original Investigation That Revealed "Near-Death Experiences."* New York: HarperCollins, 2015.

Nag Hammadi Archive. Claremont Colleges Digital Library. https://ccdl.claremont.edu/digital/collection/nha.

Nair, Balakrishnan R., William Browne, John Marley, and Christian Heim. "Music and Dementia." *Degenerative Neurological and Neuromuscular Disease* 3 (September 1, 2013): 47–51. doi:10.2147/dnnd .s35762.

Nichols, Chris. "The Stranger-Than-Fiction History of the Integratron." *Los Angeles Magazine*, November 5, 2019. https://lamag.com /lahistory/integratron-desert-dome.

Nietzsche, Friedrich. *The Gay Science: With a Prelude in Rhymes and an Appendix of Songs.* Translated by Walter Kaufman. New York: Random House, 1974.

Oliver, Mary. "Poem 133: The Summer Day." Library of Congress. Accessed June 24, 2024. https://www.loc.gov/programs/poetry-and -literature/poet-laureate/poet-laureate-projects/poetry-180/all-poems /item/poetry-180-133/the-summer-day/.

Pagels, Elaine. "The Gnostic Gospels." PBS. Accessed June 4, 2024. https://www.pbs.org/wgbh/frontline/article/gnostic-gospels/.

Parrott, Douglas M., trans. "The Sophia of Jesus Christ." The Gnostic Society Library. http://gnosis.org/naghamm/sjc.html.

Peedikayil, Hannah. "Ecological Damage on White Sage." California State University, Long Beach. April 28, 2022. https://www.csulb.edu /college-of-business/legal-resource-center/article/ecological-damage -white-sage.

Perry, Philip. "Plants and Trees Communicate through an Unseen Web." Big Think. April 25, 2016. https://bigthink.com/surprising-science /plants-and-trees-communicate-help-each-other-and-even-poison -enemies-through-an-unseen-web/.

Plato. *Euthyphro, Apology, Crito, Phaedo.* Translated by Harold North Fowler. Cambridge, MA: Harvard University Press, 2005.

———. *The Great Dialogues of Plato.* Translated by W. H. D. Rouse. Reprint, New York: Signet Classics, 2015.

————. "Meno." In *The Philosopher's Handbook: Essential Readings from Plato to Kant*, edited by Stanley Rosen. New York: Random House Reference, 2009.

Riess, Helen, and Liz Neporent. *The Empathy Effect: Seven Neuroscience-Based Keys for Transforming the Way We Live, Love, Work, and Connect across Differences*. Boulder, CO: Sounds True, 2018.

Rosen, Jody. "Welcome to the Integratron." *New York Times*, August 20, 2014. https://www.nytimes.com/interactive/2014/08/20/style/tmagazine/welcome-to-the-integratron.html.

Sagan, Carl. *Pale Blue Dot: A Vision of the Human Future in Space*. New York: Ballantine Books, 1994.

"Scientists Investigate Water Memory." The Green Times. January 24, 2013. https://thegreentimes.co.za/scientists-investigate-water-memory/#.

Sharkey, John. *Celtic Mysteries: The Ancient Religion*. New York: Thames and Hudson, 1975.

Skrbina, David. "Panpsychism." Internet Encyclopedia of Philosophy. Accessed June 4, 2024. https://iep.utm.edu/panpsych/.

Stoycheva, Valentina. "Hack Your Unconscious: Why Negative Feelings Linger." *Psychology Today*, November 13, 2019. https://www.psychologytoday.com/us/blog/the-everyday-unconscious/201911/hack-your-unconscious-why-negative-feelings-linger-0.

"Understanding Sound." National Park Service. July 3, 2018. https://www.nps.gov/subjects/sound/understandingsound.htm.

Wayman, Erin. "Why Do Babies Have Soft Spots?" *Smithsonian Magazine*, May 7, 2012. https://www.smithsonianmag.com/science-nature/why-do-babies-have-soft-spots-82746501/.

Whitman, Walt. "Song of Myself (1892 Version)." Poetry Foundation. Accessed June 5, 2021. https://www.poetryfoundation.org/poems/45477/song-of-myself-1892-version.

Wilde, Katelyn. "Wren Symbolism and Meaning (Spirit, Totem and Omens)." *Sonoma Birding* (blog). Accessed January 21, 2021. https://www.sonomabirding.com/wren-symbolism/.

"William James." Department of Psychology. Harvard University. Accessed June 4, 2024. https://psychology.fas.harvard.edu/people/william-james.

West, Martin L., trans. *Homeric Hymns, Homeric Apocrypha, Lives of Homer*. Cambridge, MA: Harvard University Press, 1998.

NOTES

NOTES

NOTES

NOTES